Exchange of Gifts

The Vision of
Simon Barrington-Ward

Simon Barrington-Ward was one of the worldwide Church's great 'bridge-builders', charting an imaginative path for Christianity from the local to the global, and from a turbulent twentieth century right into the challenges of a new millennium. Establishing a pioneering reputation as the Church Mission Society (CMS) General Secretary and then Bishop of Coventry, his long and extraordinary life spanned nine decades, combining the heart of a pastor with wide-ranging gifts as a mission theologian, lecturer, chaplain, spiritual director, ecumenist, writer, reconciler and justice advocate. He was also Honorary Fellow of Magdalene College, Cambridge.

This book – featuring both recognised and emerging voices – explores the range of concerns and lives Simon Barrington-Ward touched, his importance as a contemporary witness to an historic faith, and the inspiration and guidance his example offers to followers of Christ navigating an uncertain future. The fascinating life it documents, and to which it pays tribute, will be of interest both to Anglicans and to Christians of many different outlooks and backgrounds. Here is a figure who can unite across difference and point us towards a path of hope in an often divided world.

> This wonderful book gathers together the insights of those who knew Simon Barrington-Ward so well and who have captured the heart and essence of this most visionary man. Simon's intellect, humour and sometimes child-like simplicity are brought vividly to life along with his profound faith and trust in God, and I am delighted to commend this book to you from the Diocese that he served so fully as bishop and where he continues to be greatly loved.
>
> *The Rt Revd Dr Christopher Cocksworth*
> *Bishop of Coventry*

Graham Kings is former Bishop of Sherborne, founder of the Cambridge Centre for Christianity Worldwide, and a widely published author.

Ian Randall, a Baptist academic and writer, is Church Historian and Research Associate at the Cambridge Centre for Christianity Worldwide.

EXCHANGE OF GIFTS

THE VISION OF
SIMON BARRINGTON-WARD

Edited by Graham Kings & Ian Randall

Foreword by the Archbishop of Canterbury

Ekklesia

First published in January 2022

Ekklesia
Edinburgh
Scotland
www.ekklesia.co.uk

All biblical quotations are from the New Revised Standard Version, unless otherwise stated

Cover portrait by Peter Mennim

Back cover photo by Howard Guest, of Simon and Jean Barrington-Ward and their daughter Helen (see p.29)

Production and design: Bob Carling

Managing Editor: Simon Barrow

ISBN: 978-1-7397551-0-2

A Catalogue record for this book is available from the British Library

CONTENTS

Influences and Indicators

His Own Words

PUBLISHER'S PREFACE

Simon Barrow

While the history and development of global Christianity is very much about the energy of communities and movements, not simply leaders, we nevertheless know how certain people end up playing a vital role in helping the Christian community worldwide to think, relate, grow, change and – as this book emphasises – exchange gifts.

Simon Barrington-Ward is undoubtedly someone whose life, work and immense personal qualities have contributed enormously to such processes of mutual benefit and spiritual growth. Through this volume that continues. It is an honour to be able to play a part in helping such special gifts to go on being shared.

Part of the purpose of Ekklesia Publishing is to enable less recognised voices to find a wider public. In his activities over the years, Simon Barrington-Ward became immensely important for a large number of people, quite a few of whom have contributed to this rich and diverse collection. However, it is probably also true that his name is not as widely or instantly recognised as some of others that crop up within these pages. It is our hope that *Exchange of Gifts: The Vision of Simon Barrington-Ward* will help to change that.

It has been a great pleasure to work with co-editors Graham Kings and Ian Randall in preparing this book – in the process, renewing contact with Graham after a number of years, and forming a new bond with Ian. They and the contributors have put an immense amount of loving labour into its realisation.

Thanks are also due to Nicholas Adams for his astute comments on one part of the book. I would like to acknowledge Ekklesia Publishing's production manager, Bob Carling, in particular. His outstanding endeavours, expertise and collaboration have made this venture (and many others) possible. May the quiet wisdom shared within these pages enrich us all.

Simon Barrow
Director and Managing Editor, Ekklesia Publishing

FOREWORD

Justin Welby – Archbishop of Canterbury

There is only one sorrow, the sorrow of not being a Saint.
– Léon Bloy

Simon Barrington-Ward was a great many things to a very great many of us. In this book we hear from those to whom he was colleague, those who served under his leadership at CMS and his episcopacy in Coventry, those who knew him throughout his years as friend, and Helen, who alongside Mary, knew him as father. My guess would be that you have picked up this book because you encountered him in some capacity. For each of us, of course, that will be different. Simon has a special place in my heart and shape of my ministry, as a key contributor to my coming to faith and as my ordaining bishop who appointed me to my title parish and first incumbency. In addition he was an inspiration, mentor and exemplar of the practice of following Christ.

However, it is for the commonality of who he was for each of us that I want to give particular thanks. Simon was one who lived so transparently before the face of Christ, he became one in whom the light passed through. For each of us there will be special 'thin' places – where it feels the boundary between heaven and earth has become a fine membrane. There are locations where we particularly sense the proximity of God, geographical spaces where, sometimes to our surprise, we find God to be especially close. Often these are specific buildings or outdoor sites which we feel drawn to again and again, when we want to be on holy ground. To be around Simon Barrington Ward was to be close to a 'thin' place.

You will find this idea woven through the book – the talk of his 'luminosity' most especially when he spoke about Christ or led people in prayer. There was something of a 'heaven-touches-earth' in the simplicity of his relating – utterly even-handed with the youngest or most senior, in his ability to concentrate and give attention – to be truly present to those who were in front of him, and in his decisions for those he continually chose to put at the centre – who might otherwise have been left at the margins. Yes, I am grateful for all he did, and the things he taught me, but I am most especially thankful for who he was. He was one in whom we encountered Christ.

I am grateful then for this book – for I am reminded of things I knew and experienced, and I am glad to have the opportunity to learn things I never knew of him. But I am most appreciative of the reminder of a life lived utterly orientated around God. Lived in such close proximity to the reality of God, that those of us who encountered him in any meaningful way, sensed the nearness of the Spirit of the one who was dead but is now alive.

Towards the end of the book we learn of Simon's stated aim for his life, "I had seen my life's work to join in bringing all into the redemptive moment of this love which alone could save us". This he did by who he was. A holy one of God.

I bless the Lord for the blessings I received from his hand through Simon; it was, to slightly adapt St Peter's words at the transfiguration, 'good for us to be here'. Not, primarily, for what we received or what we gave, but for what it showed each of us could be in and through Christ.

++*Justin Welby*
Archbishop of Canterbury

INTRODUCTION

Simon Barrington-Ward: Life and Memories

Graham Kings

Simon would talk to anyone and I would usually know to whom he was talking.[1]

MARK BARRINGTON-WARD, editor of *The Oxford Mail* for 18 years, thus summed up his experience of being together with his younger brother Simon at parties. Simon was gregarious but not always fully aware, whereas Mark was more shy, but organised.

Simon's article, 'My Pilgrimage in Mission', republished as Chapter 13 below from the April 1999 edition of the *International Bulletin of Missionary Research*,[2] is very moving but he passes over various aspects of his life. In this chapter, I hope to fill in some of those lacunae, providing a setting for the rest of the book and also to contribute some of my own memories of Simon and of his nourishing, personal ministry as a pastor.

Background and Schools

Simon was born in 1930 into an erudite family with connections to the Establishment. His father, Robert McGowan Barrington-Ward, was a barrister and then an Assistant Editor at *The Times*, and later was the

---

1 My telephone interview with Mark Barrington-Ward, on 19 January 2021 (Mark died on 23 October 2021, aged 93, and his obituary was in *The Times*, 23 November 2021), and my various interviews with Helen Orr in Cambridge, Simon's daughter, have been invaluable for this chapter, as well as the following obituaries: *The Times*, 20 April 2020, https://www.thetimes.co.uk/article/the-rt-rev-simon-barrington-ward-obituary-wq8j22kxk ; *The Daily Telegraph*, 19 May 2020, https://www.telegraph.co.uk/obituaries/2020/05/19/right-reverend-simon-barrington-ward-well-liked-bishop-coventry/; *Church Times*, by Canon Paul Oestreicher, https://www.churchtimes.co.uk/articles/2020/1-may/gazette/obituaries/obituary-the-rt-revd-simon-barrington-ward ; Magdalene College, Cambridge https://www.magd.cam.ac.uk/news/bishop-simon-barrington-ward-1930-2020 , (see below, Chapter 2). Over the years, Simon provided four short autobiographical accounts of his life: 'My Pilgrimage in Mission' (see below, Chapter 13); 'Exploring the Great Exchange' (see below, Chapter 15); Anna Jeffrey (ed.), *Five Gold Rings: Powerful Influences on Prominent People* (London: DLT, 2003), 1–8; *The Jesus Prayer and the Great Exchange* (Cambridge: Grove Books, 2013).

2 Gerald H. Anderson, the editor of the *International Bulletin of Missionary Research*, had asked me, a contributing editor, to commission articles for the April 1999 edition, which focused on the bicentenary of the Church Mission Society, founded in 1799.

Editor, between 1941–48.[3] Robert was a scholar at Balliol College, Oxford, reading Literae Humaniores (Classics), was President of the Oxford Union and fought in the First World War in the Duke of Cornwall's Light Infantry, winning a Distinguished Service Order and the Military Cross for bravery.

In his sermon at Eton College on Remembrance Sunday, 2000, Simon recounted:

> My father had known that horror and that longing in the ghastly slaughter and confusion of the trenches in Ypres. I asked him once what he got his DSO and MC for, hoping to have a story to tell at school. But his face set grimly as he replied curtly, 'For surviving.'[4]

Robert's father, Mark James Barrington-Ward, Simon's grandfather, was Rector of Duloe in Cornwall, and an inspector of schools: so the ordained ministry was in the family background.

Simon's mother, Adele (née Radice), read history at Lady Margaret Hall, Oxford, and met Robert after the First World War. She was the daughter of a Civil Servant in India and was a schoolteacher. As well as Mark and Simon, Robert and Adele had a daughter, Caroline, and the family home was in a Georgian terrace in Regent's Park, London. Simon went to preparatory school near Coventry and then on to Eton College. A contemporary at Eton was Douglas Hurd, later to be Foreign Secretary. In a profile article on Hurd in 1995, Bryan Appleyard reported an intriguing link between the two:

> Hurd went for a history prize and came second to the man who is now Bishop of Coventry. The examiner said the runner-up was extremely competent and would probably become a minister, but the winner had an extra element of emotion, of romanticism.[5]

Another contemporary was John Sweet, who became a New Testament scholar and Fellow of Selwyn College, Cambridge. When Simon preached at John's funeral, in Selwyn College Chapel in 2009, he quoted a note in the online book condolences:

> a young woman recalled how, when she apologised to him for

3 Donald McLachlan, *In the Chair: Barrington-Ward of The Times* (London: Weidenfeld and Nicholson, 1971).
4 Simon Barrington-Ward, "Remembrance Sunday Sermon," Eton College, 12 November 2000, SBW papers File Sermons and Talks 1.
5 Bryan Appleyard, "Je Regrette a Thing or Two, Perhaps," *The Independent,* 18 July 1995.

the elementary nature of her naive questions, he replied characteristically, "Not at all. It's so nice to have someone ask me questions to which I actually know the answer!"[6]

Towards the end of his time at Eton, his father noted in his diary that he was glad about Simon's positive view of the church.

Simon was only aged seventeen when his father, on a cruise with his mother to recover from his ill health, suddenly died, in the harbour of Dar es Salaam, Zanzibar, and was buried on the shore there. This was traumatic for Simon, Mark and Caroline.

After national service as a pilot officer in the RAF, Simon was an exhibitioner reading history at Magdalene College, Cambridge from 1950 and graduated with a BA in 1953. The bursar there from 1949–77, Jock Burnet,[7] would be a key influence on his life. Simon contributed a chapter to a book in memory of him.

Berlin 1954: Lecturer in the Free University

In 1954, Simon taught history as a lector at the Free University, West Berlin: a learner amidst the ruins. Paul Oestreicher, Simon's Director of Reconciliation in the Diocese of Coventry, wrote in his *Church Times* obituary:

> With a group of Christians, former Nazis, and former resisters, forgiving and being forgiven, he worshipped in the Dahlem parish church where Martin Niemöller had preached sermons that went around the world, published in Britain as *The Gestapo Defied by Christ Crucified*. Eight years of imprisonment was the price that he paid. Simon's new-found Berlin friend who had been ordered to defend the city to the very last introduced him to both Nietzsche's philosophy and Brecht's plays.[8]

Cambridge 1954–60: Ordinand at Westcott House then Chaplain at Magdalene College

Returning to Cambridge, Simon trained for ordination at Westcott House, 1954–56. Surprisingly, rather than serving as a curate in a parish, he became Chaplain of Magdalene College from 1956–60,

---

6 Simon Barrington-Ward, "Sermon at the Funeral of John Sweet," Selwyn College Chapel, 15 July 2009, SBW papers computer disk.
7 http://www.cu-sparrows.net/history/jock-burnet/
8 https://www.churchtimes.co.uk/articles/2020/1-may/gazette/obituaries/obituary-the-rt-revd-simon-barrington-ward , *Church Times*, 1 May 2020.

and helped out in the vacations at a church on a housing estate in Hemel Hempstead.

The most famous Fellow of Magdalene during his time as chaplain was C.S. Lewis, Professor of Mediaeval and Renaissance English Literature. They used to go on long walks together along the River Cam to Stourbridge Common and Ditton Fields.

In his sermon in retirement, Sunday 11 October 1998, in Magdalene College chapel, Simon gave a long description of his memories of C.S. Lewis during this period, which included the following:

> If you stepped aside from the conflict and simply offered him some tentative idea of your own, he could snatch it up like a favour and whirl it round on his lance until it became a positive banner. Gradually I came to enjoy the nightly entertainment of his marvellous talk, which his writings still so poignantly recall, the rich storehouse of his reading and his skill in drawing aptly upon it.[9]

In 2014, Simon recounted this friendship with Lewis in a YouTube interview with his son-in-law, James Orr, Lecturer in Philosophical Theology, in the Faculty of Divinity, Cambridge.[10] He discussed their mutual love of George MacDonald's stories, and of reciting the Book of Common Prayer Psalms at Morning Prayer in Chapel together.[11]

In Chapter 13, 'My Pilgrimage in Mission', Simon referred to an unnamed professor at Cambridge ('at the instigation of one of our professors'[12]), who encouraged him to take up a lectureship in Nigeria. In his address at Magdalene College in 2008, 'Magdalene in the 50s and 60s: a piece of Oral History', he identified him as C.F.D. Moule, Lady Margaret Professor of Divinity and key supporter of the Church Missionary Society, who had been born in China of CMS missionary parents:

> Professor C.F.D. Moule, a New Testament scholar at Clare College and an outstanding theologian kept an eye on us College Chaplains and sent me out to Nigeria at the request of his colleague, soon to be Dean in Clare, later Professor of Divinity at Oxford, Maurice Wiles, who had been teaching in

9   Simon Barrington-Ward, Sermon 11 October 1998, Magdalene College, Cambridge, SBW papers Sermon and Talks file one.

10   "Looking Towards the End: Cambridge Memories of C.S. Lewis," Simon Barrington-Ward interviewed by Dr James Orr, 2014 https://www.youtube.com/watch?v=g_TPKVqvjnU

11   C.S. Lewis, at the time, was involved with T.S. Eliot and others in translating *The Revised Psalter* (1963).

12   "My Pilgrimage in Mission," see Chapter 13.

Ibadan in Nigeria and asked for another Cambridge man to go out and fill his place.[13]

Ibadan, Nigeria 1960–63: Assistant University Lecturer

Simon was an Assistant Lecturer in the Religious Studies Department of the University of Ibadan, Nigeria from 1960–63. Soon after he arrived another fascinating opportunity arose. His brother Mark recounts how he was offered the post of Principal of Westcott House, to succeed Kenneth Carey. Simon's mother said, 'you have given your word' to the University of Ibadan. He wisely followed her advice and stayed.

He was influenced by two key women in Ibadan: Ibribina, a prophet and leader of an African Instituted Church, and Jean Taylor, a CMS missionary doctor and university medical officer, whose father had been a Church of Scotland missionary doctor in China.

In his anthropological researches, Simon focused on the Isoko people of the Western Delta, where Ibribina led her dynamic church. He later wrote up his study of her in his key work of detailed scholarship, '"The Centre Cannot Hold..." Spirit Possession as Redefinition', in the influential 1978 book, *Christianity in Independent Africa*.[14] In Chapter 9, Linda Ochola-Adolwa, a Kenyan Anglican priest, theologian and social activist, revisits this work.

He and Jean fell in love and were married in 1963 at the Episcopal Cathedral in Edinburgh by Kenneth Carey, who had been Simon's Principal at Westcott House and was the Bishop of Edinburgh, 1961–75. They had two daughters, Mary and Helen.[15] In Chapter 1, Helen writes about her family perspectives on her father.

Cambridge 1963–69: Dean of Chapel and Fellow of Magdalene College

Mark Barrington-Ward recounts how Jock Burnet, the Bursar of Magdalene College, Cambridge, was instrumental in drawing Simon back to his alma mater and from 1963 to 1969 Simon served as Dean of Chapel and Fellow of Magdalene College. The College obituary states:

---

13 Simon Barrington-Ward, "Magdalene in the 50s and 60s: a Piece of Oral History," 6 Mar 2008, SBW papers, computer disk.

14 '"The Centre cannot hold..." Spirit possession as redefinition' in Adrian Hastings, Fasholé-Luke, *et al.*, eds, *Christianity in Independent Africa* (London: Rex Collins, 1978), 445–470.

15 Mary works in healthcare PR and Helen Orr is Vicar of the Benefices of Bassingbourn and Whaddon, Diocese of Ely.

Throughout a seventy-year association with the College, Bishop Simon was respected and admired for his intellect and his practical spirituality; and loved, too, for his warmth and his genuine interest in others.[16]

Simon and Jean lived in a house in Northampton Street, near Magdalene and also opposite Kettle's Yard, the extraordinary 'gallery-in-a-home' of Jim Ede. On 26 February 2008, Robert Wilkinson conducted a Kettle's Yard interview with Simon and Jean about Jim Ede, whom Simon first met when Simon was an undergraduate at Magdalene.[17] Jim and Helen, his wife, used to invite undergraduates to their home and influenced Simon's views on modern art. Simon introduced Jim to the works of St John of the Cross, which Jim quoted in his book on Kettle's Yard, A Way of Life.[18] He helped Jim through to deeper faith and later had the joy of confirming him.

During this period, he was influenced by two people in particular: David Watson, curate at The Round Church, Cambridge, whose renewal in the Holy Spirit introduced Simon to the beginnings of the Charismatic Movement in England, and John V. Taylor, the General Secretary of the CMS,[19] whose Africa Committee Simon chaired.

Birmingham 1969–75: Principal of Crowther Hall, CMS Training College

In 1969, John V. Taylor encouraged Simon to leave Cambridge and become the first Principal of Crowther Hall, the new CMS training college, in the ecumenical federation of Selly Oak Colleges, Birmingham, where he served from 1969–75. Simon was delighted that the college was named after the first black African Bishop in the Anglican Communion, Samuel Ajayi Crowther. In 1999 he enjoyed the three Henry Martyn Lectures in the University of Cambridge, given by Professor Jacob F. Ade Ajayi, Emeritus Professor of History, University of Ibadan, 'Mission and Empire: the Ambiguous Mandate of Bishop Crowther'.[20]

---

16 https://www.magd.cam.ac.uk/news/bishop-simon-barrington-ward-1930-2020
17 https://www.kettlesyard.co.uk/collection/recollection/interviewee/simon-barrington-ward/
18 Jim Ede, A Way of Life: Kettle's Yard Gallery (Cambridge: CUP, 1984).
19 See David Wood, Bishop John V. Taylor: Poet, Priest and Prophet (London: CTBI, 2002) and Graham Kings, 'Mission and the Meeting of Faiths: the Theology of Mission of Max Warren and John V. Taylor' in Kevin Ward and Brian Stanley, eds, The Church Mission Society and World Christianity, 1799–1999 (Grand Rapids: Eerdmans, 1999) and Jonny Baker and Cathy Ross, Imagining Mission with John V. Taylor (London: SCM Press, 2020).
20 Jacob Ade Ajayi, 'Mission and Empire: The Ambiguous Mandate of Bishop Crowther'. Lecture 1. 'Philanthropy in Sierra Leone' https://www.cccw.cam.ac.uk/wp-content/uploads/2017/07/Ajayi-Prof-Jacob-F.-Ade-252628-Oct.pdf Lecture 2. 'Crowther and Language in the Yoruba Mission' https://www.cccw.cam.ac.uk/wp-content/uploads/2017/07/Ajayi-Prof-Jacob-F.-Ade-252628-Oct.lect-2.pdf Lecture 3. 'Crowther and Trade on the Niger' https://www.cccw.cam.ac.uk/wp-content/uploads/2017/07/Ajayi-Prof-Jacob-F.-Ade-252628-Oct.lect-3.pdf

At Crowther Hall Simon introduced placements in inner-city churches and community projects. In Chapter 8, Cathy Ross, Head of Pioneer Mission Education at CMS, considers the ramifications of Simon's mission theology for training today.

In 1973, Simon watched the Oxford and Cambridge boat race at the home of an Old Etonian, George Nissen, on Chiswick Mall, overlooking the River Thames. There he met a young man, who was looking for a gap-year experience between Eton College and Trinity College, Cambridge. He suggested the 'Youth Service Abroad' scheme of CMS. This was Justin Welby's first meeting with Simon and led to his life-changing experience of teaching at Kiburu School, near Karatina, in the highlands of Kenya.[21]

London 1975–85: General Secretary of CMS

In 1975, Simon was appointed General Secretary of the CMS, a post he held for 10 years. He was very conscious of, and somewhat overawed by, following in the footsteps of two well-known and creative predecessors, Max Warren (1942–63, who became Canon of Westminster),[22] and John V. Taylor (1963–75, who became Bishop of Winchester).

In 1984, I remember him coming to dinner at our house in Crowther Hall, where Alison and I were CMS mission partners in training, preparing to go to Kenya. Carole Fallowes and Hilary Green were our other guests. Simon drifted out of the conversation, focusing on the photograph of our eldest daughter, Rosalind, aged 3, on the sideboard, which he then discussed with us. We also talked about John V. Taylor because Carole, Hilary and I had been reading his writings. Simon suggested we wrote to John to arrange a meeting in London, which we did, at the Royal Commonwealth Club.[23]

Simon introduced into CMS the theme of 'interchange': receiving from, as well as giving to, the worldwide Church. In Chapter 5, John Clark, then CMS Regional Secretary for the Middle East and later Communications Secretary, expounds this concept. In Chapter 6, Simon Barrow, CMS Deputy Education Secretary at CMS during that

---

21 Andrew Atherstone, *Archbishop Justin Welby: Risk-taker and Reconciler* (London: DLT, 2014), 16 based on an interview Atherstone conducted with Lady Williams, Justin Welby's mother, who sold 'a diamond ring she had inherited from her godmother to enable Justin to travel'.

22 Graham Kings, *Christianity Connected: Hindus, Muslims and the World in the Letters of Max Warren and Roger Hooker* (Zoetermeer: Boekencentrum, 2002 and Delhi: ISPCK, 2017).

23 Hilary and her friend, Tim Naish, had a further discussion with John about marriage and whether she should postpone going to Nepal as a mission partner or not. Hilary and Tim later were married and Simon ordained Tim in Coventry Cathedral to serve a curacy in the diocese, before they both served as CMS mission partners in Zaire and later Uganda. Hilary is now a psychotherapist and Tim is Canon Librarian of Canterbury Cathedral. Carole served in Juba, Sudan, as a teacher trainer, and later after marrying Mike Boardman, in Pakistan.

period, describes his thinking on ecumenism and mission. In Chapter 7, Sarah Cawdell, who was a CMS short-term volunteer in Uganda, outlines his theology of mission, which emanates from his monthly *CMS Newsletters*.

Twenty four of these *Newsletters* were published in his most substantial book, *Love Will Out*. In the introduction, Simon stated:

> Gradually, looking back, I begin to see [these *CMS Newsletters*] more and more as a set of variations. The theme itself an interplay, a fusion of opposites. It is a constant coming together of Heaven and Earth, universal and particular, divine and human, judgement and mercy, spiritual and material, ideal and reality, structure and community, joy and sorrow, in a whole range of varied contexts.[24]

It was while he was travelling the world as General Secretary that he first felt the need for deeper prayer and was taken by a friend to the Orthodox Monastery at Tolleshunt Knights, in Essex, headed by Fr Sophrony Sakharov.[25] There he encountered the Jesus Prayer, which was to be his spiritual foundation for the rest of his life and led to three short books: *The Jesus Prayer* (1996); *Praying the Jesus Prayer Together* (2001, written with Brother Ramon SSF); and *The Jesus Prayer and the Great Exchange* (2013).[26]

In 2014, Simon's daughter, Helen Orr, conducted a YouTube interview with him in his study and chapel at 4 Searle Street, Cambridge, about the Jesus Prayer.[27] In Chapter 12, Philip Seddon, who served as a CMS mission partner in Nigeria and later as lecturer at Selly Oak Colleges, Birmingham, writes about his use of the Jesus Prayer. He accompanied Simon to this monastery and later to Mount Athos.

Coventry: Bishop

After 10 years at CMS, Simon served as Bishop of Coventry 1985–97. He was consecrated at Westminster Abbey on 1 November 1985 by the Archbishop of Canterbury Robert Runcie, who had been Dean of Trinity Hall, Cambridge 1956–60, when Simon was Chaplain of

---

24 *Love Will Out: A Theology of Mission for today's world: CMS newsletters 1975–85* (Basingstoke: Marshall, Morgan and Scott, 1988).

25 See Rowan Williams, *Looking East in Winter: Contemporary Thought and the Eastern Christian Tradition* (London: Bloomsbury, 2021).

26 Simon Barrington-Ward, *The Jesus Prayer* (Oxford: BRF, 1996); Brother Ramon and Simon Barrington-Ward, *Praying the Jesus Prayer Together* (Oxford: BRF, 2001); Simon Barrington-Ward, *The Jesus Prayer and the Great Exchange* (Cambridge: Grove Books, 2013).

27 https://www.youtube.com/watch?v=PxttrnyBC40 See also the one hour lecture by Simon at St Paul's Cathedral in 2011 https://www.youtube.com/watch?v=JCwiyU3DVV4

Magdalene College. The preacher was Misaeri Kauma, Assistant Bishop of Namirembe, Uganda.

Simon had learned German when he had lectured in Berlin and was especially moved by his visits to Dresden, with which Coventry was twinned. Both cities had suffered devastating bombing in the Second World War. On 13 February 1995, on the 50th anniversary of the Dresden bombing, he preached in fluent German to a large congregation at the Kreuzkirche in Dresden. The following day, the heart of his sermon was published in his article in *The Times*, 'Sharing in Dresden's Sorrow'.[28]

> The destruction of 15 square kilometres of a defenceless city, packed with refugees…Any genuine military targets, such as an army barracks or factories in the suburbs, were left unscathed, and little or no damage was done to vital road junctions, railway lines, marshalling yards or bridges…The civilians had become the target. Churchill had spoken of sowing a wind to reap a whirlwind…The Litany of Reconciliation of Coventry's Community of the Cross of Nails is also prayed in the Kreuzkircke in Dresden every Friday at the hour of Christ's death.

In the General Synod of the Church of England, he served as Chair of the International and Development Affairs Committee, 1986–1996. In Chapter 3, Clive Handford, his Suffragan Bishop of Warwick 1990–1996, describes Simon's ministry in the diocese.

Simon was invited by Richard Harries, Bishop of Oxford 1987–2006, to join the small episcopal cell group which he convened, for prayer and mutual support. It met twice a year, overnight in one of their homes, for a period of 24 hours. He was a valuable member throughout his ministry in Coventry and Richard's memories include the following:

> Simon's joyous personality exuded a gentle spirituality, but not such a one as prevented him having an engagement with intellectual ideas and well thought out convictions. Particularly of course we remember him for two of his major concerns, which he shared with us: his passion for the Jesus Prayer, and his admiration for, as well as ministry to, Gillian Rose. It was also good when Jean could join us, as she did on occasions, for our

---

28 Simon Barrington-Ward, "Sharing in Dresden's Sorrow," *The Times*, 14 February 1995.

final meal together.[29]

In 1988, Simon was one of four keynote speakers at the National Evangelical Anglican Congress at Caister, Norfolk: the title of his address was 'The Saving God.' This was significant because, by some, he was not seen as a 'card-carrying' Evangelical.

In 1992 his chapter, 'The Christic Cogito: Christian Faith in a Pluralist Age' was published in the festschrift for Peter Baelz, Dean of Durham, which is republished here as Chapter 14.[30]

Paul Oestreicher comments in his *Church Times* obituary:

> If, at times, his feet left the ground, Jean, his rock, would bring him back to earth. Their hospitality, their open house, and open table were a blessing to many in the diocese and beyond.[31]

In 1992, nearly 20 years after suggesting a gap-year in Kenya to him, Simon ordained Justin Welby to serve as a curate in the parish of Chivers Coton, a working class suburb of Nuneaton, in the West Midlands. Simon said to Justin, 'You've always been with people who do things. It's time you lived in a place where people have things done to them.'[32] In 1995, Simon instituted Justin as Rector of St James church, Southam, a market town in rural Warwickshire, where he served for 7 years.

In Chapter 16, we republish Simon's sermon on Gillian Rose. She was Jewish and an ardent seeker of the kingdom of God. She was Professor of Philosophy at the University of Warwick, and had discussions with Rowan Williams over a period of ten years concerning these matters. When Simon baptised her on the day she died, aged 48, Rowan was speaking at a conference at Warwick, which she had organized.

Rowan's set of three poems, 'Winterreise: for Gillian Rose, 9 December 1995', are extraordinary.[33] Her final book was a powerful memoir entitled *Love's Work*.[34] Andrew Shanks has written the first major book on her thought from a theological point of view, entitled

---

29 Richard Harries, email to Graham Kings 4 May 2021.
30 'The Christic Cogito: Christian Faith in a Pluralist Age' in D.W. Hardy and P.H. Sedgwick, eds, *The Weight of Glory: a Vision and Practice for Christian Faith, the Future of Liberal Theology* (T&T Clark, 1991), 257–270.
31 https://www.churchtimes.co.uk/articles/2020/1-may/gazette/obituaries/obituary-the-rt-revd-simon-barrington-ward *Church Times* 1 May 2020.
32 Atherstone, *Justin Welby*, p. 70.
33 Rowan Williams, *The Poems of Rowan Williams* (Manchester: Carcanet, 2014), 68–69.
34 Gillian Rose, *Love's Work: a Reckoning with Life* (London: Chatto and Windus, 1995). It was republished by the *New York Review of Books* in 2011, with the poem, at the end, by Geoffrey Hill, 'In Memoriam: Gillian Rose', which may be found in Geoffrey Hill, *Broken Hierarchies: Poems 1952–2012*, Kenneth Haynes, ed. (Oxford: OUP, 2013), 588–591.

Against Innocence.[35]

In 1991, when she was still alive, Rowan published an essay drawing on her work, 'Between politics and metaphysics: reflections in the wake of Gillian Rose'. It was republished in his collection, edited by Mike Higton, *Wrestling with Angels*. He wrote:

> Central to Rose's concern is the philosophical importance of error and the recognisability of error. To recognize misperception is to learn; to learn is to reimagine or reconceive the self; and this in turn is to encounter the 'violence' – a crucially significant and difficult word in Rose's recent oeuvre – that is inescapably involved in our position towards others and towards ourselves. It is because this violence is always presupposed by our particular positions in any network of relations that law is required in our sociality. And the insistence on a sociality never 'mended' in a final way (another recurrent theme) is precisely what raises, obliquely but inexorably, a religious question; not the facile and tempting question of law's relation to grace, but the harder one of how the very experience of learning and of negotiation can be read as something to do with God.[36]

Simon preached a sermon in Little St Mary's Church, Cambridge in 2004 about Gillian Rose (Chapter 16) and quoted her testimony:

> When she was in hospital, strongly depending upon a
> Christian doctor whom she trusted deeply, she suddenly wrote
> him a letter and sent me a copy. I quote,
> 'You know me to be a Jew. I am also a Trinitarian ... However,
> while I feel held by God and the Holy Spirit, like many Jews I
> have a difficulty with Christ, 'to the Jews a stumbling block.'
> As a result of this week's experience I have gained Christ. For
> Christ is a stumbling block, but once you touch the hem of his
> robe with faith, you are healed. I shall be thanking God for
> this insight and gift.'[37]

---

35 Andrew Shanks, *Against Innocence: Gillian Rose's Reception and Gift of Faith* (London: SCM Press, 2008).
36 Rowan Williams, 'Between politics and metaphysics: reflections in the wake of Gillian Rose', in Rowan Williams and Mike Higton, eds, *Wrestling with Angels: Conversations with Modern Theology* (London: SCM Press, 2007), 60.
37 Simon Barrington-Ward, 'Sermon for Gillian Rose', Little St Mary's Church, Cambridge, 29 February 2004, SBW papers, Sermons and Talks, File 3 and Chapter 16.

Cambridge: Retirement as Hon Assistant Bishop, Diocese of Ely and Hon Assistant Chaplain, Magdalene College

In 1997, Simon and Jean retired to 4 Searle Street, Cambridge, not far from Magdalene College, where I remember squeezing into Simon's attic study and chapel for a discussion, when I was Director of the Henry Martyn Centre for the study of mission and world Christianity.

The previous year, I had a phone conversation with Simon and asked whether he wanted to give some of his books to the Centre (since renamed, the Cambridge Centre for Christianity Worldwide), where he could still have access to them.[38] He was delighted to give most of his mission studies books. This was the beginning of his long association with the Centre, where he served as a Trustee of the Henry Martyn Trust from 1998 and as chair 2002–4. He left his papers to the Centre, which form the basis of Chapter 4 'In The Henry Martyn Centre', by Ian Randall, Research Associate at the Centre and Church Historian.[39]

Simon served as Honorary Assistant Bishop in the Diocese of Ely for 23 years, from 1997 to his death in 2020. He had already become an Honorary Fellow of Magdalene College in 1987 and now also became an Honorary Assistant Chaplain there. This proved to be his longest period of sustained pastoral work.

His obituary on the Magdalene College website states:

> Simon continued to bring his kindness, wit, acuity and cheerfulness to the community; and when he returned to Magdalene in retirement, he found a new generation of friends – as well as many of his old colleagues and companions.[40]

He rejoiced in the friendships, in particular, of two Fellows who are Roman Catholics, Prof Eamon Duffy, Professor of the History of Christianity,[41] and Prof Nicholas Boyle, Professor of German Literature and Intellectual History and biographer of Goethe.[42] Simon enjoyed many hours discussing Hegel with Nicholas Boyle. In Chapter 10 Dr James Orr, Lecturer in the Faculty of Divinity, Cambridge, and

---

38 https://www.cccw.cam.ac.uk/
39 https://www.cccw.cam.ac.uk/wp-content/uploads/2017/10/SBW-Barrington-Ward.pdf
40 https://www.magd.cam.ac.uk/news/bishop-simon-barrington-ward-1930-2020
41 In 1997, Professor Walter Hollenweger, Professor of Mission at the University of Birmingham, gave the biennial Henry Martyn Lectures in the Faculty of Divinity, Cambridge. I remember the celebratory dinner at St Catharine's College, after the first one on 27 October. The interaction on the subject of Pentecostalism between Hollenweger, Simon and Eamon Duffy, the Chair of the Faculty of Divinity, was memorable.
42 Simon mentions Nicholas Boyle in his chapter mentioned above, 'The Christic Cogito' (Chapter 14): "It will be seen that I am heavily indebted to this article ['The Idea of Christian Poetry'] and its author. He links Hopkins with a development in which also Erich Auerbach and Hegel figure and he indeed led me to both." *The Weight of Glory*, 268, fn 5.

Simon's son-in-law, writes on 'Hegel and Holiness'.

In Chapter 2, we republish the In Memoriam articles of Dr Ronald Hyam (Emeritus Reader in British Imperial History and Archivist Emeritus) and of Professor Nicholas Boyle written for the Magdalene College Magazine and a College letter from Revd Sarah Atkins, (College Chaplain). Simon was delighted when Rowan Williams became Master in 2013, after retiring as Archbishop of Canterbury.

Simon was also Chaplain to the staff of Ridley Hall Theological College, where Christopher Cocksworth was the Principal from 2001 and who succeeded him as Bishop of Coventry in 2008. Andy Lord, who wrote Chapter 11, 'Ecclesiology, Grace and Brokenness,' first met Simon as an ordinand at Ridley Hall.[43] Simon was also member of the Chaplaincy Council of Anglia Ruskin University, serving as Chair from 2000–2006.

I remember seeing him preach at Westminster College, the theological college of the United Reformed Church, just after he had completed a week's retreat at the Orthodox monastery in Essex. He preached as one with a shining face – almost as a *staretz* (a Russian Orthodox revered spiritual leader).

The Queen made Simon one of her Chaplains in 1983 (serving till 1985 when he was consecrated bishop), then Prelate of the Order of St Michael and St George 1989–2005 and finally Knight Companion of the Order of St Michael and St George (KCMG) in 2001. He served on the Prince of Wales' advisory group on Islam.

Simon was awarded an Honorary Doctor of Divinity degree by Wycliffe College, Toronto in 1989, an Honorary degree of Doctor of Letters by Warwick University in 1998 and became an Honorary Doctor of Anglia Ruskin University in 2006.

In 1999, during a car journey together, Simon suggested that I explore being a contextual theologian as a parish priest and, eventually, that led to our move to the parish of St Mary Islington, London. After my valedictory lecture at the Henry Martyn Centre, Westminster College, he gave an astonishing summing up, which interwove Hegel and mission theology.

Simon preached on the day of Pentecost, 19 May 2002 at St Mary's. The evening before, Pentecost Eve, he led a group of us in saying the Jesus Prayer together, as we prayed for an outpouring of the Holy Spirit the next day.

Simon preached about the Holy Spirit and of a moving experience

---

43 See also Andy Lord, *Rivers of the Spirit: the Spirituality of Simon Barrington-Ward* (Oxford: Fairacres, 2021).

at Crowther Hall.

> Ugandan priest – William Nagenda? – comes to stay. Speaks
> severely to Jean and myself:
> 'You want the Holy Spirit! Holy Spirit comes not when roof is
> raised, but when the floor falls in!'

Prophetic words.[44]

After Simon's sermon people were invited to come forward for a fresh infilling of the Holy Spirit. Andrew Adigun, our organist of Nigerian heritage, had had severe problems with his hands and had been unable to play a particular piece by Chopin. He came forward and was filled with the Holy Spirit. He felt so different that, on returning home, he played the Chopin piece without any difficulty.

Conclusion

As they became frail, Simon and Jean moved into a residential home, Buchan House, in Cambridge. Philippa King, Rector of the parish of the Ascension, which includes their local church of St Luke's, took Simon by car to church each Sunday and said Morning Prayer, according to *The Book of Common Prayer*, with him each day at Buchan House. Liturgy from the depths surfaced through dementia and Philippa felt profoundly ministered to by God and Simon through the words of Cranmer and the Bible. One day Philippa introduced a German resident, who knew little English, to Simon and they conversed for hours in German.

Elizabeth Adekunle, former Archdeacon of Hackney and, prior to that, Chaplain at St John's College, Cambridge, bought their home at 4 Searle Street: a moving link back to their time in Nigeria. Their daughter and son-in-law, Helen and James Orr, bought a house on the banks of the River Cam nearby.

Full of faith and full of years, 89, Simon died of Covid-19 in Addenbrokes Hospital, Cambridge on 11 April 2020. He was a kind, intuitive and integrated seeker after mutuality and coherence and entered into the joy of his Lord. Well done, good and faithful servant.

The Times obituary mentioned:

> A slight, sharp-featured man, he would write copious notes in
> a rapid, stylised calligraphy, preferring to send handwritten

---

44 Simon Barrington-Ward, Sermon at St Mary's Islington, Pentecost Sunday, 19 May 2002. SBW papers Sermons and Talks File 2.

letters rather than have them typed.

Barrington-Ward may not have been a very systematic preacher but his ability to communicate with crowds and his joyful humanity put this humble man in the front rank of church leaders.

In retirement Barrington-Ward never lost his childlike sense of wonder or sparkling eyes.[45]

In the *Church Times*, Paul Oestreicher, summed him up:

Simon was good news. With the gospel in his heart, he was a man of joy, bubbling over with ideas: "half a dozen before breakfast", as one of his colleagues joked. The good ones would survive, the rest be forgotten. He was ever eager to learn from others. He was an enthusiast. His churchmanship? That word did not feature in his vocabulary. He had charisma, but was no more signed up to the Charismatic movement than to any other Church party. He embraced and took what was good from them all – far beyond Anglican frontiers, or even Christian frontiers. His liberality knew no bounds.[46]

Perhaps the essence of Simon's vision may be seen distilled in the title of our book, 'Exchange of Gifts'. The phrase is Simon's own. It is found at the heart of his 'Interchange Prayer', which he wrote for CMS and was printed annually in the CMS Diary:

Lord, as you have entered into our life and death
and in all the world you call us into your death and risen life,
forgive us our sins; and draw us we pray,
by the power and encouragement of your Spirit,
into an exchange of gifts and needs,
joys and sorrows, strength and weakness
with your people everywhere;
that with them we may have grace
to break through every barrier,
to make disciples of all peoples
and to share your love with everyone for your glory's sake.
Amen.

---

45 https://www.thetimes.co.uk/article/the-rt-rev-simon-barrington-ward-obituary-wq8j22kxk
46 https://www.churchtimes.co.uk/articles/2020/1-may/gazette/obituaries/obituary-the-rt-revd-simon-barrington-ward

Settings and Seasons

CHAPTER 1

Family as the Foundation

Helen Orr

Growing Up in London

GROWING UP IN THE HOME of a Barrington-Ward extrovert, such as my father, meant a constant stream of guests from all over the world.

My earliest memories are of being surrounded by fun and loving people and there, at the centre, were my parents, two relaxed and devoted people. Our home in London was fairly chaotic, with neither parent being very domestically capable. However, both were very efficient in the areas that mattered most – hospitality, fun and love.

Our elderly relation, Ivy Reid Taylor, filled in on the domestic side of things, with wonderful baking and making of magnificent meals, whilst Mum whizzed out from our doctor's practice home and Dad to CMS headquarters at 157 Waterloo Road. My elder sister, Mary, was good at helping with chores and cooking when needed and I gradually followed suit.

If someone turned up unexpectedly for tea, or supper or even to stay the night, another plate was hastily laid and a sleeping bag found for the sofa, if there was no extra bed. There was always enough room and food, whatever was required. I grew up in a house of provision and warmth, which my mother oversaw in her generous and selfless way. My Scottish mother, Jean, never bought too much and sometimes this meant 'FHB' (family hold back) as she asked us to 'fill up on bread' rather than to eat that last potato, which a guest might want. We really lacked, as the Good Book says, 'no good thing'. It was this winning partnership of my parents' relationship, and the attitude of gratitude they both embodied, that made my childhood so happy.

Mischief and Stories

Another other key word that springs to mind about my childhood is 'laughter'. My father's anecdotes and jokes, mishaps and mischief he had inhabited at school, stories of days in Magdalene and the characters they met there, were repeated often. As a young boy he had brought home a 'pewter crashing plate'. He immediately set about trying to fool his mother by offering to clear the plates that needed washing up. As he left the dining room and entered the kitchen, he dropped the joke pewter plate, which sounded like broken china. The crashing noise sent her rushing to the kitchen looking pale. On entering, she found him and his brother, Mark, roaring with laughter.

Many of his stories spawned family phrases such 'pass me the utter-butter'. This phrase came from the elderly wife of a Magdalene don, who recounted to her friends her encounter with a masseur: 'I was butter in his hands, utter butter'.

Dad cycled from Richmond into the CMS office on Waterloo Road, several miles each day. He began one particularly hot summer, during an underground tube strike. He went from thinking that cycling to work would be full of people gentling going past waving, to realising that it was a ruthless race in which it was gutting to have someone pass you as you were about to turn off, or where you could feel a whoosh of achievement as you passed someone else. As one of life's great enthusiasts, he joined a cycling club with a magazine subscription and bought all the gadgets possible to buy for his bike. He had all the gear, the clip-on pedals and shoes, the cycle shorts and helmet (before anyone was really wearing them), the speedometer and horn bell. He was just about to invest in an indicator you could strap to your arm, and which would flash red when you turned, when, thankfully, we moved to Coventry. There, although he was still known as the 'bicycling bishop,' he had to give up the daily cycle to work, as his office and home merged in the one building.

Marriage

One key, unchanging element, was the wonderfully, loving and unshakable marriage of our parents. I assumed – I realised later, quite wrongly – that when you married someone you never, or rarely, argued. I, for example, only heard my parents argue once when they were on holiday in Scotland: Mum was late with the rice for supper and Dad kept nagging her about it. Mum came out after Dad had asked for the fiftieth time about the rice, threw a cushion at him, told him to cook the rice himself, and stormed off to the bedroom. Dad looked visibly shocked, and Ivy (who was also on holiday with us) said 'go after her, dear'. I then thought it might mean divorce. When I said that to Ivy, she just laughed! Looking back on it, and knowing more about marriage since, it was one of the most compatible and peaceful unions I have ever come across.

I never tired of hearing the story of how they both met in Nigeria in Ibadan University, where Mum (with CMS) had gone out to be the university doctor and where Dad was teaching for three years at the Divinity Faculty. My mother was a handsome woman and seven men asked to marry her before my Dad, in an era when people would ask before anything really happened. She turned them all down. Her own Dad had been so extraordinary that she said she would prefer to be single than go for second best. But she felt that with my father she had found someone who, as she put it, 'could wear the trousers'. They did not even really go out when Dad asked her to marry him. This was rather unusual, but they were abroad and she would need a commitment to change her life and move back with Dad to Cambridge.

The fact that Dad wore 'the trousers' was not meant to mean that Dad did not treat my mother as an absolute equal. He always did. It simply meant it was someone whom she would trust with her life. And so it was. Dad embraced Mum's Scottish missionary background. She had been born in China before the Second World War and fled to Canada during it, before rejoining her own father back in Edinburgh. In Edinburgh, like him, she studied medicine. My own Dad said on meeting Mum's father that he was one of the most 'saintly people' he had ever met, but also good fun. I would now say the same thing about my Dad and that was no doubt what Mum saw in him too, and why she married him. A humble and godly man, who at the same time had a good sense of fun. Both my parents quite simply were, and are, 'saints'. They made everyone feel welcome and special at home and my own faith came out of the sure and certain truth that I am, and have always been, loved.

Love, Prayer and Study

The love they demonstrated was so beyond human. I never heard them say a bad word about anyone, neither of them ever swore, or used any bad language, and rarely raised their voices or rebuked us in anger. They assumed the best of everyone and never looked down on anyone. Dad would always get into a taxi and ask the driver how he was, and talk to, and be open with, everyone, something he passed on to us. Once they stopped their car because they saw a girl weeping, who had just got off the bus. We pulled up and it turned out she had left her final manuscript for her PhD on the bus. In those days, there was no laptop and that was the only copy. She got in the car and we chased the bus up the road, caught up with it. She leapt out and managed to get it back. It was selfless and unconditional love and concern for others, not just their immediate family, that struck you. Yet they both always attributed it to God and never to themselves. I noticed this from an early age.

They would sit in bed each morning, having their morning cup of tea, and pray together for a long list of friends, as they read their Bible passage for that day. They would then listen to the news on Radio 4 and go to work. Every day, a wonderful routine.

Dad's enthusiasm meant that they encouraged me in everything I tried to do and Mum's advice, 'never to say behind people's backs what you wouldn't say in front of their face', become my ideal standard at school and beyond. If someone was behaving badly, we were always reminded it was probably because they were 'insecure' and 'didn't feel loved' and it was then a task of ours to see if we could make them feel loved and secure. We are all, after all, in some ways insecure and our own security lies in God. But beyond being 'good people' my father was fully supported by my mother and was allowed to be the shining star that he was. I asked her the other day how she felt about Dad and she said that her marriage had been 'too short', a marriage that spanned decades. It was very touching to hear.

Dad had an amazing start in life. His own father had been editor of *The Times* during the Second World War, which meant he met all sorts of interesting people, from Lord Astor to Winston Churchill. He spoke of remembering going to stay with the Astors in Cliveden as a child. They had to flee to the countryside but his father had to stay in London to oversee the daily publication. His father described walking back to his club and seeing the London sky ablaze from the blitz, but St Paul's Cathedral still intact. Hearing that it had survived the blitz brought great hope to my father and his brother.

Dad never much spoke of the big blow that losing his own father when he was aged seventeen must have been to him. When I lost my closest friend at school at exactly the same age to meningitis, it was to him that I turned for comfort and not to my mother. I think this was because I knew he would understand it. Her death was just before my A Levels were due to begin. His wise, motivating words were very helpful. He talked about the choices facing me: 'Either of feeling sorry for yourself, moping about and not working, or making a difference in the world that would make her proud of you, of working hard and getting into Cambridge.' His words helped me recover and carry on. He was practical as well in his encouragements, making me do a 'specimen hour' when I was stuck on a school topic or later, at university, during an essay I was trying to write. He knew full well that sometimes the battle to work was just starting the task. From that place, many more hours would no doubt flow.

As well as his love of people, Dad also spent a good deal of time in study and prayer. He had a scholarly routine he never strayed from, which was his secret for managing his time so well. He was always up early, around seven and had a bath. He would often come up with ideas in the bath or out walking with the dogs. He would read all his sermons aloud to Mum – and to Mary and me, if we were about. He liked to test them out and then go back and scribble some last-minute notes. He was forever a seeker, moving on to the next thing with great enthusiasm. It could be hobbies such as birdwatching or the books of Kierkegaard, Dostoevsky, Tolstoy and, of course, his beloved Hegel.

Coventry

The biggest change for me, in moving to Coventry, was the visible sign, for the first time, that my father was a clergyman. Whilst he was at CMS, when friends at school asked what my father did, I could simply say he 'worked for CMS'. Most people would not know what that stood for and assumed it was something like IBM and left it there. It was not that I was ashamed of Dad being ordained, it was simply that it was not really part of our day-to-day lives growing up. He was never in a parish and, as I grew up, Mum and Dad lived in their own home in Park House Gardens, East Twickenham. There we spent many happy hours, playing by the river, or with our cocker spaniels that Mum bravely decided to breed, whilst Dad was often overseas and she was a partner in a local doctor's practice. Looking back at it, I still do not know how she juggled so many things alongside bringing up two children. Suddenly, in Coventry, we were all thrust into the spotlight and it was a big change for us all.

The house itself was huge, more like a boarding school or hotel in size. I remember the first day I went to my new school, which was just around the corner from our home in the 'posher' area of the town. As I walked past the end of our driveway a new friend joined me and asked me where I lived? I pointed back and said, 'Oh, just over there.' The response was, 'Yeah, right, sure you do!' I was too embarrassed to set her right and it was only a couple of days later, when she saw me walking back up the drive, she realised I had not been joking! That really set the tone for my time in Coventry. It was the start of, in a sense, becoming public property. When we moved from our private and idyllic childhood in London, my sister and I were immediately thrust into the limelight, as well as my father. At school, children made jokes like, 'don't swear on the Bible, swear on Helen.'

Somehow, because my father was in the church, people thought I should be a harlot or a saint – in rebellion or towing the line. I was in fact just normal and so were my parents in the way they behaved. It was this sheer normality that won everyone around to my Dad and to me. Most of my mates referred to him affectionately as 'the Bish'. We would have great parties, where we played with water pistols made from Mum's old plastic injection cases. We would fire them out of the upstairs balconies onto unsuspecting people below. Meals full of fun and laughter continued, with larger tables and more silverware. It meant Mum and Dad might have forty for lunch, when I came back from breaks at school, instead of ten. Whatever space they have had, they always managed to fill it and appreciate it. The Bishop's house became somewhere that was a home to many.

Magdalene College

His presence followed me to Magdalene, where I found a friendly and welcoming college, with people who still remembered him and some of whom knew him very well. I found out that he was the only chaplain whose college did not have a 'sit in' in the 1960s. The dons who remembered him put this down entirely to him as someone who was able to relate to the students. He made the effort to connect with every student in Magdalene so, they said, there was nothing really 'to rebel' against. With him in charge of the chapel and pastoral care they had someone to come to with all their grievances. Although Dad was a great talker and raconteur, he was also an attentive listener. When you spoke to him you felt him giving you his full and undivided attention. I could always turn to him for advice on any subject, including boyfriends, what we got up to at school and parties. Nothing shocked him and nothing was off-limits. It was always wise, kind and thought-through advice.

Recently I found his typed notes on 'Stripping of the Altars', a book I read before coming up to Cambridge. In his usual way he had sought out the book, then recently written by the Director of Studies in Theology, Eamon Duffy, and had given me a wonderful exegesis of it. Dr Duffy's new take on church reformation history was to transform the discipline. At the time he only knew my father a little, but over the years he became more than just a supervisor to me. When Dad had a sabbatical at Magdalene, a year after I had left studying there, his guest rooms were just below Eamon's own rooms. They formed a firm friendship over a good Scottish malt, which my father always enjoyed, a friendship which lasted right up until my father's death. Then, and after the move back to Cambridge, they bonded over a love of people, theology, good food and wine.

Dad would often talk about Magdalene in the days when he was there and became the youngest chaplain they had ever had. I took for granted my father's tales of C.S. Lewis (Jack, to his friends), who became a firm friend and ally in his time as chaplain. Another well-known Cambridge figure, the collector of modern art, Jim Ede, was a family friend. We would visit his home in Edinburgh on our way up to our little cottage, Culdunie, Nethy Bridge, in the Cairngorms, every year. When Jim died, I came back from Germany (on my gap year) to sing at his memorial service at Kettle's Yard, the wonderful, original home of Jim and his wife, Helen, which Dad had visited so much as an undergraduate and then as chaplain, when he had lived opposite it in Northampton street.

He and Jim prevented the little church, St Peter's, next door, from being knocked down in 1960s, when it was under threat. We all enjoyed watching Jim's book, *A Way of Life,* spring into being. He would call over with it and talk to Dad about it, as it was progressing. This was a long and painful process in the making but a thing of beauty on completion. These figures of my childhood, and Dad's stories, were something I never realised would be significant to anyone but me. And yet, the truth that so many love Lewis's work now made me realise how many interesting figures Dad had met with in his life: Nelson Mandela and Desmond Tutu (who came to stay with us in Coventry), Mother Theresa and Patricia St John, Jim Ede and Charlie Moule and even Dylan Thomas, when he came to Cambridge. He never bragged about it: they were simply friends and part of his life.

In the 1960s, when he was Dean and Mum and Dad were newly married, their entire house was given 'Jim's touch'. Mum very kindly allowed Jim Ede to arrange their furniture and objects. He encouraged them to have simple white covers and dark wheel-back chairs. He has been a huge influence on all of us, myself and my sister, in our aesthetics, and given us a real appreciation for things of beauty old and modern, from nature as well as created by humans.

Jim educated Dad and all of us into an understanding of modern art. I found myself absorbed in Alfred Wallis and Gaudier Brzeska. Dad's enthusiasm was so catching on any subject, and his love of people so immense, that he collected work by both these artists as he went through life. He also remained open and with a childlike wonder. Despite his huge amount of learning and reading he never spoke down to us, but encouraged us to learn with him. He made you feel as if your opinion mattered and also encouraged you to learn more. He would walk into a room reading out one of his sermons and ask your opinion on it and then on some Hegelian viewpoint. We were all expected to hold forth from an early age and encouraged to be fully engaged with the conversation at the table. I remember in Coventry he came back so enthused by meeting Gillian Rose at Warwick University. He loved academic and intellectual discussions but brought people with him. Gillian indeed became a dear friend of his and was, in turn, influenced by his love of Christ.

Holidays in Scotland

This routine never changed, even on holiday. In Coventry in the morning, he would write his letters and be in the study. Then we would have lunch and walk afterwards, with the dog. In the afternoon, he would have more meetings and then sometimes he would be out confirming. If we were on holiday, in our beloved cottage in Scotland, he would take the whole afternoon off to walk in the hills, not just an hour or so. His own father had always maintained that a walk wasn't really 'a walk' unless it was at least six miles. He would then come back and have tea, do a couple more hours work and then, after supper, we would gather around the fire whilst he read aloud from Sherlock Holmes, A.A. Milne, P.G. Wodehouse or John Buchan. He could change his voice to fit any character. He encouraged Mary and me to read aloud as well. We had to learn the names of the hills nearby – Mary always did this significantly better than I. We were also encouraged to learn and recite poems off by heart, reciting them on walks should a scene bring one to mind. I have continued to do this with my own children.

I felt this was perfectly normal. We had neither television nor even a telephone in our cottage in Scotland until I was around 18 years old. We went for the whole month of August and sometimes for Easter and Christmas too. We enjoyed the lack of screen time and there were plenty of other children holidaying in the valley with us so it felt like a lovely intimate community. My sister is still best friends with a daughter from one of the families that stayed in the valley too. We would build dens and make up plays and skits and we would perform them with other friends in the valley for all our parents in the evenings. We would take picnics on long walks and drink out of flasks tea that tasted of coffee and coffee that tasted of tea. On rainy days, we played many hours of card games like 'cheat' and 'beggar my neighbour'. When the dogs needing walking, Dad used to say that there was 'never bad weather – it was just badly dressed.'

There was a wonderful local church community we became part of whilst in Scotland, and Dad would often be asked to preach when we came up on holiday to give the local priest a break. His burial plot is in the Abernerthy Kirk, by Nethy Bridge, alongside a plot for my mother. They loved it so much that it became their choice as a place of rest, and they bought a plot to share many years ago.

One memorable occasion comes to mind, when my sister and I were quite small. It was a hot day and Mum was allowing us both to play outside in the graveyard, because Dad was filling in preaching in two different churches during the holidays. Suddenly, we became aware of a helicopter above and policemen on walkie talkies on either side of us saying things like, 'Capercailly to Heather Bray...come in Heather Bray.' Unbeknownst to us, an escaped convict with a gun had locked himself in the vestry. They were not exactly sure where he was, but knew he was somewhere in the church grounds and were tracking him down. Of course we were the closest people to the vestry and blissfully unaware of what was going on. Meanwhile, inside the church, Dad was about to launch into his sermon. A hand waved wildly at the back. Then, slowly, the warden walked quietly up the aisle and whispered in my father's ear, in a broad Scottish accent, 'There's a gunman in the vestry.' Dad looked up, always a good actor since his days in Footlights at Cambridge, smiled and said, 'Amen!' A rather surprised congregation, who knew nothing of what was going on behind him, were ushered out of the building, into the sunshine and safely away, whilst Dad stood in the church arch, shaking their hands on the way out. It was a much shorter sermon than they had expected. We watched amazed as the police threw smoke bombs into the vestry windows and the man eventually came out looking disheveled, with his hands up.

Royal Family

This news ended up in all the local Scottish papers, and even the national papers, including those papers taken at Balmoral. Later on that year, Dad had an invitation to Buckingham Palace for lunch. He was surprised to arrive and find a small select group of people including John Cleese, Iris Murdoch and himself. He was honored to be seated next to the Queen. She leant over and asked him what had happened with the gunman in the vestry.

He was always so amazed at how well informed the Queen was on all the goings on of her subjects and he maintained a great love of the royal family throughout his life. He was awarded a knighthood when he retired as Prelate of the Order of St Michael and St George, a happy event to which we all went. We also attended the annual Summer Garden parties the Queen would host at Buckingham Palace, where several thousand people, from all walks of life, would be invited to have sandwiches and tea or iced coffee in the wonderful grounds.

Dad was particularly fond of the Queen Mother, who taught him the card game Patience whilst he was one of the Queen's Chaplains on a weekend away at Sandringham. He was given many awards and accolades in his time but wore them all very lightly. Whatever he did, he did with fun and gusto and his sense of enjoyment was infectious.

Television and Creativity

When we got back to London from holidays in Scotland, or later Coventry, and sat and watched the television, Dad would often walk in and turn it off and say 'now go and do something creative'. Television always took a secondary place in our activities when he was around. He would continue by saying, 'My brother and I would be reading now or writing plays or drawing pictures instead of watching others doing it!' And so off we would go to do our own 'creative thing', which, for me, was often drawing or making up songs or poems. It was his own capacity to imagine what we might and could do, which made this sound like an exciting challenge and not just a rebuke.

His sparkling eye, wit, and capacity for joy, all swim around in my head. He was one of the best-read men I have ever known and yet he never made you feel as if you had not read enough. He never made you feel anything other than potentially the best you could be. It was not that we did not have the usual disagreements growing up. Mary fought our corner for the right to watch various programmes which sometimes clashed with supper and bedtime. Later, when a student on holiday at home, I was a night owl and he was a lark. He never understood my love of staying up late and working into the night, just as I could not understand his rush to be up so early. In the end we agreed to differ, but I still have the notes passed back and forth via Mum when we did not speak for a night as we both wanted to win the argument! We both inherited the B-W stubbornness too...

Taizé and the Jesus Prayer

I also decided at the age of sixteen to go 'alone with a group from my church' to Taizé, a wonderful ecumenical, monastic community in France. Mum and Dad 'happened' to go the same week as me in their car. I went on the coach from London. I joined the choir for our week in Taizé and entered into a day of silence. The time together at Taizé turned out to be key for all of us and for my father in particular. Whilst there, I enjoyed their warm showers as opposed to our cold ones in the dorm. Dad spent some time in meeting up with Brother Roger and joining in with the brothers. He even wore their vestments and went down the aisle sitting with them all one night – much to my slightly nervous gaze from the choir stalls, as I wondered if he had decided to join them and would not be coming home with us! But it was simply Dad's enthusiasm for the community that had him joining in. Dad became an enthusiast for all things Taizé. He bought the song books, the tapes, the candles and the candle holders, the icons and even the prayer stools and indeed, as a family, we all ended up being hugely influenced by the music there. We used Taizé songs regularly in our chapel at home, worshipping in harmony together. Dad commissioned a beautiful mural to adorn the chapel wall, with words around the sides, and converted it into a wonderful Taizé chapel space. The acoustics were perfect and there was something so moving about having Taizé songs and worship wafting through the heart of the house.

This love of a meditative way of life was something I recall so vividly. We went to Scotland on holiday after Dad had just been to see Brother Ramon, a wonderful saintly hermit at Hilfield Friary. Dad was as enthused by that encounter as he had been by Taizé and I could see that this was another huge step in his spiritual journey.

The 'Jesus Prayer' became an obsession for him. He wrote a book on it and then another with Brother Ramon. He was always talking about it, more and more as the years went on, and working through it. He first discovered it after visiting Father Sophrony at the Monastery of St John the Baptist in Tolleshunt Knights, in Essex. A photograph of their meeting together remained framed by his bedside until he died. As he began to draw on the Jesus Prayer more and more, it instilled a gentle quality of its own into all our lives. Dad saw it as the answer he had always been seeking in prayer, being centred and 'practicing the presence of Christ' continually as he liked to say.

Retirement in Cambridge

As my parents moved from the vast space of Bishop's House in Coventry to their small, cosy home in 4 Searle Street, Cambridge, Dad converted the attic room into his 'upper room'. He decorated it with icons, candles and prayer stools from Taizé and prayed his beloved Jesus Prayer using his prayer rope. Many a person climbed those stairs as he became a spiritual guide to so many souls in Cambridge and beyond. My mother was not as good a gate-keeper as Betty Simpson, his secretary in Coventry, had been, so he was almost too busy with the comings and goings. My husband, James, and I finally moved back to Cambridge when our children were small, in part to be close to Mum and Dad.

When we arrived, I felt he had almost exhausted himself in his helping of others. His role as Assistant Bishop in the Diocese of Ely, his spiritual direction for so many, his Honorary Fellowship at Magdalene had meant that more and more people wanted to visit and spend time with him and Mum. But they loved it and they continued right up until 2012, hosting reading parties for the students of Magdalene at their cottage in Scotland.

When I discovered Dad had been diagnosed with Alzheimer's, I wrote a poem to express my fears that his eyes would no longer recognise mine. The fact that he died from Covid-19 meant that the fears expressed in this poem never fully came to pass. As a family, we are all deeply grateful to God that he died still knowing who we were, as we sang the Taizé chant by his hospital bed, 'Jesus, remember me when you come into your kingdom.'

Dad had become a well-known figure walking up and down the tow paths by the Cam, cheering on the Magdalene boats. One of his last acts as Bishop was to come and bless a boat at Magdalene, as I stood by his side, in my clerical robes. It was somehow so natural and moving that we should both be there. A photograph of that occasion is on the back cover of this book. Our two children also came along to see the boat being blessed. It was such a happy occasion. Even as he had begun to become more frail, this was his last act before he became too sick to go out much. His role as bishop was something into which he quite naturally fell back.

That is how I like to remember him and always will: a twinkle in his eye, shining, smiling, encouraging us all on to be the best we can be, enfolded in God's loving embrace. The forgiven and forgiving sinner, who is 'failing towards' love.

CHAPTER 2

The Magdalene College Years

Ronald Hyam, Nicholas Boyle and Sarah Atkins

This chapter republishes, with kind permission, articles in the *Magdalene College Magazine 2019–2020* by two Emeritus Fellows of Magdalene College who knew Simon well, together with an extract from the 'Easter Letter to Magdalene 2020' by the Chaplain.

In Memoriam
Bishop Simon Barrington-Ward, KCMG
By Dr Ronald Hyam, Emeritus Reader in British Imperial History; Archivist Emeritus, Emeritus Fellow of Magdalene College, Cambridge.

The Rt Revd Simon Barrington-Ward, KCMG, MA. Born 27 May 1930. Educated at Eton (Scholar), Magdalene College (Matric 1950, Scholar), Historical Tripos, Pts 1 & II; Westcott House, 1954–56; National Service (Pilot Officer, RAF Regiment), 1949–50; Lektor, Free University of Berlin, 1953–54; Chaplain of Magdalene College, 1956–60; Assistant Lecturer in Religious Studies, University of Ibadan, Nigeria, 1960–63; Fellow and Dean of Chapel, 1963–69; Principal of Crowther Hall, the Church Missionary Society College at Selly Oak, Birmingham, 1969–74; General Secretary of the Church Missionary Society, 1974–85; Honorary Canon of Derby Cathedral and an Honorary Chaplain to the Queen; Bishop of Coventry, 1985–97; Prelate of the Order of St Michael & St George, 1989–2005; knighted 2001 (KCMG); Honorary Assistant Bishop, Diocese of Ely and Honorary Assistant Chaplain of Magdalene College, from 1997. Married to Dr Jean Taylor, 1963; two daughters, Mary and Helen. Honorary Fellow from 1987. Died on Easter Saturday, 11 April 2020, aged 89.

IF SIMON HAD NOT BEEN so hopeless at maths, he would never have come to Magdalene as an undergraduate. His family had close Oxford connections, and young Simon was desperate to go to his father's old college there. His Eton tutor, however, was convinced that Oxford would reject him for failing maths, and after long and difficult discussions persuaded him to try for Magdalene Cambridge. Simon won an Open Scholarship in History here in December 1948, and then had to complete eighteen months of National Service with the Royal Air Force before coming into residence in October 1950.

Simon had a famous father, Robert (Robin) Barrington-Ward, DSO, MC, a First World War hero, who became Editor of *The Times* in 1941. He married Adele Radice, of Italian descent; Simon was the middle of three children. RBW died suddenly from an insect-bite when travelling to Dar-es-Salaam in February 1948, when Simon was seventeen. Simon always regretted that his father died just when he himself was of an age to appreciate and learn from Robert's political ideas, but he was aware that his father was supportive (controversially for *The Times*) of the post-war Labour Government's social welfare reforms and promotion of Indian independence, and had long believed in evolutionary policies and 'liberating truths, at whatever cost to conventional opinion' and however painful. These formed the bedrock of Simon's social philosophy.

He was a popular History undergraduate, 'a good mixer' with many friends in different spheres. Shortly after the beginning of his second year, he decided to submit himself as a candidate for ordination, supported by the Chaplain, Tony Pearce, and his Tutor, Francis Turner, whose recommendation stressed that he was 'a man of marked intellectual ability, lively mind, wide interests, and personal charm'. However, before starting theological training at Westcott House, he spent his first year after graduation in 1953 as a Lektor at the Free University of Berlin. This was a profoundly important experience, exposing him not only to German language and literature, but also to its religion and philosophy, and especially to the influence of Hegel and the influence of Dietrich Bonhoeffer, the pastor and theologian hanged only eight years before, whose inspirational writings were starting to be published.

As Simon was finishing his training at Westcott House in the summer of 1956, Tony Pearce as Chaplain of Magdalene was spectacularly successful in being elected to a University Lectureship in Divinity. Naturally enough, he hoped and indeed expected that this could be combined with promotion to a fellowship at Magdalene. The College authorities, however, hesitated to make a tenured appointment and worried about his 'high church' Anglicanism; they denied him a Fellowship. Pearce therefore decided to resign as Chaplain and to leave Cambridge for Australia, where he became a distinguished Canon of Perth Cathedral. The College was likely to be left without a chaplain for the beginning of the new academical year, but realised that Simon was due to be made a Deacon on 30 September. He could therefore be appointed Chaplain from 1 October 1956, before his ordination as a priest, which took place the following year. If this was a gamble for the College, it was nothing less than a privileged and exciting opportunity for the youthful new Chaplain. Simon later recalled:

> From the start I loved it. I was virtually an ordained under-graduate, close to those amongst whom I was working. The Chaplain was a figure accepted by everyone... The Chapel was almost as much part of the College's life as Hall. It was packed out every Sunday evening... Everyone wore one of the surplices that hung in the Ante-Chapel.

This, and most of the other old traditions, were still in operation. All undergraduates had had to declare their religion on their application form. It was not difficult being Chaplain in such a community, and it was hugely enjoyable, joining High Table every night, and talking among others to C.S. Lewis as a Professorial Fellow.

In 1960, with Simon's five-year appointment drawing to a close, he accepted an Assistant Lectureship in Religious Studies at the University of Ibadan in Nigeria. This was another formative step for him, opening up the exciting world of Africa, of African religion, and Anglican mission. But in 1963 the College decided to try to tempt him back with the offer of a fellowship and the post of Dean of Chapel which had long been vacant. Simon accepted eagerly, and all seemed to be arranged. Then came the news that Simon was getting married. A shocked and agitated Master (Sir Henry Willink) announced this to the Fellows, suggesting that they could hardly say they didn't want him after all, just because he was no longer unmarried and wouldn't live as a bachelor chaplain in College. The Fellows learned that he had married Dr Jean Caverhill Taylor, who was practising in Nigeria, the daughter of Dr Hugh Taylor, a medical missionary who had served in China. When Simon and Jean first met, they discovered that each of them had furnished their rooms with identical curtains designed by John Piper. It was a Sign, surely?

The College was about to witness an unprecedented double pastorate. At their home in the newly-converted Northampton Street cottages, with the paired Piper curtains now on facing walls, Simon might be in the living room giving spiritual comfort and guidance to one undergraduate, while Jean was in the kitchen dispensing medical and psychological aid to another: these rooms could be entered separately, so complete privacy was assured to students seeking their complementary but equally warm-hearted and understanding practical help. But although many individual members of the College were thus helped enormously, Simon was acutely aware that the overall role of the Chaplain was much diminished. The College was quite suddenly entering a time of rapid and disconcerting change, the beginnings of an aggressive reform movement known to history as 'the Students' Revolt'. As he recalls:

> I had returned to a transformed scene. The cultural shock was far greater than anything which the vital spiritual turmoil of Africa had confronted me with.... Amid the welter of cults, enthusiasms, Utopian passions, Chapel had no place. I was part of the rejected 'Establishment'... The faith I had articulated seemed now too bland and glib. What is more, I realised I had become estranged not only from many of those I was trying to reach, but even from my former self.

It was a crisis for his ministry. He began to see the limitations of that older comfortable world which had shaped him. The framework he had relied on seemed to be falling apart around him. He began to sense something of the impatience of the rebels, to accept the need for evolving change, the need for a genuine 'death and resurrection' in the world and in Magdalene.

For a start, he embarked upon a radical redesign for the Chapel, encouraged by his friend Jim Ede of Kettle's Yard. Out went the last of the Victorian panelling; the ornately carved Edwardian altar was evicted and put into storage, replaced by a serviceable table rescued from an undergraduate room; the walls were repainted in uncompromising 'brilliant' white. Simon wanted to get rid of the Victorian glass windows which made the Chapel dark and dreary, and fill all of them (except the Pugin east window) with plain glass. This would be a major alteration, requiring Governing Body approval. The College's

Architect-Fellow, David Roberts, a Welsh Nonconformist, supported him, arguing that the Chapel was the chaplain's work-space and he should have as light and modern a facility as possible. The Governing Body was not persuaded (eventually a sensible compromise was adopted, involving the radical modification of the two worst windows, those at the sanctuary end).

As the Students' Revolt intensified, Simon thought he might usefully act as a go-between, a moderating, reconciling influence. However, a new Master and a traditionalist Bursar were nervous and sceptical about this. It was suggested to Simon that he might like to move on and further his ecclesiastical career.

Thus it came about that in 1969 Simon moved to Birmingham to become the first Principal of Crowther Hall training college at Selly Oak, the start of his momentous connection with the Church Missionary Society, of which he was appointed the General Secretary in 1974. He joined an historic line of leaders of the CMS, all of whom had biographies written about them, in recognition of the importance of their role. Simon was now right at the centre of reconciling modernisation, rejecting the old missionary authoritarianism and devising an evolving 'partnership in mission'. He travelled the world, writing a striking series of newsletters about what he found: thoroughly characteristic, stylish reflections, their regular arrival eagerly awaited. They have been published as an anthology, *Love Will Out* (1988), hailed as one of the finest statements of 'mission theology' for the late-twentieth century. As the General Secretary, he and Jean lived in a CMS semi-detached house close to the riverside at Twickenham and the bridge to Richmond. It was here that their daughters Mary and Helen spent most of their childhood.

If the General Secretaryship marvellously fitted his talents, enthusiasms and experience, the same was hardly less true of his appointment as Bishop of Coventry in 1985. It was greeted with something like a general acclamation. He received nearly 500 letters of congratulation, including, it seemed, greetings from almost everyone who was anyone in the Church of England, and many others besides. His openness to all things German, and competence in its language, was of especial value in developing Coventry's links of reconciliation with Dresden Cathedral, while his experience of Coventry itself resonated with his own spiritual vision of brokenness followed by redemption and renewal. 'Reconciliation' was now a central theme of his ministry: it was something which called for 'the sharing of the gift of forgiving love with others'. If it sometimes called for an un-popular stance in opposition to the government, he took it: his fa-ther would have been proud of him. He attacked unconscious racism, opposed the Thacherite poll tax and policy towards apartheid, and joined Archbishop Desmond Tutu in calls to free Nelson Mandela. As Bishop he chaired the International Affairs Committee of the General Synod Board for Social Responsibility, and the Partnership for World Mission, together with various other bodies.

Magdalene was the cherished thread which ran through seventy years of his life. Simon spent a sabbatical term as Bishop living in Mallory Court. His links with the College were decisively renewed and strengthened with election to an Honorary Fellowship in 1987. When the question of the admission of women to the College became a live issue he seized the chance to set out his vision of what he hoped Magdalene would become by 'transposition'. He wrote as follows:

> I am sure that it is important that the College can demonstrate that its real character and quality are able to be translated ef-fectively into contemporary terms without being in any way distorted or diminished... a mixed community in which still, more than ever even, the truly Magdalenian virtues, of humane, Christianly-rooted relationships, of a valuing of the whole per-son and not just of the intellect, can be cherished and realised, through... continuing resilience, imagination and readiness for fresh exploration.

It was no surprise when Simon and Jean decided to retire to Cambridge in 1997, and live as close to the College as they could. A house in Searle Street was found for them by Rosemary Boyle. They got to know a whole new generation of appreciative students and Fellows. During a term's interregnum in the chaplaincy, Simon was the acting Chaplain.

Simon was a man of almost unlimited imaginative insight and cul-tural breadth and refinement. Many will remember his joyful bursts of song, or his clear calligraphic handwriting, which remained un-changed throughout his life since his early teens. He had a childlike sense of fun, and could sometimes be seen in full ecclesiastical rig, speeding down Castle Hill into Magdalene Street on his drop-handled racing bike. Inevitably his shortcomings were the obverse of his vir-tues. The fluency and spontaneity sometimes meant an absence of focus and intellectual control: the sermons that went on too long, the important monographs on Nigerian religion, or contemporary spirituality, which never got written, the muddle that might overtake social engagements. But he made even vagueness seem endearing. He was in some ways a stern and committed pastor, but of great human sensitivity and sympathy, a genuine intellectual with considerable powers of critical judgment and understanding. He had an instinctive gift for kindly, unembarrassed and cheerful friendliness, and he developed into an inspirational figure who could reach out to all sorts and conditions of men and woman. There was a sheer joyful abundance in what he was able to share lovingly with so many others. It was always a joy to see Simon, whether for a long and stimulating conversation, or just briefly in passing, for you could always be sure he would greet you with his unquenchable good humour and enthusiasm.

> He was, in the fullest meaning of both words, a Catholic ecumenist, with more than a trace of the mystic.
> – Canon Paul Oestreicher

Memoir of Simon Barrington-Ward

By Professor Nicholas Boyle, Professor of German Literature and Intellectual History and Emeritus Fellow of Magdalene College, Cambridge.

Simon was Magdalene to me before I knew Magdalene. I first heard of him while I was still at school, from my future stepfather, Rockley Boothroyd (1958[?]), who told how, as he drove away from the college after graduating Simon shouted out after the departing car (won in a raffle for sixpence) 'Rockley! Read that Bible!' (which Simon had given him some weeks earlier). I was left with the impression of 'Simon B-W' as the central someone-who-knew-everyone in a sunny place peopled with characters from *Genevieve* or *Bachelor of Hearts*. When I came up to college myself, though, Simon was Dean of Chapel, having just returned from West Africa, and was already felt to be one of the intellectually more adventurous fellows. I imagine that was why my Director of Studies, Dick Ladborough, called on Simon's help when I presented him with my first essay in French, on something to do with the relation between prose and poetry. Bemused by my conceptual contortions, Dick asked Simon to work out what on earth I was saying. Simon, acutely, came to the conclusion, 'The

36

author makes in the last sentence a neat get-out from the confusion he has I think created.' On the way to that conclusion, however, he had followed every twist of my shifting definitions, remarking as he did so, in words prophetic of the whole future of our relationship: 'The synthesis is not Hegel's synthesis, quite.'

We spent over fifty years together trying to decide the meaning of that 'quite'. (I believe that when Anglican bishops gathered in conference Simon was known among them as the preacher of the gospel according to Hegel.) Simon's early, and personally decisive, time in Berlin and his openness to German culture made for a special connection between us, as did his devotion to the cause of the reconstruction of Dresden. In later years, as he ascended the church hierarchy, his occasional visits to Magdalene, and especially the sabbatical he spent here while still bishop, were delightful opportunities to hear him talk of Hegel and Nietzsche and Gillian Rose, always seeking the key that would unlock the treasury of ideas he wanted to pour into the book that would bring it all together. In the end he settled for the shortest of books on the shortest of prayers, the Jesus Prayer. Perhaps after all he did find the key he was looking for.

For a Magdalene undergraduate in the mid-1960s (the term 'student' was not then current in Cambridge) Simon and Jean's tea-parties in Northampton Street were one of the places, along with the Kingsley Club and the Writers' Circle, where serious talk was possible on anything under the sun – I remember discussing P.F. Strawson's *The Bounds of Sense* with him when it had just come out and when certainly one of us, possibly both, had yet to read it. Anything you had to tell him about a lecture you had been to, a book you had read, something that had happened to you, inspiring or otherwise – Simon would take it up with a deep desire to understand and with an ever-cheerful enthusiasm for the good cause, for any good cause, convinced, and convincing you, that it would somehow prove to be part of the great and as yet undiscerned scheme of all things. He was particularly kind to me when, like many, I suffered something of a breakdown in the approach to finals.

Simon embodied both an ideal of Magdalene and a certain reality of it too. The ideal that he communicated to us, who had little knowledge of the serious business of the college's senior members, was the ideal of a cultured society devoted principally to the affairs of the mind and the soul, but respectful of physical and practical achievement, whether in politics or mountaineering, and enjoying, in moderation, like Sir Stephen Gaselee, the pleasures of good living; a society of gentlemen, of course, but classless; of Christians, no doubt, but tolerant towards sceptics; of amateurs, yes, but so highly literate, educated, and intelligent that they could, if necessary, match or outdo the professionals.

As an image of the college it was a persuasive ideal for Simon to pass on because Simon really did embody some of the best aspects of the post-war generation in Magdalene. I have sometimes wondered whether its distinctive character resulted in some way from the undoubtedly powerful influence in those years of Francis Turner, who seems himself to have been cut from rather different cloth (I met him only once). It would be embarrassing to name other examples, living or dead, still in Cambridge or elsewhere, but they have always struck me as sharing a family resemblance with Simon. Gently refined manners; an often diffident charm; a marked sensitivity to the feelings of others and to the nuances of words that reposed, I think, on a never-stated confidence in a common culture, a culture in which everyone deserved respect for occupying their own individual place; an equally discreet but always guiding conscience; a disarmingly self-deprecating acceptance of personal limitation. Most people had only some of these qualities, but Simon had them all. He also had something else, perhaps inherited from his father, for he had some at least of the gifts of a great editor: a huge curiosity, an understanding of the peculiar gifts of very different people, a sense of how they might all be brought together for a common purpose, and a surprisingly persistent determination when he knew, or thought, he was right. He had the truly Pauline ability to be all things to all men while remaining unmistakably and unalterably himself.

Somehow he even navigated a course in the Magdalene fellowship between those he called 'the college Whigs' and the others, whom he did not label but whom I suppose logic would require one to call the Tories. It was his great strength, as it was his weakness, that he always saw the best in everyone, even when it wasn't there. Mickey Dias, who had something of the opposite failing, at least where his colleagues were concerned, often enjoyed pointing out, sometimes mischievously, sometimes more fiercely (especially in matters of college discipline) how Simon's 'cottonwool', as he called it, had blinded him to the obvious. However, as Mickey's longstanding friend, colleague, and victim, Simon repaid him at his funeral with an exceptionally generous, kind, and insightful memorial address. There were people who sometimes were irritated by Simon, but no one really disliked him, and nearly everyone loved him. Even on the darkest day it was a ray of sunshine to see that cheerful enthusiasm in his face. 'Enthusiasm' after all means 'having God inside you', and in that sense there can be no doubt that Simon was an enthusiast.

Extract from Easter Letter 2020 to Magdalene College

By The Revd Sarah Atkins, Chaplain and Fellow of Magdalene College, Cambridge.

It was Simon and Jean who introduced me to the Reading Party when I was a finalist here. Six of us undergrads were transported to their cottage, Culdunie, in the Cairngorms. It was a different frontier then, not the Southwold shoreline but a Scottish snowline. I think it's fair to say we all experienced that week with them in that place as somehow liminal. We were half in the familiar, with friends and books lugged up from Cambridge, and half on the edge of another world, a life of joyful simplicity, caught up by the glorious freedom of the wind in the mountains. Most of all, we felt that when Simon talked, when he listened, we were on the cusp of something. A veil was drawn aside. We could glimpse a reality, a joy, a hope, that had been there all along, but that we'd somehow missed.

It felt right, then, somehow, that Simon died on Easter Eve, the day when the Church stands on the shoreline of Night and Day. For many in the Chapel community this year, as we held Simon and his family in our hearts, the journey from Good Friday to Easter Day was much more poignant.

CHAPTER 3

Ministry as the Bishop of Coventry

Clive Handford

Introduction

IT WAS THE FEAST OF THE EPIPHANY, 1986. Snow was on the ground. Simon Barrington-Ward, newly consecrated, walked to his Enthronement in Coventry Cathedral. Clad in alb and gold amice, he walked alone to the front of the nave, knelt and prayed. Michael Langrish, Diocesan Director of Ordinands at the time and later Bishop of Exeter, recalls:

> The crib scene was nearby, with the three Kings offering their gifts to the infant Saviour. It was as if our new Bishop was joining them in doing the same thing.

It was a completely natural action with nothing contrived about it at all. Those who noted this and remembered came to see it as a symbol of Simon's life and ministry. Prayer, sometimes agonised, was at the very heart of it.

A Learning Curve

All new bishops find themselves on something of a learning curve. For Simon, it was particularly steep. He came with virtually no parish experience. He had never been part of a bishop's staff meeting. As his splendid, and utterly discreet, Personal Assistant, Betty Simpson, recalls, the only confirmation service he had attended was his own. The practice of anointing, which some of the parishes followed at confirmations, was a mystery to him. Betty Simpson remembers that Fr. David Bruce quietly and effectively taught him what to do. Betty's knowledge of the diocese and the wisdom and experience of Keith Arnold, the Bishop of Warwick, were of enormous importance in helping Simon find his way around and come to terms with the task to which he had been called.

Simon saw that a key part of a bishop's role was to be a leader. For that his experience as General Secretary of the Church Missionary Society had prepared him well. The distinction is sometimes made between leadership and management. Simon embodied that distinction. A leader he clearly was: a manager or administrator he certainly was not. He was fortunate to have two excellent Personal Assistants, for most of the time Betty Simpson and, for his last two years in Coventry, Christine Camfield. The latter recalls the detailed briefings that had to be provided before any meeting or engagement:

> I vividly recall a question from Bishop Simon very early on in my time with him, when he had to take a packed lunch with him to London. Before he left, he said 'Am I not to eat my sandwiches on the train?' I had a sort of cold clutching of the heart because I then realised that every detail had to be covered in his briefings. It was that question that brought home the responsibility I had in the facilitation of the ministry of the Bishop of Coventry, including when sandwiches were to be eaten!

Bishop Michael Langrish comments:

> I had a sense that he was good at delegating responsibility to close colleagues and trusting people to get on with the job. But sometimes he delegated when he should not have done, particularly when difficult pastoral decisions had to be taken, when it was often left to the Archdeacons to undertake the task.

Coventry Cathedral

Simon very much appreciated the role of Coventry Cathedral. He always enjoyed being there and had a good relationship with the Provost, John Petty. His background of teaching in Germany and fluency in the German language enabled him to take a particular interest in the work of the Ministry of Reconciliation. Canon Paul Oestreicher, its leader at the time, wrote in a sensitive obituary in the *Church Times* of how Simon was a firm supporter and loyal friend, always ready to respond positively to ideas, even sometimes before they had been really thought out.

One of the great cathedral occasions that Simon loved was ordinations.

He brought to them, as to every service, large or small, his infectious enthusiasm and warm smile. There was about him no hint of pomposity. We always seemed to have 'The Servant King' as the offertory hymn. You could be sure that Simon would go around singing it for the next two weeks.

Ordination of Women

1994 saw the first Ordination of Women to the Priesthood in the Church of England. In 1992, at the time of the General Synod vote in favour, Simon, while very much approving, was concerned for those members of the clergy for whom it would cause distress. He telephoned them all to assure them of his continued support and prayers, as well as his readiness to meet with them, individually or together. As the ordination approached, we were concerned about those who would feel that they could not receive our sacramental ministry because we had ordained women to the priesthood.

Simon and I discussed whether one of us should abstain from the ordination in order to preserve some unity within the Diocese. It was not an easy decision because we were both clearly in favour of it happening. Simon, I believe, had been from the outset of the debate. I was a slightly later convert, having been initially hesitant for ecumenical rather than fundamentally theological reasons, but by the time I moved to Coventry I was firmly in favour. In the event, we decided that for one of us to abstain would be a kind of fudge which would cloud our support for the women we wished to affirm and would have the air of living a lie. Like other bishops, we then had to live with the consequences. In the event, the Ordination was a very happy and affirming occasion. As the procession moved from the ruins of the 'old' cathedral to the 'new' (though they are technically one cathedral) we were greeted by a group of Roman Catholic nuns holding banners with the words 'Well done Anglicans!'

As expected some priests from the Catholic wing of the Church chose to stand apart and not take part in any activity involving women priests. Others continued to be involved in diocesan life but held back from sharing sacramental ministry. One or two continued to take a full part, despite their misgivings.

When the Provincial Episcopal Visitors were appointed to enable acceptable sacramental ministry for those who in conscience could not accept ours, Coventry Diocese became, in this regard, under the care of the Bishop of Ebbsfleet. The first incumbent was John Richards, formerly Archdeacon of Exeter. Simon immediately felt that John should be regarded as part of the team and be invited to staff meetings. He came at least from time to time. Simon's warm welcome and John's eirenic stance made this a positive and beneficial experience.

Staff Meetings and Shape of the Diocese

Staff meetings with Simon presiding were always fun. You never knew what interesting suggestion he might throw into a discussion. One decision was that we should take part in a Myers–Briggs Personality Types Consultation. We invited Bishop Michael Whinney to lead this. I was the only one who had done this before, on two occasions. Encouragingly, my type came out as the same each time. What emerged at the completion of the process was not just the unsurprising finding that Simon was an extrovert, but that we were each, two bishops, two archdeacons and the diocesan secretary, complementary one to another. This was a team put together by Simon and speaks both of his leadership and instincts.

When Keith Arnold was appointed the first Bishop of Warwick in 1980, the Southern part of the diocese thought they were getting their own bishop. This feeling was still around when Simon became bishop. By the time of my appointment, I think this had largely disappeared. Simon, though, was still very conscious of it and, certainly in Warwick itself, made a point of being involved in most main activities. It is true that there was at least potentially a North/South divide. I recall Keith Arnold, my predecessor, saying to me that if you drove out of Warwick House and turned left you could be anywhere in the South of England and if you turned right, anywhere in the North. It was an exaggeration that captured a real truth.

Anglican Traditions in the Diocese

Before the Ordination of Women, I did not feel that Coventry Diocese was greatly concerned about those matters of tradition that used to be called 'churchmanship'. Differences were respected but rarely if ever became an issue. I am grateful to Bishop Graham Dow for confirming this impression from his time in the Diocese as Vicar of Holy Trinity Coventry. The way it could slightly impinge on occasion was in the matter of appointments. Simon, positive as ever, was often seemingly unaware of potential complications, particularly if a fairly evangelical person was suggested for appointment to a moderately catholic parish. As the supposedly catholic member of staff, on several occasions I felt bound to question the wisdom of such a decision. I remember Simon saying 'but he says he doesn't mind wearing the vestments', to which I replied 'but that's not quite the point'.

Especially given Simon's CMS background, some people assumed that he was an evangelical. They soon found that was a far too easy assumption. I remember Simon himself saying on more than one occasion, 'am I an evangelical? I went to Westcott House'. The plain fact is that it was impossible to put a simple label on him. At the heart of his concern and motivation was a love of Jesus, a deep confidence in the work of the Holy Spirit, a love of people and a transparent desire for their good. He was certainly charismatic, as seen in much of his preaching and speaking, yet not in any partisan or churchmanship sense. In a real way, he embodied all that was best in each of the traditions while being contained by none of them.

House of Lords

When his time came, Simon took his seat in the House of Lords. He enjoyed the quality of debate and took his part in it seriously. His background in CMS, his experience of being chair of the Church of England's International Affairs Committee and of being Bishop of Coventry all enabled him to make an informed contribution. Christine Camfield recalls:

> Of the issues he dealt with in my time it is the introduction of the National Lottery that I remember the most ... I recall that he received what felt like sacks of letters ... where people on low incomes wrote pleading that the National Lottery should not be allowed because of the fear they might become drawn into spending what they could ill-afford. I recall some very poignant letters.

A lighter side came when, like several other bishops, Simon took people from the diocese, in this instance Synod Representatives, into the House at Westminster. Mike Sharman, a long standing senior layman in the Diocese, has described how, with Simon leading, they had to go through a lengthy security check. Mike observed to the Security Guard 'but he's a bishop', to which the reply came, 'Precisely'.

Thinking and Preaching

Simon never wrote a major theological work but was no mean theologian. He could more than hold his own in any theological debate. We saw flashes of it in staff meetings where we sometimes allowed ourselves to be side-tracked into more general discussion. The Archdeacon of Warwick, Michael Paget-Wilkes, was quite often the one who set Simon off while the others of us listened in wonder to the two of them. Along with this knowledge and seeming confidence, there was, almost paradoxically, a sense of insecurity and nervousness in Simon. Archdeacon Michael recalls an invitation to Simon to address the National Evangelical Anglican Congress at Caister, Norfolk, in 1988. Simon was very diffident as he approached the occasion but went on to deliver a powerful and much acclaimed speech.

One year, Simon was invited to preach the next year's sermon at the annual Shakespeare Festival in Stratford-upon-Avon. To say he took the invitation seriously is an understatement. He bought the complete New Arden Shakespeare and took the best part of a year to write the sermon. Even Betty, his ever loyal PA, did quietly observe that it was a bit excessive, but that it was a good sermon. Others of us were quite a few times telephoned to ask if we could take over one of Simon's engagements.

A longstanding interest of Simon was philosophy, and particularly that of Hegel, whose dialectic in many ways informed his approach to life. Bishop Kenneth Cragg wrote a semi-autobiographical book, *Faith and Life Negotiate*. That may be a summary for Simon too. His own philosophy, with its Hegelian origins, he developed through his friendship, spiritual and intellectual, with Professor Gillian Rose, a Jewish Philosopher. This was very special for Simon. Their discussions and explorations led to Simon baptising Gillian. She was by then seriously physically sick. She had planned her baptism for 9th December 1995 to coincide with a seminar organised by her Department at Warwick University. The idea was that friends and colleagues should come to the hospital after the seminar to have a party and celebrate her baptism. In the event, Simon was able to baptise Gillian just before she died. He then had to go out and tell the friends who were already gathered for the party that Gillian had just died. Christine Camfield has written:

There was shock but, of course, there was also joy because Gillian had been baptised as she had wanted, and because Bishop Simon had had the privilege to be the one to baptise her.

I record this because it is another window into the heart and mind of Simon, moving from a mutual love of philosophy to a sharing of the love of God in Christ.

Bishop Graham Dow kindly brought to my attention part of Simon's sermon at his enthronement. Prefacing it with the observation 'Simon's heart was for the gospel, the transforming work of the Spirit and the Bible. It was only a matter of time before these emphases took a firmer place in the diocese'. He then quotes from the sermon:

> Like every great work of art and vision, the new Cathedral brought into its wholeness the very fragments and ruins of the old. Out of the sole sore loss and brokenness was fashioned a new harmony, a new richness, the sign of a healing and reconciling influence that was to reach out all over the world. That is what God's new love in Christ can do for us if only we will yield ourselves to Him. The ruins of our very gifts and failure can be made new and brought into a greater pattern.

Bishop Graham added 'it would not be an exaggeration to say that his sermons were an amplification of that theme and they often made similar poetic use of imagery'.

To observe Simon in the act of preaching, be it in the Cathedral or a parish church, was almost always captivating. Starting gently, the sermon increasingly gathered momentum into a crescendo, not in terms of volume but in intensity of delivery. With it went the facial expression, so often radiant. One could not doubt the sincerity conveyed both in the enthusiasm and the challenge which was always there. As in the other aspects of Simon's life, the love of God and the joy of the Gospel shone through.

Character

If there could be one word to characterise Simon it might well be 'yes'. That was his instinctive response to all sorts of people and ideas. If something new was suggested, Simon was nearly always ready to run with it. The role of those close to him was quite often to challenge or urge caution. On not a few occasions, a priest would propose something which Simon would immediately seem to embrace. It was then left to people like the archdeacons or me to follow up. The priest would say 'the bishop says...' to which we might respond, 'well, yes, but it's not quite as straightforward as that.'

Bishop Mark Bryant who at one time was Vocations Development Advisor and Diocesan Director of Ordinands, and later Bishop of Jarrow, has written:

> Throughout my time as DDO, Bishop Simon was always immensely encouraging and supportive. At times I wonder if he accepted what I said too unquestioningly. Very early on in my time in the diocese I went to him with a proposal for an ordinand whose path to ordination had not been entirely straightforward ... Bishop Simon's response was simply 'Mark, I think that is a wonderful idea. Let's do it!' History may suggest that my proposal was not one of my best!

Bishop Mark adds:

> There was always the sense that he wanted to see the very best in people. Archdeacon Ian Russell always said that he hoped Bishop Simon would be standing by his side on the Day of Judgement ... he (Simon) was always certain that if this person was given a second chance he would turn out good.

Several bishops learned to be a little wary of Simon's references.

Pastoral Care

Many people, particularly members of the clergy, have been grateful for Simon's pastoral care. It was so clearly the natural response of a pastor's heart, offered quietly, sensitively and confidentially. Nigel and Celia Adams, both ordained by Simon and serving their whole ministry before retirement in Coventry Diocese, have said that their overriding memories of Bishop Simon are of his pastoral care, his kindness and humility. Many would say the same. Nigel Adams tells of his wife, Celia, being diagnosed with cancer early in 1993. On the day of her operation for the removal of the cancer, Simon came for a Confirmation Service at Holy Cross Wyken, where Nigel was Team Vicar. At the end of the service Simon insisted that Nigel go immediately to the hospital. Nigel adds:

A few weeks later, on Easter Day, when Celia was recovering at home, Bishop Simon telephoned from the cathedral where he had just presided at the Eucharist to say that he was just leaving there to come and visit her. When he came he gave her a card showing Christ the Healer and she later had it made into an icon which, to this day, hangs by her side of our bed. Celia will always remember him as someone who gave out lots of love and sympathy.

One knew that one was listened to and remembered.

The spontaneity that often characterised Simon's pastoral response is seen in an incident shared by Bishop Mark Bryant:

> One year, at the end of the Maundy Thursday Chrism Mass, Bishop Simon was standing in front of the glass screen and people were milling around and a young couple came into the Cathedral. She was heavily pregnant and they looked as if they lived on one of the more challenged estates in the City. Simon saw them and went to speak to them and you could see his face lighting up as he spoke to them with what I am certain was deep love and concern and then what seemed to happen was that he enveloped them both in the folds of his cope and prayed with them. I often wondered what they made of what, from a distance away, looked like a very significant encounter.

Prayer

Simon's first public appearance in Coventry, the Enthronement, began with prayer. It was prayer, often deep and agonising, which one knew undergirded all he did. At the bedrock was the Jesus Prayer coming out of Orthodoxy and first met in an Orthodox monastery. After Coventry, in 2001, he published *Praying the Jesus Prayer Together* with his spiritual friend, Brother Ramon.

Simon carried in his pocket a tiny notebook. In it he would jot down a name, a problem or a situation for his prayers. Bishop Mark Bryant speaks of an occasion where they had to make a decision about an ordinand who was giving real cause for concern.

> When I met with Simon early the next morning he was greatly concerned about this man and his well-being and it was clear that he had been up at 4 am wrestling with God and praying

about this man seeking to do what was best for him.

I knew a bishop who whenever one met him seemed to say 'I do want you to know that I am praying for you'. Perhaps it was an unworthy thought, but I used to find myself wondering if he did. Simon never said that, but you knew that he was.

Bishop's House and Jean

Bishop's House had its own character. Jean, Simon's Scottish doctor wife, in a sense presided over it in a way that matched Simon's, at once brilliant yet quite scatty, but always welcoming. Christine Camfield has noted, with fondness:

> There was a sense of living in a community, because of the integration of domestic and official areas, with boundaries completely blurred. Bishop Simon's razor-sharp intellect and absent mindedness matched Jean's own intellect and absent mindedness. Together, this resulted in countless episodes of staff having to retrieve items of lost property – a sermon or a mitre – that had been carted off with laundry, destined for the airing cupboard, or from behind the chest freezer.
>
> Then there were the dogs Holly and Caspar. The latter was rather a rogue. We used to enjoy Jean's excellent soup at lunchtime but brought our own sandwiches. On one occasion I found that Caspar had eaten mine.
>
> Jean and Simon were very hospitable and great fun. The staff were invited at Christmas to look in if they wished. We nearly always went and joined Simon, Jean and their daughters, Mary and Helen. Our daughter, Catherine, still has a vivid memory of standing by the tree with its twinkling candles and Simon singing 'we will rock you' with that radiant expression on his face.

Conclusion

David Urquhart, the current Bishop of Birmingham who was Vicar of Holy Trinity, Coventry from 1992 to 2000, has written movingly:

> Simon influenced me at crucial moments in my life, as a new Christian working with BP, in my membership of the Church Mission Society, and in discerning a vocation to ordination. He and Jean were an essential force for prayer, wisdom and

hospitality in the parish of Holy Trinity Coventry and in the wider diocese. Simon was graced with enthusiasm for life and the good news of Lord Jesus. He was a man of stimulating, imaginative intellect, focused on the mission of God, profound prayer, good humoured friendship and boundless energy. Whether at the pulpit or lectern, in the streets of the city, on the highland hills or by a humble hearth-side, Simon was for me a true companion on the Way.

I am very grateful to the colleagues who have kindly shared their memories of Simon with me in preparing this chapter. There will be many memories that others too could bring, but space forbids their recounting here.

What would Coventry say of Simon its Bishop? Surely, as of Daniel, 'O Man greatly beloved'. He was indeed a man with a very large heart, who walked very close with God.

CHAPTER 4

In the Henry Martyn Centre

Ian Randall

ON 1 NOVEMBER 2003, Simon Barrington-Ward preached a sermon in All Saints Church, Lolworth, outside Cambridge. He began by saying that recently he had been reading a letter from a young man just ordained, who was a curate attached to Holy Trinity Church, Cambridge, and in charge of Lolworth parish. The letter, written to one of the curate's College friends, mentioned difficulties in composing effective sermons. The young man, Barrington-Ward continued, was Henry Martyn (1781–1812), a Fellow of St John's College, Cambridge, one of the top mathematicians in the University and one of its finest classical scholars. Barrington-Ward went on to speak of Martyn's vision of spiritual awakening, one that was indebted to the Evangelical Revival and to the preaching of Charles Simeon, Vicar of Holy Trinity.

Martyn was ordained in 1803. He was working, said Barrington-Ward, on Persian and Arabic, a Hindustani Dictionary and a Bengali grammar, and all of this was put to good use when he went to India and then Persia. The 2003 sermon, to commemorate the bicentenary of Martyn's ordination, was a classic example of Barrington-Ward's detailed knowledge of historical developments and his ability to communicate these in ways that brought events to life.[1] It was also a sermon that connected with an involvement which Barrington-Ward took up when he returned to Cambridge in 1997: the Henry Martyn Trust and Centre.

The Henry Martyn Trust

It was through the energy of John Barton, who was Vicar of Holy Trinity, Cambridge, from 1877 to 1893, and had previously been a

[1] Sermon for the Bicentenary of Henry Martyn's Ordination on 22nd October 1803, on All Saints Day, Saturday 1st November 2003, at All Saints, Lolworth. The text was Ephesians 3:17–19.

missionary in India, that the Henry Martyn Trust was formed in 1881. The date was significant. It was the centenary of Henry Martyn's birth. The new Trust, which had influential backers, was able to buy land next to Holy Trinity Church in Market Street, Cambridge, and the foundation stone for a Hall, the Henry Martyn Hall, was laid on 2 December 1886. The Order of Service for the occasion stated: 'To the inspiring memory of Henry Martyn, scholar, evangelist, confessor and Man of God, a later generation of his own Cambridge dedicates this home of Christian converse and counsel.' The purpose of the Hall was to be a meeting place in which the missionary vision that had inspired Henry Martyn could be shared. Speakers at the dedication of the Hall referred to Simeon, whose ministry 'changed the tenor' of Martyn's life and led him 'to consecrate himself to the high and holy calling of a Christian missionary'. The Hall would not only remember Martyn and what he believed, but would, as one speaker said, be 'an effectual means of creating and keeping alive in Cambridge that missionary spirit which has made Martyn's name so deservedly a household word among us'.

In 1898 the Trust also established a Library, housed in a part of the Hall, and over the decades of the twentieth century up to the 1970s the Hall and the Library were used by many students and others in Cambridge. The work was expanded in the 1980s with the appointment of an Overseas Advisor, John Cooper, who encouraged students contemplating international mission. A further, very significant development took place in 1992, with Graham Kings being appointed to the new post of Henry Martyn Lecturer in Missiology in the Cambridge Theological Federation. He expanded the Henry Martyn Library as a resource for the study of mission and world Christianity. In 1995, the Library and the office of the Lecturer moved to Westminster College and there was an official opening there on 22 January 1996. In 1998, the centenary of the Library, was celebrated and the name changed to the Henry Martyn Centre (in 2014, it was renamed the Cambridge Centre for Christianity Worldwide – CCCW). In 1999, the Centre was established as an associate member of the Cambridge Theological Federation and in affiliation with the Faculty of Divinity of the University of Cambridge.

Simon Barrington-Ward and the Centre

When Barrington-Ward retired in 1997 and moved back to Cambridge, it was natural that he would be drawn into work connected with world mission. He was happy to respond to an approach from Graham Kings to be involved with the Henry Martyn Centre. As one of the Henry Martyn Trustees from 1998, Barrington-Ward's vast experience and wise advice were much valued. From 2002–2004 he was the chair of the Trustees. As always with him, he was an encouraging presence.

David Ford, who was Regius Professor of Divinity in the University of Cambridge (1991–2015) and who in this role was a Henry Martyn Trustee, writes of his memory of Simon Barrington-Ward as:

> a quiet presence, and very affirmative (what a smile he had!) of what we were doing, especially of the big changes Graham Kings was initiating. One recurrent impression was how, for all his gifts in one-to-one interpersonal relationships, he also really understood the importance of institutions and organizations. I was always aware and grateful for the fact that he knew what it was to carry institutional responsibility. He might have seemed quite apolitical, but time and again I appreciated his understanding of what it takes to get things done in an organisation, how paths from conception to action are rarely linear, and how much depends on consultation and trust-building over time. And every so often he could be the person who, when called upon, put the weight of his presence in favour of something, which therefore was carried.[2]

On occasions he would make a point forcibly; for example, in discussions that took place from time to time about the role of the Henry Martyn Hall. There was awareness that with the Centre being based at Westminster College, the Hall was no longer at the heart of the work of the Trust. Also, it was a drain on the Trust's resources. There were those who were interested in buying the Hall, but it was the view of Barrington-Ward and others that the Hall still had a part to play. Barrington-Ward argued at one stage that 'we should on no account even contemplate selling the Henry Martyn Hall, which is a vital asset to the Trust'. He was 'totally opposed to such a sale on both strategic and financial grounds'. His view was that it could again be a centre for 'recruitment' for world mission. The Trustees decided unanimously not to sell, although the passage of time would mean that meetings previously held in the Hall came to be held in Westminster College or the University Divinity Faculty. Barrington-Ward also chaired the

---

2   David F. Ford, email to Ian Randall, 7 June 2021.

Henry Martyn Library committee, which helped to give a much higher profile to the Library, as an integral part of the Centre.

The friendships in the Henry Martyn Centre led to other connections. Again, David Ford writes:

> Simon was both adventurous and faithful at the margins of the institutional Church. I was deeply involved with a little place of retreat in central Wales, now called the Monastery of St Barnabas the Encourager, begun in the early 1990s by a remarkable husband and wife, Bryan and Dorothy Scrivener. I introduced Simon, and also Donald (A.M.) Allchin, to the Scriveners, who wanted to consult about what sort of community they could become. Simon visited them in Wales, gave advice about such matters as the use of their chapel and how they might understand themselves in relation to the history of communities of prayer, and gave his episcopal blessing to their development. He succeeded, together with Donald Allchin, in helping them to evolve into a unique sort of community that was simultaneously deeply related to Orthodox, Quaker, Evangelical, and Black Pentecostal forms of Christianity, while yet remaining recognisably Anglican.

The Henry Martyn Centre Archive was expanding considerably in the 1990s and into the twenty-first century. A range of Barrington-Ward material was presented to the archive by Simon and Jean in 2000. One box of Barrington-Ward material in the archive, with 63 items (folders SBW 1-3), has been fully catalogued. The cataloguing was done by Carol Pickering. The largest part of this section of the archive (SBW 1) comprises letters to Simon or Jean or to both. The letters are virtually all dated in the 1970s and 1980s. There are also some miscellaneous papers (SBW 2) gathered by the Barrington-Wards. The third section in this box (SBW 3) comprises papers found within books which Simon donated to the Henry Martyn Library at that time from his personal library.

By far the largest element in the current Barrington-Ward archival holding in the Centre is in four large boxes, deposited more recently. Although this holding needs arranging for future researchers, for the purpose of offering insights that have come out of what I am calling my 'archival delvings' I have drawn from these boxes, looking especially at material from the early period up to 1975, rather than the period after Barrington-Ward became the CMS General Secretary.

Because the material has not been catalogued there are no footnote references. I have grouped the material here under periods and themes.

The Archives: the Move to Nigeria

The post Barrington-Ward applied for in Nigeria was Senior Lecturer in Church History, Department of Religious Studies, University College, Ibadan. The archive has his application. His referees were Sir Henry Willink. QC, Master of Magdalene College, Owen Chadwick, Master of Selwyn College and Dixie Professor of Ecclesiastical History, University of Cambridge, and C.F.D. Moule, Fellow of Clare College and Lady Margaret Professor of New Testament Studies, University of Cambridge.

The application referred to providing teaching for the University of London BD and a BA in Theology. When a chaplain at Magdalene, Barrington-Ward had taught courses in Early Church History in the University of Cambridge Theology Tripos. He stated in his application that he would like to do research on the Church in Nigeria, with a view to wider historical study of Christianity and Culture. This fitted with the Department's emphasis on studying Christianity in Africa and in particular in Nigeria.

A letter of 2 August 1960 offered Barrington-Ward the Ibadan post. The appointment was for three years from 1 October 1960. He would, the letter stated, need to be vaccinated against smallpox and yellow fever. One of the letters as he prepared to move was from the influential historian John Walsh, in Oxford, who wrote on 11 August 1960:

> I suppose this Sunday will be your last at Magdalene. I give thanks for your ministry there, and that you have not preached the word there in vain, but have brought with God's grace many to His knowledge.

Walsh was thankful that as Magdalene Chaplain, Barrington-Ward had nurtured 'a living cell of Christ's kingdom on earth'.

Barrington-Ward entered a very different world in Nigeria, which had just become independent. He described a University College that dated from 1948, having been set up with British Colonial Development and Welfare funding, and having received £1 million from the Cocoa Marketing Board. There were 1,000 students in Arts, Science, Medicine, Agriculture and Veterinary Science. The College's library had 105,000 volumes. Ibadan, about 90 miles from Lagos – on a tarred road – had a population of about half a million. Only 1,000 were Europeans. Barrington Ward had particular responsibility for teaching 60 students of Religious Studies.

It is evident in the archive how much Barrington-Ward's contribution in Nigeria was appreciated. One letter, from an African, speaks of Barrington-Ward as having more of a spiritual impact in the College than any others of the – mainly European – staff. Barrington-Ward showed a determination to understand African culture and spirituality. In the archive there are extensive hand-written lecture notes he wrote and used. They concentrate on the history of Christianity in the context of Nigeria and more widely of West Africa. There are also notes of sermons he preached in the College's 'Resurrection Chapel'. One letter speaks of how he 'brought the presence of Christ when he preached'. He led what were 'moving services of worship', and called people to commitment. There are references to his love for people and readiness to listen and help where possible. These and other qualities, said one correspondent, have made 'an indelible imprint on my mind'. Another wrote: 'I cannot fully explain my gratitude for your kindness and hospitality.'

In touch with Cambridge from Nigeria

The correspondence in the archive shows that Barrington-Ward kept in close touch with events in Cambridge. His closest friend at Magdalene was the Bursar, J.F. (Jock) Burnet, and Burnet's side of the correspondence offers many insights, although Barrington-Ward's side does not seem to have been preserved. They enjoyed discussing books. There is also reference to Nigerians whom Barrington-Ward was commending to further their studies in England, perhaps at Magdalene. Others with whom Barrington-Ward was in touch included Nathaniel Micklem, the retired Principal of Mansfield College, Oxford. Micklem wrote to say that he had very much appreciated a letter he had received from Barrington-Ward and he hoped to see him in the summer of 1961.

The summer of 1961, which Barrington-Ward spent back in England, involved some heart-searching on his part. He was invited by the Westcott House Council to be the Westcott Principal, succeeding Kenneth Carey. This was an adventurous move by the Council, since Barrington-Ward was only thirty-one. The process of thought and prayer on Barrington-Ward's part included consultation with family and others, and although his letter to the Council does not appear in any documents in the archive, the reply is there, from E.C. Ratcliff, Regius Professor of Divinity in the University of Cambridge and chair of the Council. Ratcliff wrote on 31 August 1961:

> I will not pretend that the decision which you have reached is not a disappointment to us. You explain your decision so fully, however, that one can entirely understand and appreciate if one still regrets it. From what you have written, I can see the issues before you: it would have been something of a betrayal of Ibadan had you accepted our offer and you would not have had a peaceful conscience at Westcott House. All I can do then is to wish you all blessing and happiness in the work in Ibadan.

Among others with whom Barrington-Ward kept in touch was Kenneth Carey, then Bishop of Edinburgh. Carey had hoped that Barrington-Ward might have followed him at Westcott, but wrote on 31 August 1961 to say that he had 'no doubt now' that Barrington-Ward's decision was right. He continued:

> It's painful for Jock and me in particular. But your letter makes it clear that you couldn't have looked God in the face if you had agreed to come to Westcott... So now, be at peace and don't let the devil give you after-thoughts. It's decided.

Maurice Wiles, Dean of Clare College, Cambridge, had taught in Ibadan and was helpful in discussing Nigeria. Another person in the conversations was Robert Runcie, then Principal of Cuddesdon, who wrote to say that a talk Barrington-Ward had given at the College had done 'a power of good'. Runcie affirmed the 'difficult decision' that had been made about Westcott. Barrington-Ward had also kept the Principal at Ibadan, K.O. Dike, informed, and on 9 September 1961 Dike wrote to Barrington-Ward, who was staying in Oxford, to thank him for his letter explaining that he had refused the Westcott principalship. Dike, recognising it had not been an easy decision, said: 'I congratulate you all the more for your courage in sticking to what you consider to be the right decision in this matter. I am looking forward very much to your return to Ibadan.'

'Christ's ministry in Nigeria' encouraged from Cambridge

Having re-committed himself to the three-year contract at Ibadan,

Barrington-Ward settled back there. Again, the archive offers insights. Although he wanted to spend as much time as possible with Africans, there were opportunities for relaxing with staff colleagues. There was also a demanding level of correspondence. One of those in Cambridge, who at times plied Barrington-Ward with questions and at other times surprised him, was Jim Ede, the art collector. In one letter, Ede described an experience during morning prayer when he felt there was a 'ghostly' Simon kneeling beside him. Simon in this encounter looked 'an older and a wiser man'. In another letter Ede said he had been thinking how wonderful it would be for those who would hear the words, 'Well done thou good and faithful servant', but for him the thought that he might be told by God he was 'good' might make him disbelieve in God. Ede discussed his reading with Barrington-Ward. This included Meister Eckhart, Bernard of Clairvaux, and John Baillie on *The Sense of the Presence of God*. Ede reported that his reading made 'all denominations seem a bit arrogant', although beliefs were important. Love was 'beyond all'. These sentiments echoed Barrington-Ward.

The second year at Ibadan saw parts of Nigeria experiencing a State of Emergency. There was a serious economic downturn. On political matters, Simon was in correspondence with his brother Mark, then editor of the *Uganda Argos*. He was also in touch with Lt Col. G.C. Grimshaw, who had a post in London as Secretary for Overseas Visitors, about welcoming African students who came to the UK. Further letters about Barrington-Ward's future also feature in the archive in the middle of his second year at Ibadan. The most significant was on 5 February 1962, from Sir Henry Willink, Master of Magdalene, who stated that if Barrington-Ward wanted to come back to Cambridge there could be a possibility at Magdalene as Dean of Chapel and a Fellow. Willink wrote that he would 'encourage the Fellows to feel as I do, that we should try to get you back here'. He concluded by asking Barrington-Ward to consider this.

February 1962 saw Barrington-Ward in serious consultation with others about this challenge. Kenneth Carey was unequivocal: the need for an effective Dean of Chapel at Magdalene was great. Also, Carey considered that the need in the University of Cambridge generally was pressing, as the Christian leadership present in the University in the 1950s was not as strong in the 1960s. C.F.D. Moule voiced a similar opinion. Barrington-Ward's gifts would, in Carey's view, contribute significantly in Cambridge in 'the next five rather critical years'. Carey's advice, which turned out to be prophetic, was '*Reculer pour mieux sauter*' – go back to jump further. Writing at the end of February, Jock Burnet wrote that he 'did not flatter himself that he could guess what the Holy Spirit was up to', but suggested that it had been necessary for Barrington-Ward to go to Nigeria and it was now right for him to come back to England 'because in the long run you will do more for Christ's ministry in Nigeria by persuading others to go there'. Striking a rather more reserved note, Maurice Wiles wrote that he had been talking to Max Warren, who felt that prospects back in Cambridge were are 'not at all bad' if Barrington-Ward returned.

The Return to Magdalene

Events moved quite rapidly behind the scenes. Burnet wrote in one letter about his dream coming true, to have Simon doing work in Magdalene 'of tremendous importance'. He said that the College did not expect that Barrington-Ward would be content to stay for more than five years, 'but some of us hope that you might be drawn to the life for longer'. Barrington-Ward was still concerned that he might be 'avoiding the cross' by leaving Nigeria, but Burnet reiterated his view that there would be more people going to Westcott for ordination training and more going to Nigeria if Barrington-Ward's influence was at work in Cambridge. Barrington-Ward replied to Willink officially, and there is the response from the Master, dated 27 April 1962. He wrote that there was 'great joy among the Fellows, to whom I reported your decision at a Governing Body last night, that you, D.V., will be with us again in 1963'. Willink echoed Burnet in saying that there was work Barrington-Ward could do for Africa from Cambridge.

Over the late spring and summer of 1962, the arrangement at Magdalene had not yet been made public, but the Master and the Bursar both believed that it would leak out. Barrington-Ward himself had some continued anxiety about the move, and Kenneth Carey had to reassure him that the decision to return to Cambridge was right, and urged: 'don't worry about it any more'. Simon was not returning alone, but with Jean. The archive has many letters of congratulation on their engagement and marriage. One letter from a colleague in Nigeria said that Simon needed to be 'congratulated for being so lucky as to have been chosen by this angel on earth'.

The official announcement of Barrington-Ward's election to a Fellowship at Magdalene and appointment as Dean of Chapel came in October 1962, with an announcement in *The Times*. The last year

Barrington-Ward spent in Ibadan was one in which he seems to have experienced mixed emotions. On the one hand there was encouragement gained from affirmation by others. Letters spoke of him – and this was to be a recurring theme – as a 'spiritual father'. He especially appreciated letters from African students, such as one who wrote, 'despite colour we are one'. On the other hand, there were those who suggested that if he had stayed on at Ibadan he could have accomplished more. A letter on 24 February 1963 from Solomon Odunaiya Odutola, Bishop of Ibadan, was particularly blunt. He wished that Barrington-Ward had spoken to him, as Bishop, about the future. The Bishop's view was that Nigeria needed people like Barrington-Ward, but now he was seen as having 'carried coals to Newcastle by going back to Cambridge'.

Another source of anxiety – referred to obliquely – had to do with the Department. One letter spoke of Barrington-Ward 'doing the charitable thing by leaving the field to an older man who is probably coming to the end of his career'. Given the worries Barrington-Ward had evidently been feeling, Burnet wrote on 7 April 1963 to offer further assurance, emphasising once more that 'what you can do for Nigeria in Cambridge will ultimately be far more than you can do for Nigeria in Nigeria. I will eat any sort of hat if this is not true.'

Experience of Renewal

In the three years in Nigeria, Barrington-Ward became deeply committed to understanding African history and culture. On return to Cambridge, he found that the whole society at home had changed and that an experience of breaking and remaking, which had been present before, was again crucial. He found help in charismatic renewal. Correspondence in the archive does not make much reference to this, but in typical fashion Barrington-Ward began to wrestle with the meaning of what was happening in his own thinking and experience and to include it in his lectures. His handwritten lecture notes in the archive give ample evidence of this. Barrington-Ward began to look for models of renewal in history that would be relevant to societies in Britain and elsewhere in the contemporary world.

His notes look at specifically Pentecostal denominations, notably Assemblies of God, Elim, and the Full Gospel movement and others. He noted that there were members of Pentecostal churches who did not speak in tongues; in Chile, he observed, a majority of Pentecostal members and even some pastors did not do so. He then looked at renewal in Anglican, Baptist, Methodist, Presbyterian, Roman Catholic and other Churches. He suggested there were gifts given for use in worship and ministry ('given freshly, like the manna') such as wisdom, knowledge, healing, miracles, prophecy, discernment, tongues, and interpretation of tongues. He saw the Ephesians chapter 4 gifts of apostles, prophets, evangelists, pastors and teachers as more permanent. Not surprisingly, he drew attention to insights from Africa, where, he wrote, healing and religion have always been linked. The gift of healing through prayer was 'complementary to general medicine'. On exorcism, he referred to the Maasai in Tanzania where women were 'used in exorcising evil spirits through the Word of God'.

Barrington-Ward insisted that it was Christ who 'gave gifts to the church'. These were, in St Paul's teaching, 'gifts of grace not rewards'. As gifts, they could 'cut right across natural ability'. Thus a person did not need to be a linguist to speak in tongues. Barrington-Ward's view of the baptism of the Spirit was that 'we are nowhere commanded to be baptised in the Spirit, but to be filled'. He was adamant that the New Testament did not portray 1st and 2nd class citizens (Spirit-baptised or not) in the kingdom of God.

For him, 1 Corinthians 14:39–40 was a key text, with Paul's call to 'be eager to prophesy and do not forbid speaking in tongues', and for this openness to operate 'together with good order'. He saw preaching and prophecy as distinct. When a word of prophecy was given, he added, it 'is not always 100% accurate'. With prayer for miracles, he suggested two models of petitionary prayer: Matthew 21.22: 'Ask in faith and you will receive'; and 1 John 5.14–15: 'Ask according to God's will and you will receive.' There were two keys in this area: discernment and making sure God received the credit. In response to the objection that these forms of worship and ministry are 'not our custom', Barrington-Ward went back to the Bible as his authority. At the same time, he warned against despising 'the old familiar things'. His notes ended with a prayer: 'Lord Jesus when you returned to heaven, you gave gifts to men. Pour out on us afresh your very precious gift of Him who brings your risen life to thirsty souls and bodies, even the Spirit of God.'

The Community of Crowther Hall

In 1969, a new opportunity opened up for the Barrington-Wards, as John V. Taylor, the General Secretary of CMS, invited Simon to lead the new CMS Training College at Selly Oak, Birmingham, named

Crowther Hall. From 1969 until 1975, Simon and Jean threw themselves into this work. The archive has many letters from former students, who went on in most cases to serve with CMS. They gave reports to the Barrington-Wards about their mission situations. It is striking how many expressed appreciation not only of the training they had received but also of the friendship offered by Simon and Jean. The medical advice Jean had given was mentioned by several. Crowther Hall was described by some as 'A Christ-centred community', led by a couple with gifts of 'fostering love in community'. Although the letters from the Barrington-Wards to the former students are not in the archive, it is clear that these letters brought encouragement in challenges that were faced.

A selection of letters in the early 1970s shows that from Crowther Hall individuals and families had gone – for example – to Iran, North and South India, various part of Africa, and Turkey. Barrington-Ward suggested to one student who had a science degree that he consider teaching science in Africa. This became a reality, but the challenges were considerable: a letter back said the school had not heard of a test tube. Another former student, a Scot from Fife, was in Uganda, and reported on the East African Revival. Barrington-Ward was to give a great deal of attention to this Revival. A fellow staff member at Crowther and a Ugandan pastor who came to stay both brought a vision for deeper relationships, a vision that owed much to the Revival.

There was something of a creative fusing, for Barrington-Ward, of this African Revival movement and charismatic renewal. The latter was present at Crowther, as it had been in Cambridge. One former student, Mary Ingle, wrote in 1972 from Turkey, recalling that on her last day at Crowther, Dennis Bennett, an American who was one of the Episcopal leaders of the charismatic movement, had come to speak, and she was happy to hear that the students in 1972 were 'such a good group'; and, she added, 'several baptised in the Spirit!' Although most who trained at Crowther were with CMS, some were with the Wycliffe Bible Translators and one went on Operation Mobilisation's ship, the *Logos*.

In March–April 1973, Barrington-Ward undertook an extensive tour to visit CMS missionaries and others, presaging his travels as CMS General Secretary. He wrote notes, as he always did, describing his experiences – on this occasion in Bombay, Delhi, Varanasi, Bihar, Calcutta, Nagpur, Bangalore, Karachi, Lahore, Rawalpindi, Peshawar, Kabul, Tehran, Beirut and Cairo. His most impressive encounter in India, he wrote, was with Mother Theresa. He spoke of her work as fusing spiritual depth and material compassion. Her advice, which seemed to apply to those training for mission, was: 'Teach them to love and send them out among the people and let the people teach them. Then they can reflect on what they have learned.' From his further experiences in parts of the world outside Europe, Barrington-Ward began increasingly to emphasise global perspectives. The West, he said, 'lives with excess consumption, waste and pollution. We have to live in cheerful protest against it.' He also suggested that there were problems with the West setting the agenda for global development.

During 1973–74, correspondence took place between Barrington-Ward and Robin Baird-Smith, of the publisher Darton, Longman and Todd (DLT), about the possibility that Barrington-Ward might write a fairly small book that spoke to what Baird-Smith called 'the renewed interest in the theology of the Holy Spirit'. It was agreed in an exchange of letters that this book would explore how 'the Holy Spirit affects prayer and worship'. It would be for general readers; DLT was publishing more 'technical' books in this area, by Simon Tugwell and Gordon Strachan. Baird-Smith visited Crowther Hall and for a time it seemed that the book would go ahead. The title was to be *Possessed by Love,* although one advisor commented that charismatics were seen in many places as 'extremely divisive', and their 'love' would need explaining and defending. One of the books Barrington-Ward consulted at this stage (which is in the archive) came from an ecumenical group in South India that took in Anglicans, Eastern Orthodox, Moravians, Pentecostals, Presbyterians and Roman Catholics. It was entitled *The Witness of the Spirit and Charismatic Renewal* (1972). Despite the hopes for a book by Barrington-Ward, it was not written, but much valuable thought had been stimulated.

Conclusion

There is a great deal more than I have outlined here that can be drawn from the Barrington-Ward archival holdings in CCCW, and I hope that one day a PhD student will take advantage of them for a thesis on his work. The content of his lectures, as can be seen from his hand-written notes, was profoundly theological and missional. He ranged across the world and across the centuries. They would repay study in themselves. Here I have traced some of the characteristics that can been seen in parts of the archive in the period 1960–75. The letters – even if these are largely from others to him – show his desire to always learn from others, to foster deep friendships, to look out for strategic opportunities and to seek to understand the movement of the Holy Spirit in the world. There is much more that can be examined for the period of his General Secretaryship of CMS, with many letters and many detailed reports as he travelled. These supplement his printed letters. Much of the material has the power to speak today. In one lecture he called for a faith that was 'not the tired custodian of the ruins of an outworn culture but the leaven of a new life of love'. This was echoed at the conclusion of his 2003 sermon at Lolworth, when he gave this blessing: 'Now to Him who by the power at work within us is able to accomplish abundantly more than all we can ask or imagine, to him be glory in the church and in Christ Jesus to all generations for ever and ever. Amen.'

Church and Mission

CHAPTER 5

Interchange and Partnership at CMS

John Clark

Introduction: Personal Memories

I FIRST MET SIMON in the summer of 1973 in Tehran. As Principal of Crowther Hall, he was paying his first visit to Iran, a major mission field for the Church Missionary Society. Simon was later to become a valued support and adviser to Bishop Hassan Dehqani-Tafti during and after the travails the diocese had to pass through at the time of the 1979 Iranian Revolution. I had been approached to take on management of the publishing sector of a newly formed inter-church publishing and bookshop company, drawing together the historic publishing and bookshop work of the Presbyterian and Anglican/ Episcopal Churches in Iran. I had been advised to apply to CMS to return to Iran under its auspices and this was a chance to introduce myself to him. I found him bright and supportive to a young man who was rather daunted by the reputation of the great CMS.

Having applied to CMS I was selected for training at Crowther Hall during Simon's last term as Principal in the autumn of 1974. I had actually seen him in the train to Birmingham but was hesitant about approaching him, as he was deep into a book entitled *Depth Psychology and Religious Belief,* about which I then knew nothing. But we did meet on the bus to Crowther Hall! That term at Crowther was immensely invigorating personally, spiritually, and emotionally. So much of that flowed from Simon himself for he brought a warmth, an inspiration, and a sparkle to his leadership of the community, to worship and to meetings. In one-to-one sessions one felt one had his full attention. He carried those same gifts into his time as General Secretary. But those of us there were aware of the nervousness and anxiety he felt at taking on the General Secretaryship.

When I became Regional Secretary for the Middle East and
Pakistan in May 1980 I worked under Simon until his appointment
as Bishop of Coventry, for three years of that time as part of the team
of Secretaries. The Secretaries would meet on Thursdays each week,
under Simon's chairmanship, and twice a year in winter and summer
for four days at St Julian's Coolham. These were times of great stimu-
lation, debate and ideas that led to changes and to action. He would
normally respond positively to ideas put to him, often without assessing financial consequences. Harry Moore, Home Secretary, used to
comment wryly that his role was to follow after Simon to say 'No' to
commitments he had made.

A noticeable feature of the obituaries to Bishop Simon Barrington-
Ward has been the omission of any significant reference to his ten-
year term as General Secretary of the Church Missionary Society. This
may be because the writers knew him best as Bishop of Coventry. But
the omission is important for it fails to recognise that Simon was in
the ranks of the great General Secretaries of the Society. It was under
his leadership that what had been formed in 1799 as 'A Society for
Mission to Africa and the East' added to that calling to become a
Society also engaged in Mission in Britain and a proponent of the role
of the voluntary society in Partnership in Mission.

In this chapter I want to consider: the challenges Simon faced; his
vision for Interchange and its practical outworking; his clarification
of the aims of CMS; the inclusion of Mission in Britain as an aspect
of CMS and the consequent restructuring of CMS' national office; the
principle of Partnership leading to the development of Partnership
for World Mission Partnership House and the term 'mission partner'
in place of missionary; the ordination of women; the role of the voluntary society; and the development of membership structures for
CMS.[1]

Challenging Role in the Mid-1970s

Simon took on the role of General Secretary of CMS in January
1975. In many ways he was an obvious choice to succeed two influential leaders of the largest Anglican evangelical missionary society
in the Church of England and Anglican Communion – Canons Max

---

1   I have drawn on my chapter, 'CMS and Mission in Britain: The Evolution of a Policy' in Kevin Ward and Brian Stanley
eds, *The Church Mission Society and World Christianity, 1799–1999* (Grand Rapids: Eerdmans, 2000), 319–343.

Warren (1942–63) and John V. Taylor (1963–74) on his appointment as Bishop of Winchester. Son of an Editor of *The Times*, educated at Eton and Magdalene College Cambridge, of which he became a popular Chaplain, Dean of Chapel and Fellow, he had seen the value of CMS work (as well as meeting his wife Jean, a CMS missionary) when he had lectured in Religious Studies at the University of Ibadan Nigeria. He had successfully managed to establish Crowther Hall as a new missionary training centre for CMS, set amongst the missionary and educational training colleges at Selly Oak, Birmingham. He not only had the background but also the warm, compassionate personality, a gift for informality and a desire to listen and learn from others that brought a freshness of touch, a lightness of spirit and vitality drawn from a deep spirituality, to the role.

It was a challenging time to assume the leadership of a large organisation. CMS was in the throes of discerning what the role of a voluntary Anglican missionary society should be in a rapidly developing Anglican Communion in which local Anglican leaders were taking over so many of the roles formally held by missionaries.

Max Warren had been an adviser to Archbishop Geoffrey Fisher on the establishment of independent Anglican Provinces overseas. One consequence for CMS was merging CMS work into that of the local church. This included handing over institutions (largely medical and educational) to local leadership and ownership, dismantling the structures of CMS missionary committees and CMS representatives to be replaced by indigenous leadership. It was well expressed by Bishop Hassan Dehqani-Tafti, the first Iranian Bishop on his appointment in 1961 who told Max Warren that he did not want a separate CMS representative or CMS Committee in Iran: all missionaries were to come under local church leadership.

Under John V. Taylor that process had continued as new independent Anglican Churches were formed. New structures were developing in the Anglican Communion to provide forums for discussion and guidance. For example, alongside the Lambeth Conference of Bishops, the Anglican Consultative Council, formed in 1968, was intended to be the pan Anglican Forum in which episcopal, clergy and lay representatives of the newly forming provinces could meet for discussion and decision. New patterns of relationships between churches and voluntary agencies were being formed.

In the search for direction for CMS John V. Taylor had a vision of the Society becoming a 'Community of Commitment' for Mission and

Service. This did not win acceptance, but he did establish a General Council at which representatives of CMS Associations (members groups) could both gain an overview of CMS activities and provide overall guidance to the Standing Committee and Secretaries. One of his bequests to Simon was the development of this membership structure as a means of involving CMS members in the oversight of the Society and not just recipients of information, prayer concerns and requests for donations.

One of the traditions into which Simon entered was that of the monthly *CMS Newsletter*. Started at the beginning of the Second World War by General Secretary W. Wilson Cash to keep in touch with CMS members it had been developed to a level such that it had become vital reading for many Church of England bishops and clergy. John V. Taylor had continued to write a monthly newsletter. Both he and Simon referred to their 'terror' at entering into the tradition of the *CMS Newsletter*. The reading for, and the writing and constant revision of, successive Newsletters in Simon's spidery black ink was always in the background of his ministry.[2]

Financially the country was going through a period of inflation rising to double figures and reaching over 25% due to the tripling of oil prices, following the October 1973 Arab–Israeli War. Costs at 157 Waterloo Road were under tight control, so much so that the blank sides of used carbon copies of memos and correspondence were reused for further copies. It was only the decrease in the number of CMS missionaries (despite campaigns such as that for 150 new missionaries) that enabled the Society to avoid significant financial deficits.

Interchange

Simon made clear at his first General Council of CMS members that one of the guiding themes of his general secretaryship would be Interchange. It is summarised in the Minutes of that meeting:

> The idea of giving and receiving, of exchange, of interchange had become for him [a] dominant theme... of people entering into one another's worlds... a network of glowing fire, of grace, of shared joy and pain... CMS was emerging as an informal personal movement of giving and receiving... The new impetus that was coming through this theme of interchange called for

---

2   See Chapter 7 below.

a right balance between emphasising our continuing role as a 'sending' agency and the new possibilities of enabling people to make a contribution here.[3]

This theme of an exchange of gifts, insights and experiences through which the Holy Spirit could flow was to run through his time at CMS. Theologically he drew it from the exchange of love within the three persons of the Godhead flowing out into God's world in and through God's people and practically expressed in outflowing mission.

Its roots can be seen in Max Warren's book on *Partnership* and John V. Taylor's writings on the Holy Spirit, *The Go-Between God*,[4] both of which spoke of the importance of relationship and the personal. But Simon expressed the principle by providing two practical foci, which would influence other aspects of CMS' calling. The first was the Interchange Programme 'to bring notable Christians from one country to another to share their insights into the Gospel with those in another.'[5] The visits were mainly, but not solely, to Britain. In 1975 there was one visit and for 1976 the budget was increased fourfold.

The 1976 Report of the CMS Standing Committee described existing CMS activities as aspects of interchange, for example, interchange in multifaith communities…interchange from Britain through widening the age range for volunteer service and through a number of visits by senior staff, interchange through bursars.[6]

All were seen as means by which this exchange could take place.

The distinctiveness of the interchange programme was that those invited had come to give, not to bring news or report on CMS overseas, but to share what God was doing in their churches, to lift people's spirits and encourage witness and mission in this country. For many this was the first time they had met with Christians of another culture. Organisational practicalities were handled initially by expanding the bursaries department to cover 'interchange visitors' under Dr Hugh Sansom. Interchange visitors could be those whom Simon met on his overseas visits or recommended by CMS staff on their visits. I recall visiting the Revd Elias Chacour of the Greek Melkite Church in his village of Ibillin during the Israeli invasion of Lebanon

---

3 General Council meeting of CMS, 18–20 April 1975, minutes, 16.
4 John V. Taylor, *The Go-between God: The Holy Spirit and The Christian Mission* (London: SCM Press, 1969).
5 General Council Paper April 1981, item 6, 'Mission in Britain: Information Paper,' 2.
6 Clark, 'CMS and Mission in Britain', 336.

in 1982. Author of the book *Blood Brothers,*[7] he was working for reconciliation between Israeli Jews and Palestinians. He agreed to an interchange visit sponsored by CMS and spoke with great effect on reconciliation and the Israeli–Palestinian conflict during his first visit to the United Kingdom.

A second stage can be seen in the longer-term appointment of a Nigerian Chaplain, the Revd Ken Okeke, to assist English Churches in welcoming Nigerian Christians to their congregations. However, it rapidly became clear that there was a need for extensive pastoral work among Nigerians in this country, particularly in London and this became the focus of the ministry initially largely funded by CMS and supported by a small committee. Such appointments went through a number of titles from 'long-term interchange visitors' to 'joint appointments' until well after Simon's time they became in 1988 'mission partners in Britain'.

But longer interchange appointments also included returned missionaries. Roger and Pat Hooker, who had served in India, were appointed to engage with people of other faiths. Christopher Lamb led a joint inter faith project with BCMS. And I well recall a visit by local vicar, the Revd David Wickert, to a lunch with CMS Secretaries in the Waterloo Road offices at which he challenged us about what CMS was doing in mission in Waterloo when so many office workers left the area every night. Simon felt convicted and responded with alacrity that the Society had a responsibility to support the local parish. Soon the Revd Tim Naish was appointed to the staff of St John's Church, Waterloo, to assist in mission in the parish.[8]

A complementary approach was taken with the appointment of the Revd John Ward as Members' Training Secretary. Here the intention was to draw on the members of the Society in Britain and to assist them in their local situations to engage with others.

This emphasis on Interchange was to contribute to the decision that CMS should engage in Mission in Britain.

Clarifying the Aims of CMS

Just as his predecessors had sought to redefine CMS' role in the light of changes in the world and the development of the Church in what was then known as the Third World, so Simon led a review of the

---

7 Elias Chacour with David Hazard, *Blood Brothers: the Dramatic Story of a Palestinian Christian working for Peace in Israel* (Grand Rapids: Baker Books, 1984).
8 Canon Tim Naish is currently Canon Librarian of Canterbury Cathedral, having previously served with CMS in Zaire and Uganda, and lectured at Ripon College, Cuddesdon.

broad aims of the Society at the beginning of his service. The result of that review and many discussions was formally adopted by General Council in 1980 and laid out for popular publicity in a film strip *Aiming to Share*.

The three overlapping circles of a Venn diagram contained the words 'Sharing in spreading the gospel'; 'Sharing in the renewal of the church', 'Sharing in creating a society based on gospel principles' to highlight Simon's and CMS' understanding of 'holistic', all of life, mission. At the centre, where the three circles overlapped, was placed a cross as the source from which all Christian mission derives: the self-giving, sacrificial death of Jesus Christ for the whole world. But around the diagram was an outer circle, with the threefold repetition of 'Interchange' separated by the words 'people', 'resources', 'insights'. The filmstrip took the form of Simon travelling across the world and discovering examples of Christians in action to illustrate the points in the Venn diagram.

This restatement of how CMS regarded mission provided a framework for speaking about the work of the society as well as assessing requests for grants and for missionary personnel as to where, and how well, they fitted the pattern of 'Aiming to Share'. It was a clear, timely restatement of the text on the front of CMS offices at 157 Waterloo from Mark's Gospel: 'Go forth to every part of the world and proclaim the good news to the whole creation'.

Mission in Britain

It was during Simon's time that CMS took the decision to move from being a Society that worked overseas to one that also engaged in mission in Britain. In one sense the Interchange Programme, bringing people to encourage British Christians in their mission, was a harbinger. But it was an open letter asking for help from the Revd John Holden, formerly a CMS missionary in Uganda, and then vicar of Saints Peter and Paul in Aston, Birmingham, one of the largest urban parishes in the Church of England, that set the ball rolling.

In preparation for General Council discussions and decisions Simon produced a paper outlining current CMS involvement in Britain,[9] such as support for missionaries who had returned to this country, the interchange programme, community relations work, a joint interfaith project with BCMS under the Revd Christopher Lamb. It was made clear that CMS would seek to make a contribution that

---

9   'Mission in Britain: Discussion Paper,' CMS General Council, 23–26 April 1981.

would distinguish it from (and not compete with) other Societies and Organisations such as the Church Army or the Church Pastoral Aid Society, in that it was based on 'the principle of interchange – namely the gaining of Christian insights through crossing cultural barriers.'

There was a two-year process of discussion and discernment for this was a major development for a Society formed for mission 'to Africa and the East'. It was not anticipated that it would be a large-scale involvement but as Simon put it to the General Council, where the decision was taken in 1982, it would also be a response to the challenge churches overseas were increasingly making to CMS about 'what it was doing in its own country, for some of them felt that the West was possibly in greatest need of mission work today.'[10] CMS would not decrease its primary calling to mission overseas, indeed overseas work would be strengthened and 'in the context of interchange there would be mutual enrichment'. And at that meeting it was resolved that the CMS Standing Committee should instruct the Secretaries to set up 'fresh initiatives in mission in Britain'.

Restructuring CMS in its National Office

One of the consequences of the decision to undertake mission in Britain was that a restructuring of the staffing arrangements in CMS' offices at 157 Waterloo Road was needed. Simon engaged Charles Handy, a consultant in organisational behaviour and management, who asked probing questions about the role of the society to assist the Secretaries to work out the best structure to facilitate that role. In essence it became clear that CMS had moved from solely sending people and money overseas to become an agency of brokerage, namely in the exchange of people, finance, resources and insights in five regions of the world: South and East Asia; the Middle East and North Africa; West Africa; East Africa and the Sudan; and Britain.

So, in 1983 Simon oversaw one of the most substantial central office reorganisations. In place of an Overseas Division of four departments for mission in Asia, the Middle East and Africa and a Home Division covering all work in Britain, five separate Departments were formed for the five regions listed above, alongside three departments: for finance and administration; personnel; and communications. These were set up to cover the three resource areas of money, people and information. It was what was termed a matrix organisation in which decisions were taken at the intersection of region and resource.

---

10 CMS General Council Minutes, 15–18 April 1982, 1–2.

It involved major changes for the Home Division now renamed Britain Region. The Home Division had previously been responsible for sharing news, raising funds and recruiting missionaries, but now was to take on responsibility for mission in Britain. The Area Staff Team's role was developed to include assisting members in mission in their localities stimulated by news from overseas.

Partnership

The word 'Partnership' dominated discussion of the relations between Churches and mission agencies of the Anglican Communion in the last three decades of the twentieth century and it was significant alongside 'interchange' in Simon's time as General Secretary.

The increase in independent Provinces in the Anglican Communion raised the issue of their mutual relationship and support, as many of the new Provinces came from areas of great poverty. The concept of 'Partnership' became the overriding theme. A 1963 Anglican Congress in Toronto used the phrase 'Mutual Responsibility and Interdependence' as key to the new relationships. With experience the practical outcome in the 1970s was to set up a process of Partnership in Mission in which different churches would hold consultations with partners (namely other Churches of the Communion) to determine mission priorities and how they would be resourced by partners.

This raised issues for the Church of England. International mission relations involving people and funds were undertaken by the missionary societies as distinct from the governing structure for the Church, the newly formed General Synod (1970). The solution was the formation of the Partnership for World Mission in 1978 as the forum in which the recommendations of Partners-in-Mission consultations in different Churches of the Anglican Communion could be considered and Church of England representatives appointed for consultations. The PWM Committee had representatives of General Synod and the General Secretaries of the nine major mission societies. It was with some caution that some agencies agreed to take part, fearing a takeover by the Church structures. But Simon was always warmly supportive of improving relations provided the varied callings of the different societies were respected and pressures for the Societies to become a Board of Mission, under Synod oversight, for the Church of England, were resisted.

Under the Chairmanship initially of Bishop David Brown of Guildford (himself a former CMS missionary in Sudan) Church of

England representation at Consultations, and responses (through the mission agencies) to priorities identified in the Partners in Mission Consultations, were worked out. But these discussions also helped identify areas for closer cooperation.

The first Secretary of PWM was Canon David Chaplin, who came from the Anglican Communion Office, where he had set up an extensive programme for the different churches of the Communion to hold consultations. Simon was concerned that when David retired he be replaced by someone who could raise the profile of world mission in the Church of England and he persuaded Bishop Pat Harris, former Bishop of Northern Argentina, to leave his parish of Kirkheaton to take on that role.

Under One Roof, which became Partnership House

Out of the closer co-operation that arose from the PWM discussions emerged the vision for the Church of England world mission agencies being based in one building, which would act as a kind of World Mission Centre for the Church of England, with the PWM Secretary as the host. Simon was an enthusiastic proponent. In his last two years as General Secretary the plan was finalised by which CMS Headquarters, renamed Partnership House, would become that building. USPG, needing to sell their offices in Tufton Street, agreed to move into the building as did Rwanda Mission CMS. The offices of the Anglican Consultative Council, a tenant of USPG, also agreed to move with them. The PWM Office was located on the ground floor to welcome visitors. The work to transform and refurbish 157 Waterloo Road began in Simon's last year with CMS and USPG sharing the costs of what was to take eighteen months to complete.

Mission Partners

It was in the early 1980s that CMS Secretaries began to question whether the term 'missionary' as a noun to describe those who served overseas with CMS, particularly in the Islamic world, was still useful. It smacked of imperialism, of go-it alone white people seeking converts, when in fact this was contrary to the modern reality of (British) Christians working alongside Christians of another Church and culture engaged in witness, mission and service relevant to the local context.

By the summer of 1983 it was agreed to discuss, alternative descriptors. Suggestions like 'co-worker' or 'colleague' lacked the element of outward look implicit in the term 'missionary' but it did contain the element of shared working. I well remember the discussion at a Secretaries' residential weekend at St Julian's where the term 'mission partner' emerged. It was preferred to a phrase using the word 'companion' (e.g., 'mission companion' or 'companion in mission') because of the significance of the word 'partner'. 'Mission partner' retained the sense of looking outwards and engagement in the term missionary but added the element of partnership, working alongside local Christians. It was agreed to use the term for a limited period subject to review. That review never happened as the term rapidly gained wide acceptance and has been used by CMS ever since. It has also been taken on by many other mission societies. It has even been applied anachronistically to those who served with CMS in the nineteenth and early twentieth centuries.

The Ordination of Women

In the late 1970s the question of the ordination of women grew in importance in the Church of England. It was important to CMS because one of its missionaries, the Revd Joyce Bennett, was the first English woman to be ordained deacon (1962) and priest (1971) by Bishop Baker of Hong Kong. It was an issue that Simon took up with conviction. As campaigns in the early 80s by the Movement for the Ordination for Women (MOW) and debates took place in General Synod, he felt it important that CMS should take a clear position in support of women's ordination. It was controversial for the evangelical world was seriously divided on the issue and support for women's ordination could have lost parish support for the Society. But he produced a clearly argued theological and practical case for CMS taking a position on the issue which he took through Standing Committee such that CMS' decision in favour of women's ordination was a notable milestone on the road to ordination to the diaconate in 1988 and to the priesthood in 1992.

The Role of the Voluntary Society

CMS has always maintained the principle of the voluntary society in contrast to those who would have preferred the missionary arm of the Church of England to have been an agent, or Missionary Board, of its national structure, the General Synod. Simon was a warm supporter of the voluntary principle but in an Anglican ecclesiology the voluntary movements should be sufficiently far from central structures that they could express their distinctive callings, but close enough to ensure they could influence and draw from those structures.

Simon's considered statement on the role of the missionary society came in one of his Newsletters *Missionary Movements: A New Phase*. He was clear that:

> the missionary order or society is simply one expression of a missionary spirit which exists in the local church and the Church universal. The society becomes a kind of sign or sacrament of the Church as a whole, just as the Church is a sign or sacrament of the coming kingdom-community. The society by the particular commitment and dedication of its members should point the local church itself to its own essential character as a committed community.[11]

Drawing from the examples of covenanting bands in the Old Testament, and the monastic and itinerant orders, he argued that voluntary movements could serve as ginger groups holding the wider Church to its missionary calling. He went on to call for the development of many such voluntary initiatives across the churches of the world. This theme was to be taken up by his successors leading in the twenty-first century to the establishment of CMS Africa and CMS Asia, and the networking group Faith2Share linking a number of such movements.[12]

Membership and Members' Council

Simon emphasised that CMS had been a membership society from its early days. He sought to develop John V. Taylor's initiative to renew and reinvigorate the CMS membership by giving members a greater role in decision making in the Society through a General Council. That Council would be drawn from the CMS Associations across the country who would send representatives to an annual residential meeting. At those meetings news from the regions was shared, often visitors from overseas spoke and key policy issues, such as the decision to undertake Mission in Britain or to support the ordination of

---

11 Simon Barrington-Ward, 'Missionary Movements: A New Phase' *CMS Newsletter* (435, September 1980) republished in Simon Barrington-Ward, *Love Will Out: A Theology of Mission for Today's World, CMS Newsletters 1975–85* (London: Marshall Pickering, 1988), 183–197. Quotation from 189.
12 https://churchmissionsociety.org/about/church-mission-society-the-big-picture/ https://faith2share.net/network/connected-networks

women, could be debated and voted on.

The meetings involved several hundred members and provided opportunity for Simon himself to inspire and lift the spirits of those who attended. The national gatherings lasted for some years before the decision was taken to move to Members' Councils in the different regions of the country. The intention was that more members could participate as the meetings were more locally rooted, involving less travel and expense. But they required a committed core of members to plan and organise them.

Conclusion

I remember Simon telling the team of Secretaries that he had been appointed Bishop of Coventry, just before the public announcement. Some years previously he had turned down an invitation to become Dean of Ely. He explained that Archbishop Runcie had told him that if he turned down the See of Coventry there would be no other offers! He was sorry to leave CMS but had completed ten years as General Secretary and needed a new challenge. As Secretaries we were sad to see him go but recognised that the years had taken their toll. He had been such a warm, inspiring, and genuine person, a friend and colleague. He had seen the Society through challenging times and given it a new purpose. It was smaller in numbers but equipped with new aims, for the new era of Mission in Britain and Partnership in Mission. We had been privileged to work with one of the great General Secretaries of the Church Missionary Society.

CHAPTER 6

Bold Humility: an Evangelical–Ecumenical Spirit

Simon Barrow

As a young person seeking my way in the world, and still finding my feet in faith as in life, I was extremely fortunate to work with Simon Barrington-Ward for three years.

This was during the final period of his General Secretaryship of what, at that stage, was still called the Church Missionary Society (later Church Mission Society). My five-year tenure in the education department at CMS headquarters also coincided with the involvement of Diana Reader Harris. She was the first woman to become President of the Society in 1969. This was the same year as the training of women and men was integrated at Crowther Hall in Selly Oak, with Simon as its pioneer. Her concern for global development issues and for tackling poverty as a key component of Christian mission (she was also chair of Christian Aid from 1978–1983) clearly influenced Simon. It was one that I was therefore enabled and encouraged to address, from a world church education perspective.

Liberationist Perspectives

I recall vividly that, within a little over a week of arriving at CMS headquarters in Waterloo Road, London (early in September 1982), I found myself sitting in Simon Barrington-Ward's office, surrounded by books and papers. We shared a sandwich lunch and entered into what turned out to be a deep conversation about the nature of the church and its mission, confronted – as ever – by multiple challenges, both local and global. The week before, Education Secretary Richard Handforth had left a magazine article on my desk. It was an interview with Simon in CMS's regular members' publications, *Yes* (to which I will return), and came along with two books: Ian Fraser's

Reinventing Theology as the People's Work,[1] and *Putting Theology to Work,* edited by Derek Winter.[2] The latter contained papers from the 1980 Fircroft Consultation of European and Latin American theologians, in which Richard had been a participant. 'You'll find these interesting, I think,' he said. 'You might mention them to the General Secretary when you meet him, too.'

Those were prescient words in more than one sense. Ian Fraser and his pioneering work with base ecclesial communities (*comunidades eclesiales de base,* CEBs) became a significant influence on me, not least when I became Secretary of the Churches' Commission on Mission of Churches Together in Britain and Ireland (CTBI) more than a decade later. Derek Winter – with whom I shared a commitment to liberationist perspectives – later became a CMS Area Secretary, and ally on educational and theological issues, too. Meanwhile, Simon himself proved to be open, insightful, gracious and encouraging of this interest in the emergence and significance of contextual theologies. His personal gentleness was accompanied by a deep passion for 'breaking open the Word, and being broken open by it,' as he once memorably put it. This meant hearing and being confronted by the gospel through different voices, not least those of poor and oppressed peoples. The CMS interchange programme became a valuable vehicle for this, bringing into the Society's orbit people from whom it might otherwise have remained distant (for reasons of geographical remit, among other things), such as courageous Jesuit priest and theologian Jon Sobrino, who spoke at a packed meeting in Waterloo Road in 1982.[3]

Back in 1979, Simon had also acceded to Asia Secretary Malcolm Warner inviting Lakshman Wickremesinghe (a Sri Lankan bishop and human rights activist who had earlier served a curacy at All Saints Church, Poplar, in the East End of London) to give the CMS Annual sermon.[4] The politically-charged take on mission and evangelism in his address had a very powerful impact on me when Simon gave it to me to read, sensing that it would connect with me. It was far from universally welcomed at the time. But Simon, though not entirely comfortable with aspects of its pungent radicalism, stood by the

---

1   Ian Fraser, *Reinventing Theology as the People's Work* (London: USPG, 1980).
2   Derek Winter (ed.), *Putting Theology to Work* (Fircroft College, Birmingham, UK, 1980).
3   Jon Sobrino, *Christology at the Crossroads: A Latin American Approach* (SCM Press, London, UK, 1978). My own copy bears an inscription from the day I met him at a meeting at CMS headquarters: 'To Simon, With great hope for liberation, Jon Sobrino.'
4   Lakshman Wickremesinghe, *Mission, Politics and Evangelism: the 1979 CMS Annual Sermon* (London: Church Missionary Society, 1979).

need to hear it and engage with what it said. Tragically, Lakshman Wickremesinghe died of a heart attack in 1983, a year after I had the honour of meeting him during his sojourn in London. One of the several messages read out at his memorial service was from the CMS General Secretary.

Meanwhile, the year before I arrived at CMS headquarters, the Annual Sermon had been delivered by another pioneer, J. Andrew Kirk.[5] In some sense this built on what Lakshman Wickremesinghe had said, though they were of rather different theological temperaments. Andrew's theme was world development and addressing poverty and inequality, viewed through a biblical lens.[6] Though his background was with the church in Latin America (an area of the world with which CMS had few links at that stage), Simon recognised him as an important 'bridge person' within the evangelical world, challenging it to take justice issues and liberation theology seriously. Andrew latterly became a mission theology consultant for CMS, and another important interlocutor in my own personal evolution out of a similar background. In particular, he joined Diana Reader Harris in encouraging both Simon, and the Society as a whole, to engage with debates around the Brandt Report.

Written by the Independent Commission on International Development Issues, first chaired by Willy Brandt (the former West German Chancellor) in 1980, this called for a substantial transfer of resources from the North to South.[7] Simon saw in it not just a call to greater global equality, but a parallel to the kind of transfer and exchange of resources and insights which was what Christian mission now needed to be about, he believed. Brandt seemed a little too reformist and ameliorative for me at the time. But the interest it evoked opened the door to producing some educational resources from CMS addressing these questions – both theologically, and in terms of the development work it supported and encouraged.

Listening, Reconciliation and Prayer

Looking back, I retain a sense of tremendous gratitude that Simon was willing to take time out of his busy schedule to talk at length to a relatively junior member of staff. But that was the measure of the

---

5   J. Andrew Kirk, 'My Pilgrimage in Mission', *International Bulletin of Missionary Research*, Vol. 28, No. 2, 2004. http://www.internationalbulletin.org/issues/2004-02/2004-02-070-kirk.pdf

6   J. Andrew Kirk, *Some Biblical Reflections on Development Today: the 1981 CMS Annual Sermon* (London: Church Missionary Society, 1981).

7   Willie Brandt, ed., *North–South: A Programme for Survival* (New York: Macmillan, 1980). Online summary here: https://www.sharing.org/information-centre/reports/brandt-report-summary

man, and of his commitment to nurturing those around him, not least the young. One of the most remarkable things about Simon, and a key element of that kindness and gentleness of spirit which marked all his relationships, was the desire to listen across the generations. That included, in my case, those of us who might have been deemed – from a more traditional CMS viewpoint – to possess a more rebellious temperament. For him, holding to Christ was central. But as to everything around that, he allowed the Spirit to blow freely, even when this took him out of his own comfort zone.

When Simon left CMS, one of those paying tribute to him was an old and unexpected friend, Maurice Wiles, who had preceded him as lecturer at the University of Ibadan. Wiles was Regius Professor of Divinity at University of Oxford for 21 years, an alumnus of Ridley Hall (where Simon was subsequently chaplain), and a controversial advocate of liberal theology within the Church of England and its Doctrine Commission. He and Simon were many oceans apart theologically. But they were still able to recognise the affection of God in each other at a key turning point like this; and to do so with gratitude. For this was an era when, thanks to Simon and his immediate predecessors, the Society was open to a wide range of voices and experiences across the expansive economy of the church. Because of this, CMS was able to bring together people of different backgrounds and formations, operating with that spirit of faithful generosity which marked what was still honourably known in some circles as 'liberal evangelicalism'. At every point, his ministry was one of hope expressed through reconciliation.

All of this was bound together for Simon by prayer and devotion. His heartfelt contributions to proceedings at the Chapel of the Living Water were frequent when he was around headquarters. You soon realised that the humility and hesychasm of the Jesus Prayer was central to his very being. Equally important was the fact Simon's mind was broad and inquiring, as one quickly discovered in conversation with him. He evinced an eagerness to go on learning, a keenness to discover fresh patterns and possibilities, and a deep desire to see the practical engagements of the church shaped by a spirituality which was at one and the same time generous and faithful, committed and adventurous.

Following on from the towering leadership provided by his immediate and renowned predecessors, Max Warren (1942–1963)[8] and

---

8   See, for example: Max Warren, *Partnership: The Study of An Idea. The Merrick Lectures* (London: SCM Press, 1956).

John V. Taylor (1963–1973),[9] Simon was conscious of the weight of their legacy and the continuing responsibility it carried. He was also desirous of helping CMS to forge the kind of paths in partnership which would be adequate to the demands of the Christian gospel in a decolonising (if far from fully post-colonial) environment.

Indeed, among the issues I brazenly raised in my first conversation with Simon was the vexed 'moratorium on mission' question, which had caused a minor storm in the 1970s. I had become aware of it partly because my own father had been a CMS missionary in Kenya in 1954 (four years before I was born), before returning home through ill health. It was from my conversations with him, and wider reading, that critical questions about the nature of mission started to arise for me. Was the gospel as we understood it essentially colonially dependent? If it was not, but had inherited that framework to a large degree, how could new gospel-based relationships and understandings arise in a radically changing missional context? Faced with such an existential challenge, John Gatu, then General Secretary of the Presbyterian Church of East Africa, had issued a strongly-worded moratorium on all foreign missionaries and funds back in 1971.[10] The immediate reaction to this abrupt, controversial action had been heated. It provoked a lively debate about the nature of the Christian enterprise. In so doing, it marked a symbolic end of the colonial mission paradigm, and initiated the start of what could be described as a postcolonial era in global Christian praxis.

Challenge, Partnership and Possibility

I think my raising of the moratorium question took Simon a little by surprise. The existence and shape of CMS eleven years on from the articulation of that challenge did not seem to have been notably influenced by the debates which had raged in ecumenical circles. That included those taking place in the Commission on World Mission and Evangelism (which had succeeded the International Missionary Council in 1971), and at the 1975 World Council of Churches Assembly in Nairobi, on the theme 'Jesus Christ Frees and Unites'.[11] But Simon was nonetheless alive to the painful issues of a Western-shaped and dominated mission agenda. He genuinely wanted to find a way beyond its wrongs and limitations. However, he felt that the

---

9   David Wood, *Poet, Priest and Prophet: Bishop John V. Taylor* (London: Churches Together in Britain and Ireland, 2002).
10   Robert Reese, 'John Gatu and the moratorium on missionaries', *Missiology: An International Review*, 1 October 2013. https://doi.org/10.1177/0091829613502143
11   World Council of Churches, 'Jesus Christ Frees and Unites', 5th Assembly, Nairobi, Kenya, 23 November–10 December 1975. https://www.oikoumene.org/about-the-wcc/organizational-structure/assembly#past-wcc-assemblies

asymmetries of power (about which he was aware, but which his establishment background made him uncomfortable towards) would be better addressed by new approaches to interchange and partnership ('a flow of people, resources, money, insights and experience'). He saw this as the path forward, rather than a severing or reversing of relationships which, for him, amounted to much more than the inequalities, distortions and failings that Gatu and others were pointing out.

This was a more comfortable view than anti-colonialists, and some closer to the edges of the church, might have found easy to accept, but it was wholehearted and sincere. In that interview for *Yes* magazine in 1981, which I mentioned earlier, Simon articulated and summarised his viewpoint in the following way to CMS Media Secretary Wallace Boulton:

> By means of this exchange, we work together with Christians all over the world, with three aims in mind. We work at sharing the gospel. We seek together new patterns of church life and witness; all it is understood by 'renewal'. And thirdly, we join with others in working out new patterns of society, closer to the gospel society as we see it in the New Testament. Well, that is really something to work at in the next ten years.[12]

This stance illustrates two aspects of Simon Barrington-Ward's time and influence as General Secretary of CMS. The first is what could be termed 'evangelical ecumenism' – wide relationships rooted in a profound commitment to the transformative power of the gospel. The second is 'bold humility' – a phrase with many and varied roots, but popularised in theological circles by doyen South African missiologist David Bosch, who explored it in his 1982 CMS Annual Sermon, 'The Scope of Mission',[13] among other places.[14] What it meant for Simon was that, far from scaling back the activities of the Society during a period of emerging upheaval (Thatcherism and Reaganism were re-writing the world political and economic order, and epochal changes were stirring in Southern Africa and Eastern Europe), he wished to strengthen and recast them. He wanted Christian mission to move decisively out from under the shadow of colonialism, and he

---

12 Wallace Boulton, 'Living with Questions: An Interview with Simon Barrington Ward', *Yes* magazine (London: Church Missionary Society, 1981) https://churchmissionsociety.org/wp-content/uploads/2020/04/CMS_OX_Yes_1980-1981_02_3-4.pdf

13 David J. Bosch, *The Scope of Mission: the 1982 CMS Annual Sermon* (London: Church Missionary Society, 1982).

14 David J. Bosch, *Witness to the World: The Christian Mission in Theological Perspective* (Atlanta: John Knox Press, 1980).

wanted CMS to play its part in achieving this. But he felt that humility about the tasks (and shortcomings) of the church could be accompanied by daring, rather than retreat.[15] Secondly, therefore, Simon saw some combination and synergy of the evangelical spirit with the ecumenical one as necessary – indeed essential – for this to be possible. Alongside this came an understanding of the church as a global, interactive community. One rooted in local realities and specificities, but united by its purpose of announcing, embodying and prefiguring the transformative arrival of God's new domain. All of this needed to happen in, through and beyond our present ideas, structures and endeavours, he firmly believed.

This was an inviting and energising vision, for sure. Simon always sought to surround himself with those who shared its excitement, and who could contribute fresh ideas and energy (as well as a respect for biblical and church traditions) to the enterprise. At the same time, he had a major task on his hands in enabling and encouraging CMS's staff, funders and supporters to grasp this all-embracing understanding of mission as pioneering partnership – what Bosch once called 'the church crossing frontiers in the form of a servant'.[16] Communication and education were central to that task, as Simon well understood. He urged those of us engaged in those activities to do everything we could to get the message across. He wanted the membership structure of CMS to be strengthened and extended, and the mechanism he and his team of Regional Secretaries came up with for that was the development of Members' Councils. These would be, in Simon's aspiration, laboratories for the sharing of inspiration and information, linking the tasks of 'mission in Britain' to those of 'mission across five continents'.

In practice, however, the effort to further restructure took a huge amount of time, money and energy, when the reality was that all three of these were slowly ebbing away. Moreover, a number of vocal CMS members tended to see the new structures as a layer of bureaucracy rather than as a motor for change. Key positions within the emerging organisation soon began to be dominated by people who – not necessarily out of ill will – used them to solidify their own roles and varied understandings of what the key tasks and priories should be. Then, at the same time, there was the powerful British Region (parallel to Africa, Asia and the Middle East), brought about by a previous

---

15 See also: Willem Saayman and Klippies Kritzinger, *Mission in Bold Humility* (Eugene OR: Wipf & Stock, 2013).
16 For more about Bosch, his influence and legacy, see: Kirsteen Kim, 'Postmodern Mission: A paradigm shift in David Bosch's theology of mission?', *International Review of Mission*, 89/353, April 2000.

wave of reform, and headed up by the force of nature that was Betty Pointon. She recruited an assistant and a deputy, harboured youth work within her orbit, and kept her operation somewhat separate from both communications and education as discreet activities within CMS headquarters.

These disparate elements of what some saw as a rather misshapen whole did not work easily or logically together. Flow charts could be produced, but working relationships sometimes struggled to give them tangible impact and meaning. At this point, Charles Handy, an Irish author and thinker specialising in organisational behaviour and management, had a particular influence on Simon – especially the book *Understanding Organizations*.[17] The idea that had emerged was to create a 'matrix' system of working across CMS operations at headquarters and within Britain. This meant that a function like education would simultaneously sit within communications and cooperate with locally-based Area Secretaries (whose role was promotion of CMS and support for members), but also link across the other world regions. Regarding the latter, Regional Secretaries attempted both to support relations with the churches across the world, and to maintain channels of contact with missionaries (soon re-labelled 'mission partners') whose job was seen as equally relational – but who were often working in fairly traditional roles: in education, health, evangelism, development, engineering, etc.

Since he had an embracing mind, which revelled in concepts and diagrams as well as narratives and ideas, Simon Barrington-Ward could see all this working in his head. But the reality did not square easily with the intention, and because he was a highly revered figure, Simon was not always told so directly. For example, I remember one Members' Council meeting where he came to speak. As ever, he gave an inspiring talk and biblical reflection. Then there was a Q&A session with members to find out how the new approach was working. There was a polite response, with one or two subtle barbs which he did not really seem to pick up on, such was his natural enthusiasm. But as soon as Simon left, the moaning and complaining started. This was a weekend event, so it was not until a few days later that I bumped into Simon in the corridor at 157 Waterloo Road. He was most enthused by what he had seen and heard. It was left to me to try to explain that there were, unfortunately, some real problems – and that the reality of the situation (and of the power dynamic) was that

---

17 Charles B. Handy, *Understanding Organizations* (Harmondsworth: Penguin, 1976).

people would tend to direct complaints at 'ordinary staff members' like me, not at the much-loved General Secretary.

This was difficult for Simon to hear. It was so mainly because he liked to think of everyone as equal, and so did not wish to consider someone like me as being in a 'lesser role' in the eyes of others (though this was, of course, entirely the case). Also, he wished, understandably, to focus on the positive. In addition, it was painful for Simon to have to confront the growing financial challenge which the Society was facing, and which would require significant economies. On the one hand, legacies were dipping significantly, and on the other hand, live giving was not growing sufficiently. At a tense staff meeting in late 1984, Simon sought to help us all face this uncomfortable reality. He did so with great feeling and humility, in terms of the difficulties we faced. Ever the trade unionist, I spoke against redundancies, arguing the Keynesian case that if the vision was right, investment rather than cuts would be needed to re-energise and re-galvanise CMS. In truth, and with hindsight, the writing was on the wall for the size and scale of operation being envisaged, and also for the type of 'mission organism' that the General Secretary envisaged in a fragmented and globalising environment.

I do not write this in a critical or negative spirit. Simon Barrington-Ward was one of the kindest, most generous and most sincere people I have ever met. His understanding of the gospel was embracing and life-giving. His vision of mission was all about developing and sharing that abundant life, and it was accompanied by a real concern for social and economic justice. But organisational development and (the inevitable) institutional politics were not Simon's greatest strengths. Handy might not have been quite handy enough, and trying to re-engineer an already complicated structure with an eroding resource base and a reluctant or confused crew was always going to be a tall order.

Moreover, its underpinning faith in a God of surprises and fresh possibilities was not always deeply enough shared in practice to overcome the barriers and blockages it faced in institutional terms. The issue was not, at the end of the day, Simon, but (to a significant extent) the increasingly impossible role he had come to occupy – something which amounted to at least three jobs in one. In these terms, Simon Barrington-Ward will be seen, I believe, as the last in a 'great generation' of church mission leaders whose primary gift was envisioning, inspiring and theologising, but who ended up managing increasingly struggling organisations on dwindling income in a changing and divided world, marked by growing technological complexity and economic inequality. Navigating mission under the enervating conditions of neoliberalism arguably requires a quite different skill-set to enhance and utilise the theological, encouraging and pastoral ones Simon demonstrated in abundance. Equally, the language being nurtured within mission theology circles felt, at times, increasingly out of touch with a world where aggressive forms of both religion and disbelief – not just unbelief – were on the upswing.

A Creative and Imaginative Thinker

Despite these difficulties in managing a church agency through the processes of change, it is very important that we recognise and honour the abiding spiritual and missiological legacy that Simon Barrington-Ward bequeaths to us. Though they were not always the polished literary gems he craved (overly conscious as he was of his father's senior newspaper role, and the gilded pens of his predecessors), his *CMS Newsletters* remain important. They are a source of continuing insight within contemporary debates and explorations as to the nature of the church and its calling. These, together with his other writings (less in volume than they perhaps deserved to be, such was his commitment to practice), are rightly noted and documented in this book. I was not immediately within the circle of advisers who Simon regularly engaged when he was working on the text of a Newsletter – which was not really news, but more of an extended essay-cum-sermon-cum-intellectual investigation. They were often lengthy in gestation, as he wrote and re-wrote, anxious to do justice to the wealth of insight and experience he was always keen to draw upon. That said, he consulted me, and others outside his closest circles, on quite a few occasions, and he always tried to listen and respond with diligence.

In particular, I recall lively discussions about re-encapsulating CMS' aims using the famous Venn diagram – which came with the added twist that the diagrammatically-unrelated Henry Venn was CMS honorary secretary from 1841 to 1873, and a leading 19th century Protestant mission strategist. Simon wanted the greatest possible headline economy ('evangelism', 'renewal', 'justice'). He then sought to communicate these core ideas through the more expansive medium of the Newsletter, as well as across a range of publications and educational initiatives. The issue that animated him was how the lived

Word (the gospel as it addresses us in flesh and text) the reforming church (the organic, structural and inspired community called to bear the Word), and transformative action (translating this lived gospel into changed social and interpersonal relationships across society) could feed off and sustain one another. From Simon's vantage point, this was about embodying the wholeness of God in Christ through the persuasive and interruptive power of the Spirit. The very shape of his understanding was essentially Trinitarian, therefore. He also talked more and more about the philosophy and practice of 'inter-change' between people and churches, which he was as keen as ever to resource both from a New Testament perspective, and from the range of communicative and relational possibilities that lay within, and on the liminal edges of, CMS's networks.

Among other things, it was a conversation about the history and direction of CMS in these terms that partly led to my involvement with author Jocelyn Murray in the final arrangement and editing of her short history of CMS, published in 1995.[18] Once again, that was a moment full of those unexpected connections and possibilities in which Simon revelled. For Jocelyn, a notable Africanist, historian and missiologist (and former CMS missionary in Kenya), was based at the London Mennonite Centre. She became a valued friend. It was also through the Centre that I ended up meeting my future wife, Carla J. Roth, whose family were firm friends of Jocelyn, too. She was later a witness at our wedding in 1995. In addition, the Anabaptist and peace church tradition was one that shaped me a good deal, and about which I enjoyed some valuable exchanges with Simon. In some ways he could not fully embrace its theological pacifism, but he came very close.

By a wonderful synchronicity of the Spirit, the last connection I had with Simon came when, in 2012, he was invited to give the commencement address at Goshen College,[19] the Mennonite liberal arts university in Indiana, which my wife attended in the 1970s, and which my mother-in-law, Alice Roth, had worked for, before going on to be Vice President of Global Ministries at Mennonite Board of Missions. My father-in-law, Willard E. Roth, recalls in his personal archives:

---

18 Jocelyn M. Murray, *Proclaim the Good News. A Short History of the Church Missionary Society* (London: Hodder & Stoughton, 1985).

19 Simon Barrington-Ward, 'Becoming What You Are: Exploring the Great Exchange'. Goshen College commencement address, Sunday 22 April 2012. See Chapter 15 in this volume, and 'Graduates challenged to become ambassadors of reconciliation' in *Goshen College News*, 23 April 2012: https://www.goshen.edu/news/2012/04/23/goshen-college-graduates-challenged-to-become-ambassadors-of-reconciliation/

My spouse and I were invited to drink tea and munch Welsh cakes with the commencement speaker and his spouse. Bishop Simon Barrington-Ward kindly penned his autograph with the words 'Every blessing!' on the title page of his 2011 paperback *The Jesus Prayer: a way to contemplation*. The retired Anglican bishop had been chosen by the graduating millennials because they admired his ability to integrate this ancient practice into his daily routine as well as to communicate that devotion with clarity and conviction. Why did they know? During a London-based term they took a day trip to Coventry where Bishop Simon won their hearts with his winsome manner and jargon-free piety.[20]

A Legacy of Humility and Hope

From conversations with others in and around CMS, I know that quite a few found Simon's trains of thought difficult to follow at times. As devoted sub-editor Pauline Bower and librarian Jean Woods each recalled, he crafted long, sometimes syntactically awkward (or innovative, depending on your viewpoint!) sentences. He leaned on literary or poetic allusions that spoke strongly to him. He enthused about what he was reading or praying about at any given time. He waxed lyrical about the ideas, stories and possibilities which grabbed and motivated him. In short, his Newsletters required work to appreciate, and those around him were not always willing or able to put that effort in. G.W.F. Hegel, Gillian Rose and David Bosch are not for everyone, and habits of mind within the church are not always as adventurous or engaged as they might be. But at the core of everything Simon said, wrote and did was a disarming simplicity and integrity.

When he left CMS to become Bishop of Coventry, in 1985, it was recalled that earlier that year I had signed a farewell card for a CMS colleague left at the headquarters reception desk, 'Simon (the lesser)', in order to distinguish myself from the General Secretary. When I returned later, Simon had, of course, spotted this and had delightfully signed himself 'Simon (the least)'! This entirely genuine combination of diffident humour and modesty communicated volumes to people, even among those who perhaps struggled to trace his latest ideas, explorations and impulses in written form. Its evangelical–ecumenical call to a vocation of bold humility is well summed-up in a

---

20 Willard E. Roth, *The Jesus Prayer* (personal archives, retrieved and sent on 7 March 2021).

telling paragraph from Simon's later contribution on 'The Christic Cogito: Christian Faith in a Pluralist Age' (Chapter 14 below). This was published in a 1991 collection on Anglican and Christian futures, *The Weight of Glory,* brought together by Daniel Hardy and Peter Sedgwick.[21] There Simon wrote:

> The Christian task now is to let the Cross of Christ through the action of the Spirit be planted deep within the consciousness of all faiths. But the only way to do this is to plant the Cross again in the heart of the consciousness of Christians themselves. We need a more far-reaching repentance and a self-criticism, a deeper humility, a costlier readiness for long- term loving. We need to learn what it means to take up the Cross and follow, to be 'crucified with Christ' as we are 'plunged into the life' of worlds in crisis. To such a witness (*martyria*) these worlds are open.

This very much confirms that 'the global Christ', if I can put it that way, remained at the centre of Simon's vision throughout his life, developed and expounded in different ways and in varying contexts. Though he could not embrace a specifically pluralist ideology of religion or belief,[22] the Christ he followed and worshiped with such dedication was no imperial overlord, but the invitational Word of God calling people of all conditions and beliefs to servanthood, reconciliation, sacrificial humanity and universal love. May his memory continue to enrich us all along those paths.

---

21 Simon Barrington-Ward, 'The Christic Cogito: Christian Faith in a Pluralist Age', in Daniel Hardy & Peter Sedgwick, eds, *The Weight of Glory: A Vision and Practice for Christian Faith* (Edinburgh: T & T Clark, 1991) (Chapter 14 below).
22 Nicholas J. Wood, 'Confessing Christ in a Plural World': The Whitely Lecture, 2001–2 (Regent's Park College, Oxford, 2002) https://biblicalstudies.org.uk/pdf/whitley-lectures_2nd-series/2001-02-whitley-lecture_wood.pdf

CHAPTER 7

The CMS Newsletters

Sarah Cawdell

Introduction

As with his predecessors as CMS General Secretary, Max Warren and John V. Taylor, Simon Barrington-Ward wrote regular newsletters as a way of communicating within CMS. By the time Barrington-Ward became General Secretary, in 1975, these were a well-established feature of CMS life. Barrington-Ward wrote 93 in all, each four pages or more in length, and his own sense of their significance can be seen in the fact that he published a selection of the letters in a book, *Love Will Out* (1988). In the introduction to the book, he wrote that 'almost to my own surprise, a coherent theme has been weaving itself through the whole sequence, over ten years'. He saw 'an interplay, a fusion of opposites', which issues in the 'bringing together into one of the Creator and the creation in the crucified figure of Jesus Christ, disclosing himself through the Spirit'.[1] There is no doubt that the newsletters provided an outlet for Barrington-Ward's creative thinking and were a way of generating and sustaining the ethos of the CMS. They also provide for us a record his experiences. He was aware that he was in in a unique position to reflect on Christian communities throughout the world, seeing them from outside, in their culture and context, and also knowing them intimately from inside by an active relationship with the members of the Society. In this chapter I will follow, in three sections, the three main themes of *Love Will Out*.

The Personal at the Centre

A major concern for Barrington-Ward, was to do all he could – for himself and for members of CMS – to encourage a deepening per-

---

1 Simon Barrington-Ward, *Love Will Out: A Theology of Mission for today's world: CMS newsletters 1975–85* (Basingstoke: Marshall Pickering, 1988), vii.

sonal relationship with God who is himself personal. In his first news-letter he referred to what would be an ongoing theme: interchange. He believed that Christians in the West needed to move away from institutional forms and to learn, through interchange across national boundaries, 'the language of the heart'.[2] The Church was never to be tolerated as an obstacle to this learning, but always, in whatever nation it was found, to be challenged to reformation. He wrote early on in his second newsletter about African visitors who had summoned CMS members 'to live within the parable of our own New Testament faith'. This meant, said Barrington-Ward:

> ...to be caught up in the movement of God into his future and to be ready for the suffering and for the losing hold of our past securities which this will involve, ready for a death and a res-urrection. But we are above all to be receptive to the power of the Spirit, 'the power of futurity'. We must be ready for those surprising miracles which come to people who give up living imprisoned in the strength or weakness of their own past.[3]

The personal journey God in Christ was inviting people into was one of risky living and also of experiences of liberation.

The emphasis on the personal did not imply individualism. Barrington-Ward was emphatic on this point. His participation in a small Christian community – a house group, but more than a house group – in Berlin in his early life remained a determinative experience for him. In a 'double number' newsletter in September 1975 he wrote on 'Rediscovering the Body'. He ranged across African indigenous Churches, Latin American Pentecostals, the Jesus family in China, and the East African Revival to argue for the central place of com-munities with mutual commitment. He had a vision for what might happen 'if all over the world, wherever there are churches, or house groups, or tiny gatherings of Christian people, their faith became ac-tive in love'. He saw what he termed genuine Christian revival in the body of Christ as 'always earthed, working its way outwards from a central experience through material, social and even political means'. A missionary society such as CMS could, he believed, play a small part in the 'rediscovery of the Body' through exchange of ideas, infor-mation and experience, often through personal meetings.[4]

---

2   'The Break-up and the Break-through', CMS Newsletter January 1975, No. 388.
3   'Life from the Future', CMS Newsletter February 1975, No. 389.
4   'Rediscovering the Body', CMS Newsletter September 1975, No. 395. See also Barrington-Ward, Love Will Out, 65–72, entitled 'A New Belonging'.

In his thinking, Barrington-Ward was clearly seeking to develop the membership of CMS in new ways. At the foundation of the Society, Josiah Pratt spoke of the need to begin on a small scale, and the penny a week associations of twelve members was the bedrock which had been overlayed in the years of CMS work. In the early newsletters Barrington Ward often referred to gatherings of small groups, using a concept that was more associated with the Free Church tradition – 'cells of dissent'. For him the dissent was against the norms of the world. As he put it in October 1977, referring to a visitor he called Ahmed:

> Little organic groups of the kind that might gather in Ahmed's courtyard or in my sitting room and within which each member is cherished and confirmed in his own being. Each group at home and welcoming to anyone without exception, but yet having its own intrinsic character its roots in God in Christ, its own essential theme.

In this letter he pictured such groups, scattered through the world, 'like burning fragments setting so many others ablaze'. They offered the opportunity to experience alternative patterns, 'not only of self but of the structure of society'. This kind of evangelism meant communicating 'a way of praying, a way of being'.[5]

It was this spiritual vision, beginning as far back as Berlin and nurtured subsequently, that was at least partly behind the development of local small CMS groups, nascent communities, around Britain. Barrington-Ward wrote about this in the newsletter in 1982. One bishop from Asia told him about problems in the diocese and how he had summoned a little group of his most intimate circle of clergy and lay leaders. They began by repenting of wrong attitudes to each other. They prayed for one another and laid hands on one another. From this gathering 'a movement of renewed faith and love' seemed to grow and pervade the congregations, the clergy and indeed other parts of the Church.

In other situations, Barrington-Ward reported, small groups were praying quietly for years. From these a movement 'spreads outwards in a way that touches and transforms the whole life of the Christian community' and draws others in. He spoke of 'some fresh apprehension of Christ, breaking in upon the group or the individual'. In typical fashion he added examples from across the world – Sadhu Sundar Singh in India, a woman in the slums of Manila, healing and exor-

---

5 'Love Will Out', CMS *Newsletter* October 1977, No. 413.

cisms in the Anglican Church in Nigeria – to illustrate renewal that could happen. He was more and more convinced that small-group relationships were 'the real dynamic of mission' and he saw CMS as one of God's 'leverage points' in this process.[6] Under Barrington-Ward, CMS encouraged the development of groups that were the first workings out of the missional community which CMS has been becoming.

A particular concern Barrington-Ward had for the followers of Islam led him to an extended exploration of 'the personal centre' in September 1976. He wrote about a Sudanese friend in Khartoum who had 'struggled his way from Islam to Christ by way of membership of the Muslim Brotherhood'. This friend spoke of young Muslims 'looking for God to be with them as a friend. They are hungry for personal communion'. The 'wise' friend, as Barrington-Ward described him, added that 'in the Sudan there is a latent faith, a latent Christ, a latent Church'. In the same newsletter Barrington-Ward cited a missionary in the Middle East who had recently written to him to observe: 'I sometimes wonder whether in God's grace the conversion of the House of Islam may not come from the established Churches at all.' This missionary suggested, using an image that appealed to Barrington-Ward, that just as Jesus was revealed to Thomas through his wounds, he might be revealed to Islam through 'contemporary wounds', which included deaf and other handicapped people who were often given little space in the Eastern world.[7]

As General Secretary, Barrington-Ward worked out his commitment to relationship and to community by building up the CMS as a community of disciples. His style of leadership, in contrast to Warren and to some degree Taylor, was one of moving forward together, of collaboration. He was inspired by the pattern of the Church after Pentecost: the disciples and followers of Christ drawn to work together, recognising and sharing their varied gifts and ministries under the direction of the Holy Spirit in a way which had not been possible when Jesus was among them as their leader.[8] This development throughout his time at the Society led to one of the most significant changes which he brought about: to change the title of workers in the field from 'missionaries' to 'mission partners'. The idea of exchange, again of interchange, was key, and he developed this theme in a prayer and a vision diagram which became widely used in the Society. This was the Venn Diagram, recognising the importance of

---

6 'Leverage Point', CMS Newsletter July 1982, No. 448.
7 'The Personal Centre', CMS Newsletter September 1976, No. 404.
8 Simon Barrington-Ward, in an interview with Sarah Cawdell, December 1997.

Evangelism, Renewal and Justice in the work of the Society, and all of this held together by Interchange: Interchange between churches in different places, but also that divine exchange of hope for despair, of life for death, mediated by the cross. Barrington-Ward returned to these themes, for example reporting on conferences in 1980 which seemed to miss the 'whole gospel'. He wrote of needing 'local renewal and an evangelistic movement in congregations', 'a new mission from the Third World to the West', and 'a movement with the imagination and public will for change'. For him this was the 'kingdom-community', one 'to which Jesus calls his followers'.[9]

Entering the World of Others

From his three years in Nigeria, Barrington-Ward learned what it meant to enter into the world of others. His reflections on this period were published as 'The Centre Cannot Hold'.[10] Observing a very different culture to his own, one on the edge, where life was fragile, he noticed the development of 'spiritual cult' in response to the unsettled times in which people were living. He argued that it is at times of catastrophic change and upheaval that people are open to new understandings of the divine. In very varied settings, he remained convinced that it is in the uncertainty in moments of disintegration and change that we find the opening to a fuller relationship with God. To go back is death, but the future, though unknown, can be life through participation in the cross and resurrection of the Saviour. Nostalgia, and desire for the familiar, were not only temptations in the Western churches. Barrington-Ward wrote of a visitor who had recently toured small Anglican Churches in East Asia and had commented that these small minorities expressed a sense of isolation and loss. There was a fear that having 'lost' control of schools they would 'lose' hospitals. Some lamented the passing of the days of 'great missionaries', although one senior Church leader commented in more subtle tones that 'when the British departed, we were forced to recognise that God and our patrons were not necessarily one and the same'.[11] Barrington-Ward saw it as a task for the CMS to put such struggling people in touch with one another so that in the world of another they might be mutually encouraged and strengthened in their discipleship.

In dealing with the colonial past, Barrington-Ward recognised

---

9 'In Search of a Whole Gospel', *CMS Newsletter* October 1980, No. 436. The conferences he attended and reported on were a World Council of Churches conference in Melbourne and a Lausanne Conference in Pattaya.
10 Simon Barrington-Ward, 'The Centre Cannot Hold: Spirit possession as redefinition', in Edward Fasholé-Luke, *et al.*, eds, *Christianity in Independent Africa* (London: Rex Collings, 1978), 445–470.
11 'Paths to Resurrection', *CMS Newsletter* April 1978, No. 417.

the conflicts and problems inherent in the colonial enterprise. He did not hesitate to own the damage done, while remaining grateful for the gifts of relationships in the post-colonial era. He was more interested in the relationship of the gospel to the changes brought about by Enlightenment, industrial and other revolutions across the world, seeking to move away from a nostalgic retrospective outlook which was a form of escapism in the face of apparent disintegration. In March 1975 he quoted a missionary in India who described someone who had been alienated by 'the bleak Christian doctrine' he had been taught by missionaries and had instead embraced communism. 'Christian evangelists have taught doctrine where they should have taught Christ' was the lesson to be learned. Barrington-Ward had his eye on how there could be fresh initiatives, building on the rubble, rather than rooting around in it. He concluded his March 1975 newsletter with a vision in which 'the church everywhere can be reshaped so as to convey freshly and clearly through its life, love and worship the immediate reality of the one infinite universal Person'. In such a movement, there could be new discoveries, in which people with 'our transient patterns of belief and action, central or peripheral, may yet hope to find in him the centre of a new world still in the making'.[12]

Part of the life of those who were with CMS as mission partners in various parts of the world, was to both receive and give from their link parishes. In Barrington-Ward's mind, this giving and receiving encouraged a fundamental recognition that we are all fellow disciples wherever we are, links in the chain of love which the cross has stretched around the world. Barrington-Ward encouraged recognition of the significance of what was happening in other places and sharing of insights.

An example he gave from India was of a group of Christians who had 'left CMS' and now, as a Christian Ashram, 'just lived a life of prayer and worship, farming a little, dispensing a few medicines and receiving visitors who came in search of all kinds of help'. A visiting government official was puzzled, and spent an hour or two talking about their experience of God and the meaning of Jesus. As he was leaving, he remarked: I see now that you are not missionaries. This is spiritual work!' The official later explained that missionaries were 'admirable people'. It was good to have had them, 'But they are always trying to do things to people.' He saw the Ashram as just 'being there for God'.[13] For Barrington-Ward, to enter a different space was

---

12 'Divided Worlds – the Way Through and Beyond', *CMS Newsletter* March 1975, No. 400.
13 'A Third Way', *CMS Newsletter* March 1977, No. 408.

always a work of God and was done in prayer. He spoke of Christian prayer as 'the most profoundly potent transforming power'. It was 'participation in a central purpose, a sharing in a movement of love'. This enabled movement into a new reality.[14]

Although this offered such possibilities, Barrington-Ward recognised the cost of such a living and active relationship with Jesus. It meant living through disintegration on the way to new opportunities, with others, for the self-revelation of God, and a developing knowledge and love of God. Key to his relationship with God was a sense of utter dependence. In 'Call to Prayer', in January 1977, he spoke of the way in which the Orthodox monks on Mount Athos in Greece had kept up a continual round of praise since the ninth century. He highlighted what he called 'a surrender of grace, something through pain and weakness'. This led him to the words of what was for him a concept held closely to his heart, namely the Jesus Prayer in the Orthodox tradition: 'Lord Jesus Christ, Son of the living God, have mercy on me, a sinner.' Or in its simpler form, 'Lord Jesus Christ, have mercy on me'. This 'longing', he said, 'is never separated from a pleading and a yearning on behalf of the whole creation'. In other words, this dependent relationship was not a way of retreating from the world. He associated with the Jesus Prayer a book by the leader within the charismatic movement, Arthur Wallis, entitled *Pray in the Spirit*. Barrington-Ward affirmed Wallis's view that prayer involves an act of faith 'by which we surrender ourselves to be freely at the disposal of the Spirit'. This was intimately related to Jesus Christ, 'the wounded man at the heart of God' (a favourite theme for Barrington-Ward) since Jesus was, like the Spirit, a Witness, an Advocate.[15]

The conjunction of Orthodoxy with the modern charismatic movement was typical of the way Barrington-Ward entered many different worlds. As General Secretary he travelled widely, and his newsletters show the degree of his openness to others, and willingness to learn and interact wherever he went. He did not seek to impose a 'CMS way' or method, nor to insist on Western cultural influences. Rather he recognised that as God was incarnate in Bethlehem, in Galilee and in Jerusalem, so the gospel must be embedded in each culture and place where it is preached. He reflected carefully on the voice of Christ speaking into each place, seeing both the abilities and the failures of the carriers of the Gospel, learning from the past, but always hopeful and enthusiastic about the future in Christ.

---

14 'Prayer: A Double Rhythm', *CMS Newsletter* December 1976, No. 422.
15 'Call to Prayer', *CMS Newsletter* January 1977, No. 407.

In a newsletter on 'Disciples' he talked about Mrs Shanti Solomon, an 'Indian missionary to this country', who had said: 'People are no longer converted to a doctrine; they can only be attracted to a way of life'. She saw the Church presenting Christianity, the system, 'and not Christ as a Person' or as 'life in the Spirit'. In this newsletter Barrington-Ward also drew from Juan Carlos Ortiz in Buenos Aires, with his book *Disciple*, and linked this with Dietrich Bonhoeffer's *The Cost of Discipleship*. He argued that Ortiz and Bonhoeffer were 'wonderfully alike in one central stress', portraying the 'devastating antithesis between Christian life and the pleasantly bourgeois respectability which so often passes for it'. The authentic Christian life was a response to the call of Jesus 'to follow him at whatever price'.[16]

Christ for the World

This is the title of part three of *Love Will Out*, and, as the first chapter within that, Barrington-Ward wrote about 'Missionary Movements: A New Phase'. In the newsletters he wrote in an informed way about faith and culture in the Middle East, Russia, India, South America, China and Japan, and various parts of Africa. He often commented, too, on the current affairs in the Church across the world and on very diverse religious life. On the subject of other faiths, he valued the insights of Max Warren, who urged a 'theology of attention', which encourages the missionary to look at first, and listen to, followers of other faiths.

There was opportunity for the Christian, as Barrington-Ward saw it, to be open to what he called 'points of entry' (this was in relation to Islam) and to respond in love. He wrote about the insights of Muslim scholars and also of about the experiences of Muslims he met through friends. One of these, a widow, was deeply concerned about her son who was ill and spoke of the power in all the Names of God. She then added 'a hidden Name, a great unknown Name', and asked Barrington-Ward for prayer for her son in that Name, which she had heard was the Name of Jesus and was powerful.[17] With such opportunities, Barrington-Ward recognised the need for Christians to take the place of service, the lowest place in the communities they inhabited, so that Jesus, who took the lowest place for us, might be fully made known. He related a story from Hassan Dehqani-Tafti, Bishop of Iran, which offered a powerful example in the Islamic context. After the death of Hassan's father, his brothers were quite unsure

16 'Disciples', *CMS Newsletter* December 1976, No. 406.
17 'Response to Islam: Points of Entry', *CMS Newsletter* February 1976, No. 400.

that he could be admitted as a Christian to the mosque to attend the funeral. After debate it was agreed he could slip in at the back. He experienced, he said, the joy of being 'at the lowest place'.[18]

Barrington-Ward's understanding of Christianity and mission in relation to other faiths was open and inclusive: whilst in no way denying the uniqueness of Christ's offer of salvation, he did not condemn or deny the good in other faiths, but sought for Christ in them. He was always eager to learn from, as well as able to gently critique, other cultures, and by his example and his writing he set the CMS in a place of humility: not so much doing good to those being served – although that was included – as always learning and seeking ways to see more of God alongside one another. This set the tone for the further development of mission as being 'from everywhere to everywhere'. He rejoiced in the crossing of cultures. For him it was a process of becoming more open to the divine self-revelation as encountered in the variety of people and cultures. Christ, he believed, is a 'sign for all faiths' (as he designated one of his newsletters), Christian, Muslim, Buddhist , Sikh, and the true calling of Christians was 'to go out beyond the frontiers of what we have walled around as the church into a dynamic interaction with the spiritual quest of others in the whole intermingling of cultures which increasingly characterises our time'. There God in Christ, in his fullness, he continued, 'will only begin to be adequately disclosed to us and in us as we are ready to receive him with and alongside seekers of all faiths'.[19]

The way in which the churches had taken Western ways to other parts of the world was a concern for Barrington-Ward. After a visit to Japan he spoke of how the Christian Churches in Japan had been 'influential purveyors of Western education, popularising at least a notion of Christianity through, for instance, carols and Handel's *Messiah* at Christmas'. This seemed, however, 'too alien' a community for the Japanese to join. Nonetheless, as he always did, Barrington-Ward looked for signs of hope, and in Japan he found these in examples such as the episcopal (Nippon Sei Ko Kai) housing estate church which its own members built up with their own hands. He saw the congregation sitting on tatami (mats) on the floor and heard of how house meetings were multiplying, 'touching many lives in the freshly integrating way'.[20] Barrington–Ward was always delighted when he found instances of the gospel being presented to cultures without baggage from the presenting culture. For him this was, as he put it

18 'Response to Islam II: Broken Circles', *CMS Newsletter* March 1976, No. 401.
19 'A Sign of all Faiths', *CMS November* 1984, No. 463.
20 'A People Between', *CMS Newsletter* April 1980, No. 433.

in April 1981, looking at Kenya and New Guinea, the 'Credibility Test'.[21]

It is striking, reading the newsletters, which often contained reports of Barrington-Ward's travels, to see the way in which he connected with the mission partners of CMS in so many parts of the world. Even when he could not visit, he was reading their letters, and in his newsletters he often quoted thoughtfully from their descriptions of their experiences, expanding those and bringing them to bear on the thinking of the time. He reflected on the decade of the 1970s in which Christian Churches across the world had embarked on a 'demanding and exhilarating enterprise of real meeting and joint mission'. He turned, as he often did, to the East African Revival movement, 'now so significant for the whole world', and reiterated its basic themes of 'mutual confession and shared re-empowering', suggesting that these needed to become 'the cry of each of us in costly partnership with the other'. He was not content with international gatherings that were at a surface level. For him real relationships had to go deeper, to changes of heart.[22]

The newsletters reflected on the world for the members who were prepared to grapple with Barrington-Ward's often demanding thinking. He drew on contemporary culture from across the regions of the world – expressed in drama, books and music – to bring together the understandings from widely different cultures and to demonstrate the richness of an incarnate faith: Jesus made known in East Africa or the East End of London, in Mexico, Kenya or Japan, by the same means of the faithful witness of his disciples. His insights from the world of art and culture, with narrative and artistic interpretations, opened new possibilities in understanding and experiencing the love of God. Above all, he spoke of people. Sometimes it is a phrase which is striking in a newsletter. Barrington-Ward spoke of an African friend who was a former Muslim, but then offered the phrase 'a fulfilled Muslim', as this friend had become a disciple of Christ, and Barrington-Ward further spoke of the way the friend told his story 'with the characteristically gentle dignity and courtesy which he had brought from his Islamic culture into the refining fire of his devotion to Christ'.[23]

Barrington Ward's newsletters demonstrate again and again that he was always willing to engage with those of other cultures and faiths, in order to share their riches and so have the right humbly to share the riches of the Gospel. Such courtesy underpinned the culture

---

21 'Credibility Test', *CMS Newsletter* April 1981, No. 440.
22 'Not Even Meeting?', *CMS Newsletter* March 1981, No. 439.
23 'Way through the Ways', *CMS Newsletter* January 1982, No. 445.

of interchange which characterised Barrington Ward's work in the CMS: bringing people of difference together to learn from one another and to be open to the presence of Christ at work in the midst of them. Barrington-Ward's profound awareness of his own brokenness, his humility in knowing himself to be dearly beloved of God, opened his heart and eyes to see God in all, to be aware of Jesus Christ, the wounded man in the heavens, reaching out to all humanity. In this way Barrington-Ward lived and ministered – open to God in every circumstance, believing that the self-revealing nature of God would mean that people of all faiths and none would find a welcome at the cross. He recognised that fear, arrogance and ignorance have too often led to the proclamation of religion rather than faith, and structures rather than freedom. His starting point therefore was not the Church, but the person, Jesus Christ. His love alone should direct the Christian and will attract the seeker after truth. He never denied the uniqueness of Christ, but neither did he constrain the expression of the faith to the structures of the Church. Christ was for the world.

Conclusion

Through the newsletters, as well as in other ways, Barrington-Ward linked up people in a cycle of interchange. His vision was always to keep the personal at the centre. He wanted to connect the people on the frontiers, the explorers, believing as he did that as people stepped into the space occupied by others new discoveries were made. At the end of *Love Will Out* he wrote about the cry that might come, 'If only we in the Church, in the midst of the world, could start all over again.' Then, he continued, 'as we kneel there dumb and broken, we shall be filled with a strange joy'. The secret revealed was that God out of his 'ever-glorious, ever-undying radiance' can say to anyone, in any place, that a new start is possible. 'Behold I make all things new'.[24] This outlook is embodied in the prayer that was the CMS prayer for a number of Barrington-Ward's years as General Secretary:

> Lord, as you have entered into our life and death and in all the world you call us into your death and risen life draw us now we pray by the power of your Spirit into an exchange of gifts and needs, joys and sorrows, strengths and weakness with your people everywhere that with them we may have grace to break

---

24 Barrington-Ward, *Love Will Out*, 243.

beyond every barrier, to make disciples of all nations and to share the good news of your love with all mankind, for your glory's sake. Amen.

CHAPTER 8

'A Fellowship of the Unlike': An Aspiration for Theological Education

Cathy Ross

Introduction

I CAME ACROSS THIS PHRASE, 'fellowship of the unlike', in a story that Simon Barrington-Ward relates in his 'My Pilgrimage in Mission' article in 1999.[1] This image immediately resonated as it articulates a vision and a dream for theological education for which I long.

Barrington-Ward uses the phrase to describe the community envisaged by a prophetic woman leader and trader, Ibribina, in the 1880s in Nigeria. She had been filled with the Holy Spirit in a mission church. Subsequently she learned how to read from the local CMS missionary so that she could read, translate and interpret the Gospels.

> She saw in 'Jesu' Krisi' a new love, a new all-pervasive Spirit power, the possibility of a new people, a fellowship of the unlike, bonding together all tribes, all ethnic groups, both black and white, into a new society. Here the rich would care for the poor and the strong for the weak in what was to be a new heaven and a new earth.[2]

The movement grew enormously, not only drawing in young people of all ethnic groups but also creating conflicts with the elders until after World War One. Barrington-Ward describes how the Church Mission Society (CMS) missionaries came in to tidy things up to conform to a tidier, colonial mindset: 'The CMS shaped and trained the new church to fit in with the wider colonial world. A much more individualised, spiritualised faith seemed appropriate along with a largely

---

1 Simon Barrington-Ward, 'My Pilgrimage in Mission,' *International Bulletin of Missionary Research*, Vol. 23, No. 2, April, 1999, 60. See Chapter 13.
2 ibid., 61. See more in Chapter 10, by Linda Ochola-Adolwa.

utilitarian education.'[3] This seems to describe so much of what has happened in theological education over the years and still today.

In this chapter I would like to lay out a vision for theological education that could model and be 'a fellowship of the unlike', a diverse community, 'a new society.' To do this I will explore the concepts of theological homelessness, the double-edged sword of our context and history, the pedagogy of plantation and what the Ibribina possibility might call us to today.

Theological Homelessness

At CMS I am part of a team who have been training pioneer leaders for ten years. Our training is accredited by the Durham University Common Awards programme.[4] Over the years we have discovered that the paradigms within which they have learned and understood theology have not equipped them well. One striking metaphor that is quite commonly used is that they feel like the rug is pulled from under their feet, sometimes leaving them destabilised, unsteady and wondering what happens next. They then begin a journey of moving from a world where theology is a content to be downloaded, learned and imparted – and perhaps even defended – to a world where theology is more like a process with which the community engages together. This shift is challenging but opens up new horizons for the way we all conceive of theology in practice. We have come to think of this process as a kind of 'theological homelessness' that needs to be experienced and embraced in order to find a new way home.

One of the very first exercises we do with students is to invite them to complete two statements in as many ways as they like and to stick them on the wall. The statements are 'Theology is...' and 'Theology is not...' Invariably a whole set of negative associations with theology come up for discussion – theology seems to have a bad reputation! These associations cluster around themes of academic irrelevance, lack of connection with real life, insistence on right belief systems and doctrines, and that theology is about power, control and oppressing others. Theology, as many of the students have experienced it, seems to be neither life enhancing nor life-giving. It does seem to reflect the utilitarian approach that Barrington-Ward refers to and also an approach that requires conforming to certain (colonial?) expectations.

But as we press into this exercise, another picture begins to emerge

---

3   Barrington-Ward, 'My Pilgrimage', 61.
4   https://pioneer.church missionsociety.org/

that is more aspirational, and certainly more hopeful of theology that connects to life as we live it and experience it. Theology can be an adventure or a quest; theology is communal and conversational; can ask questions; and can explore friendship with God, with one another and with the world. This signals the start of a journey for students, an adventure of the imagination or a treasure quest to find ways of speaking about God, the world and their own context that make sense. This whole experience generates a kind of theological homelessness.

Leaving home is risky. Sometimes you even have to leave without knowing where you are going. Consider Abraham who, by faith, obeyed when God called him to leave home, 'He went without knowing where he was going.' (Heb. 11:8). Barbara Brown Taylor suggests that the practice of getting lost is a valuable spiritual practice. She cites Abraham and Sarah as good examples and claims that 'the Bible gives no reason for God's choice of Abraham and Sarah except their willingness to get lost.'[5] We resonate with this idea of getting lost as it forces us to experience discomfort, and to be open to new possibilities. It also heightens perceptions and encourages us to see things in new ways.

Getting lost and letting go can be followed or accompanied by a sense of loss and grief and feelings of being unsettled or unsure – the theological homelessness. This can be painful. It may leave us stranded between two or more worlds. It forces us to look at our theological upbringing with new eyes. However, a certain amount of theological discomfort may be a good thing. Certainly the themes of exile, pilgrimage and even homelessness are biblical themes. As noted, our ancestor, Abraham, was uprooted from his home by Yahweh to discover new things about God. The people of Israel were forced to adapt to new cultures and strange ways while in exile. And Jesus knew pilgrimage and homelessness, beginning in his mother's womb. An African proverb expresses it well, 'The person who has not travelled widely thinks their mother is the best cook in the world.' While leaving home can be painful, it also sharpens our senses, forces us to ask questions, and confronts us with dissonance. We believe that it is in the dissonance and discomfort that authentic learning begins to take place. As students begin to wrestle with new and different ideas that may challenge formerly cherished beliefs, this is when the questions emerge, vistas are opened, horizons expanded. This is also when

---

5 Barbara Brown Taylor, *An Altar in The World* (London: Canterbury Press, 2009), 73.

we begin to understand that every home has its context.

The Double-Edged Sword

Context is everything. At CMS we are learning in the context of a British-founded Anglican mission society, now based in Oxford. This context is vital to acknowledge and to reflect on. It is also vital that we are attentive to the global context. Barrington-Ward was aware of this both in his context at Magdalene College, Cambridge, where he tried to develop the 'Ibribina possibility' in the chapel community there, and then at Crowther Hall, the CMS training college in Selly Oak, Birmingham. He wrote of his time there:

> I was to lecture on how the CMS had started in 1799 as a movement of reparation for the evils of the slave trade and East Asian commerce, to bring the hope of a new gospel life to Africa and the East, and how after Venn's death it lost its way. Venn's vision of a euthanasia of mission – that is of bringing mission agency control of the African church to an end – was neglected. The CMS itself became a vehicle of white dominance over the churches it had helped to found.[6]

We live with this legacy today and we need to pay attention to it. This legacy and context constitute a double-edged sword – and I use that metaphor intentionally, with all its connotations of conquest, violence, power, patriarchy and colonialism.[7] The positive side is the legacy of global engagement. We work hard at exposing students to theologies from other parts of the world with which they are less familiar. Historically violent events such as the conquest of Latin America, aspects of European colonisation, slavery, apartheid, oppressive dictatorships as well as a range of rich indigenous theologies, inform much of Majority World theological reflection from which we learn and grieve over. Gambian scholar Lamin Sanneh has reminded us that we live in a world of polycentric Christianity and that 'world Christianity is not one thing but a variety of indigenous responses through more or less effective local idioms, but in any case without necessarily the European enlightenment frame.'[8] Scottish mission historian Andrew Walls alerted us more than twenty years ago to

---

6   Barrington-Ward, 'My Pilgrimage', 62.
7   This also calls to mind the reference in Hebrews 4:12–13 about the word of God being living and active and where everything in all creation is laid bare before God. This may also be a timely reminder of needing to expose and lay bare the harmful aspects of colonialism.
8   Lamin Sanneh, *Whose Religion is Christianity? The Gospel Beyond the West* (Maryknoll: Orbis, 2003), 22.

the reality that Christianity is primarily a non-Western religion, that our twenty-first century faith will require robust scholarship from the soil of Africa, Asia and Latin America, and that the 'most urgent reason for the study of the religious traditions of Africa and Asia, of the Amerindian and the Pacific peoples, is their significance for Christian theology; they are the substratum of the Christian faith and life for the greater number of Christians in the world.'[9] Malawian missiologist, Harvey Kwiyani tell us that by 2050, 45% of the world's Christians will be in Africa.[10]

So we work hard at exposing students to theologies and people from other parts of the world. We encourage them to engage in theology as a global conversation and to appropriate a theology without borders. In our own UK context, many of our students are living and working in contexts with people on the edges and outside the church. Their journey involves border crossing and home looks very different when you look back from across a border. The world starts to look a lot bigger than they had seen when they were at home and the horizons more expansive. Of course, our faith is a border-crossing faith and is most alive, creative and renewed in the process of border-crossing encounters.

The negative side of this metaphor is how this legacy of conquest, violence, power, patriarchy and colonialism has impacted theological education (and mission) and I shall explore this using a slave plantation metaphor from African–American scholar Willie James Jennings.

The Pedagogy of Plantation

Our students appreciate this global perspective and indeed many say that this is a unique aspect of studying at CMS. However, as Barrington-Ward has reminded us there is a dark side to this global engagement which has haunted CMS for centuries. The first African bishop, Bishop Ajayi Crowther, consecrated under CMS auspices, died in 1891, quite literally, from a broken heart, when arrogant and earnest young missionary men refused to work under his leadership.[11] We are part of a long and painful history of colonialism and this has impacted how we engage in theological education and mission. As Barrington-Ward wrote, 'The CMS shaped and trained the new church to fit in with the wider colonial world. A much more

9   Andrew Walls, 'Old Athens and New Jerusalem: Some Signposts for Christian Scholarship in the Early History of Mission Studies.' *International Bulletin of Missionary Research*, 21, no 4 (October 1997), 153.
10   Statistic cited in class at CMS, 22 June 2021.
11   See Jehu Hanciles, *In the Shadow of the Elephant: Bishop Crowther and the African Missionary Movement*, Crowther Monograph (Oxford: Church Mission Society, 2008).

individualised, spiritualised faith seemed appropriate along with a largely utilitarian education.'[12]

Willie James Jennings writes powerfully about theological education and claims that, because of this painful legacy, it is distorted. Moreover, he argues that the whole of Western education is distorted and that it has been for centuries. In his book, *After Whiteness*, where he claims that the role and purpose of theological education is to cultivate belonging, he explains that instead theological education has become an exercise in mastery.[13] Literally it was the master training the master's son to run the plantation efficiently, to maintain order, to categorise, delimit, define and maximise the efficient use of slaves' bodies. However, he offers some hope by stating that theological education has the resources within it to reframe Western education beyond this distortion. According to Jennings, there are two things that form this distortion. The first is the image of an educated person which is 'a white self-sufficient man, his self-sufficiency defined by possession, control and mastery.'[14] The second is that many respond to this image by promoting a homogeneity 'that aims toward a cultural nationalism.'[15]

These factors result in hegemony and homogeneity, neither of which are Gospel values and neither of which will lead us towards 'a fellowship of the unlike' but rather towards the individualised faith and utilitarian education that Barrington-Ward describes. Jennings explains that white self-sufficient masculinity does not refer to a particular person but rather it is a way of organising life that distorts our identity and the possibility of a richer life together. Moreover, whiteness does not necessarily refer to skin colour but rather to a way of being in and operating in the world; a way of seeing the world and inhabiting the world. He explains how colonialism meant that whiteness was projected onto the rest of the world. European Christians and missionaries projected a meaning onto the world that was very different from many of the cultures they were living in. They challenged the vision shared by many indigenous peoples about their sense of identity, their sense of well-being and relationship with the land, creation and the place.

These early Europeans in new places defined, they designated, they divided ancient tribal groupings, they created borders with straight

---

12 Barrington-Ward, 'My Pilgrimage', 61.
13 Willie James Jennings, *After Whiteness, An Education in Belonging* (Eerdmans: Grand Rapids, 2020).
14 ibid., 6.
15 ibid.

lines, and they developed racial categories. They challenged and destroyed the deeply held beliefs and practices of indigenous peoples. For indigenous peoples, the place is in them – they are the place, the land, the creation. I know this from my own country, Aotearoa/NZ, where the Maori define themselves according to their place, their mountain, their river or sea and their tribe. In the Maori language, the word for land and placenta, *whenua*, is the same. Maori are the land. The land is them. Jennings explains that the early missionaries brought a very different understanding of how to be in the world:

> This crucial educational hope was to disabuse Native peoples of any idea that lands and animals, landscapes and seasons carried any communicative or animate destiny, and therefore any ethical or moral direction in how to live in the world. Instead they offered peoples a relationship with the world that was basically one dimensional – we interpret and manipulate the world as we see fit, taking from it what we need, and caring for it within the logics of making it more productive for us;[16]

Therefore when theological education becomes an exercise in possession, control and mastery, it sets out to maintain order, to categorise, delimit, define and maximise efficiency and productivity. Indeed, it becomes what Barrington-Ward called 'a largely utilitarian education.' Mission has played its part in this, as it has so often been framed by or located in white colonialism, and this was how the colonial masters saw the world. This is the pedagogy of plantation.

So mastery is a slave metaphor, straight from the slave plantation. Jennings believes that this metaphor has influenced Western education. Education is about mastery and control. It is literally about slave owners training their sons to sustain any colonial holdings with power and control. In the USA, educational institutions are literally built on former plantation land or with endowments from slavery. We know that the same is true in Britain also.[17] This is more than just an economic worldview. It relates to how we organise our world,

---

16 Willie James Jennings, 'Can White People be Saved? Reflections on the Relationship of Missions and Whiteness', in Love L. Sechrest, Johnny Ramírez-Johnson, and Amos Young, eds, *Can 'White' People Be Saved? Triangulating Race, Theology, and Mission, Missiological Engagements* (Downers Grove: IVP Academic, 2018), 33.

17 https://www.uncomfortableoxford.co.uk/ The Uncomfortable Oxford Tour is an excellent way of learning about Oxford's uncomfortable history including its links with the slave trade. One of the stops on the Uncomfortable Walking Tour is All Souls College, where its connection to wealth generated from slave plantations in the Caribbean is explained. The College's Codrington library is named after a plantation owner. The online tour shows a photo of a young black man outside the college with the words 'All Slaves College' painted on his body. To address the legacy, the College recently changed the name of its library to 'All Souls College Library' and created an annual scholarship for students from Caribbean nations. They also mounted a plaque outside the library that reads: 'In memory of those who worked in slavery on the Codrington Plantations in the West Indies.' The plaque is not visible to most people as it sits behind a door closed to the public.

how we inhabit our world – a world of efficiency and control for the sake of the master and the master's sons. This, he claims, is replicated in places far removed from the history of the slaveholding USA because we have all been formed in this way: 'an ecclesial reality inside a white patriarchal domesticity, shaped by an overwhelming white presence that always aims to build a national and global future that we should all inhabit.'[18]

The slave legacy of theological education is deeply embedded in our imaginations. If you think this is extreme or just a North American problem, then think again. Look at the portraits on the walls of many theological institutions in Britain. These are a very good visual representation of 'white patriarchal domesticity.' Look at the teaching staff or faculty and then at the so-called 'domestic staff', the architecture of the buildings, the timetabling, the curricula, the libraries and the books on the shelves, the resources required to gain access to many articles that are behind paywalls. And then look at the hidden curriculum around Common Rooms, sports, etiquette around meals and drinking, dress codes, clubs, notice boards, offices, invited speakers and scholars, and air time in the classroom; there is a kind of assumed 'contextlessness' to much of this formation. This could be the utilitarian education Barrington-Ward referred to and much of this seems a far cry from his 'fellowship of the unlike.'

Things are changing, with the advent of movements such as #BLM, Rhodes Must Fall, #MeToo, Extinction Rebellion, the momentum around decolonising the curriculum, and the ongoing discussion about statues brought to a head with former slave trader, Edward Colston being unceremoniously dumped in Bristol Harbour. We are slowly becoming aware how white privilege and white supremacy have skewed and distorted theological education for so long. Malawian missiologist Harvey Kwiyani claims, 'Many white Christians' Jesus do[es] not know how to relate with black and brown people apart from oppressing them – 600 years of church history can testify.'[19] He maintains that mission, as we understand and practise it today, is a European creation and that we need to learn to engage in mission – and in theological education – without an attitude of superiority.

One of our students challenged us recently:

The interesting thing to me then is just how much this module

---

18 Jennings, *After*, p. 82.
19 Harvey Kwiyani, 'Mission after George Floyd: On White Supremacy, Colonialism and World Christianity', *ANVIL, Faultlines in Mission: Reflections on Race and Colonialism*, Vol 36, Issue 3, 2020. https://churchmissionsociety.org/anvil-journal-theology-and-mission/anvil-journal-of-theology-and-mission-volume-36-issue-3/

[Theologies in Global Perspective] is making me question everything. One of the questions I have repeatedly asked in the sessions is why amazing people continue to work towards improving an institution so clearly steeped in colonialism, patriarchy and a whole manner of other issues when they could create something new (a contrast community as Jennings puts it). All of the speakers have had examples or given glimpses of alternative systems that seem to work better than the time honoured traditional way of doing things and yet they continue to seek to be part of and change the system.[20]

For this student the most exciting alternative they had heard of was The Circle of Concerned African Women Theologians, which has been such an important space for women to do theology together communally. It draws on women from all backgrounds, culture and religions. Although this group is for women only, by encouraging a diversity of cultures, religions and background and by being a loose and flat collective, perhaps this is coming a little closer to 'a fellowship of the unlike.'

The Ibribina Possibility

How can we hope for the Ibribina possibility of 'a fellowship of the unlike' bonding us into a new society with all our diversity, complexity and differences? How do we learn to live together? How do we create this kind of learning community?

We need to be hospitable and make the learning context a hospitable space. North American educationalist Parker Palmer explains that our learning spaces need to be welcoming. 'A learning space needs to be hospitable not to make learning painless but to make the painful things possible, things without which no learning can occur...'[21] African–American scholar and social activist Gloria Jean Watkins, better known by her pen name bell hooks, positions herself as a learner in the classroom. She does not ignore the power dynamics, but insists that 'we are all equal here to the extent that we are equally committed to creating a learning context.'[22] She stresses that it is everyone's responsibility and she acknowledges that the agenda may need to be changed so we can follow the energy, the heat in the room to learn together. She reminds us that we are embodied beings

---

20 Used with permission.
21 Parker Palmer, *To Know as we are Known: Education as a Spiritual Journey* (San Francisco: Harper One, 1993), 4.
22 bell hooks, *Teaching to Transgress: Education as the Practice of Freedom* (New York: Routledge, 1994), 153.

and that we bring our bodies as well as our minds into the learning space. She makes a plea for 'passion in the classroom',[23] so that we enter the learning space as whole person and not with a mind/ body dualism. She names this passion as 'eros'. This is not meant in a sexual sense but rather in terms of an energy or passion that propels us towards learning as an adventure. It is an energy that drives us towards discovery and wholeness as well as towards co-learning and co-creation of knowledge. One student noted that she thinks people no longer seek out experts who impart information to them (a master-save model?), but rather people prefer to join in learning together.

Eros and the erotic are picked by up Jennings, who says these have been distorted by whiteness. But we can start again and reimagine this erotic power. Both hooks and Jennings offer us a way forward which is mediated through the concepts of eros and the crowd. Hooks tells us that eros can be a powerfully motivating force and 'that it can provide an epistemological grounding informing, how we know what we know … and to use such ways … to invigorate discussion and excite the critical imagination.'[24] Jennings believes that theological education 'has as its fundamental resource erotic power, and that power finds its home in the divine ecstasy in which God relentlessly gives Godself to us, joyfully opening the divine life as our habitation.'[25] However, this is power that we can enter only through participation. And here is the promise and the challenge. With whom do we participate? Is it with 'a fellowship of the unlike' or with the like in our own echo chambers?

Jennings' metaphor of 'the crowd' that surrounds Jesus in their desire for God is an intriguing one. He says that Jesus attracted crowds and that he often gathered people who preferred not to be together. Jennings reminds us of God's power to end hostility and to draw us and all of creation into reconciliation – a movement that we do not control but one that will recreate and reform us. This starts with community, the crowd.

For this to happen we need to be in shared spaces so we can share life together. It means gathering together those who may even prefer not to be together – perhaps 'a fellowship of the unlike'? So what might this mean for theological education – if we could gather together people who would prefer not to be together? Jennings insists that we must be willing to live toward a different formation of place

---

23 ibid., 194.
24 ibid., 195.
25 Jennings, *After*, 151.

and space. 'We fight against... the segregation that shapes our worlds, and we work to weave lives together.' He goes on to explore the concept of forming a contrast community. These communities 'must be formed on the actual ground *in neighbourhoods* and living spaces.'[26] It is in our shared living spaces, in our friendships, in being together in the same space and in conversations that learning and change can happen. Imagine a learning community who welcomes all, across all the lines that might divide us – a contrast community that is formed on the actual ground, in neighbourhoods and learning spaces – so that we experience the gifts and challenges that we can offer one another.

In this discussion I have focussed on ethnic diversity to explore 'a fellowship of the unlike'. Of course, diversity has many faces – cultural, racial, ethnic, gender, sexuality, differently abled, neuro, age, and class, to name some, and many of these have been unmasked by the Covid-19 pandemic. The pandemic and movements such as #MeToo, #BLM, Extinction Rebellion have challenged us as to how we live in the world. Roman Catholic, lay theologian Janet Soskice reminds us that God is love, and that, 'We learn love through the reciprocity of our human condition, through being in relation to others who are different from ourselves...'[27] Difference is built into our DNA right from the creation story. At Pentecost we see an outpouring of the Spirit so that many cultures and languages are praising God in their mother tongues. The Jerusalem Council in Acts 15, the Peter and Cornelius story, the shared meal table, are all powerful stories of coming together in difference and diversity. And of course we have the beautiful vision in Revelation 7.9 of all types of people worshipping before the throne.

Andrew Walls describes what he calls the Ephesian moment.

> The Ephesian letter is not about cultural homogeneity; cultural diversity had already been built into the church by the decision not to enforce the Torah. It is a celebration of the union of irreconcilable entities, the breaking down of the wall of partition, brought about by Christ's death (Ephesians 2.13–18). Believers from the different communities are different bricks being used for the construction of a single building – a temple where the One God would live. (Ephesians 2.19–22.)[28]

We are in experiencing an Ephesian Moment today. The Christian

---

26 Willie James Jennings, 'Can White People be Saved? Reflections on the Relationship of Missions and Whiteness', 43.
27 Janet Soskice, *The Kindness of God, Metaphor, Gender and Religious Language* (Oxford: OUP, 2008), 51.
28 Andrew Walls, 'The Ephesian Moment', *The Cross-Cultural Process in Christian History* (Maryknoll: Orbis, 2002), 77.

world is experiencing greater diversity that it has ever known before and this offers us new possibilities in our theological education and learning. Harvey Kwiyani makes a compelling argument for this in his latest book, *Multicultural Kingdom*, where he argues that diversity is a blessing. 'God gives us gifts in the form of the different other who comes bearing some of what we need to thrive. It is God who brings us together. Diversity is God's gift to us. What matters is what we do next.'[29] What matters is what we do next. Do we have the courage and the intentionality to seek out, to welcome, to listen to and learn from diverse people in our learning spaces? Diversity can be an abstract concept that we read about, learn about and quote statistics on. Encountering diverse people is not and that is how we learn. Ultimately it does come down to eros and the crowd; that embodied passion and energy to learn, shared living spaces, life together – in all its complexity, misunderstandings, defensiveness and pain as well as in our joys, celebrations, parties and friendships – participating in actual learning spaces together. It really is about being face to face with those unlike us, 'a fellowship of the unlike'. I think Ibribina would have loved this line from British performance poet Kae Tempest who says, 'I can see your faces and I love people's faces.'[30]

---

29 Harvey Kwiyani, *Multicultural Kingdom, Ethnic Diversity, Mission and the Church* (London: SCM, 2020), 106.
30 http://www.kaetempest.co.uk/videos/kate-tempest-peoples-faces-audio

Influences and Indicators

CHAPTER 9

Ibribina and the Isoko Tribe Revisited: The Emergence of Women's Leadership in Times of Social Change

Linda Ochola-Adolwa

Introduction

IN '"THE CENTRE CANNOT HOLD" ... SPIRIT POSSESSION AS REDEFI-
NITION' (1978), Simon Barrington-Ward provides insights into the
significant upheavals experienced by the religious and social institutions of the Isoko in Nigeria from the 1890s to about 1910.[1] He presents the key challenges to the culture. First, there was the economic
upheaval from the palm oil trade, which introduced a new way of
life with new sources of wealth and power outside the traditional
framework. Second, he draws attention to the political upheaval from
military excursions that were conducted to stop some of the cultic
practices. Published in the volume *Christianity in Independent Africa*,
Barrington-Ward's article provides an authoritative account of the
context in which new spirit cults began to emerge. In his conclusion,
Barrington-Ward states that culture abhors a vacuum and that from
time to time, when various circumstances and events undermined the
authority of societal institutions, spirit cults at the periphery would
jostle for domination as the society struggled to redefine itself.[2]

The insights Barrington-Ward offers into the emergence of a woman as a leader in the religious arena, within the context of the lived experiences of women among the Isoko in the 1880s, provide the focus
for my reflection in this chapter. Adrian Hastings, in 'Were Women a
Special Case?', notes that gender analysis has often been overlooked

---

1 Simon Barrington-Ward, '"The centre cannot hold ..." Spirit possession as redefinition', in Adrian Hastings and Edward
   Fasholé-Luke (eds), *Christianity in Independent Africa* (London: Collins, 1978), 445–470.
2 Barrington-Ward, 'Spirit possession as redefinition', 469.

117

in the focus on other aspects of the implications of Christian conversion. He points out that the early converts saw the opportunities that Christianity offered to women and that even though the Church finally followed the societal pattern of male domination, the potential for liberation offered within Christianity continued to attract African women.[3] I reflect here, more broadly, on how in times of social change, the societal structures and power relations are disrupted in such a way that women's self-understanding, as well as access to and control of spiritual and material resources, provides opportunities for their emergence as leaders.

Part of my motivation for this study lies in my own experience of the post-election violence in Kenya in 2007–8.

Having been born in Kenya and having lived here all my life, I was extremely disturbed by the social disintegration and violence that took place on a scale that surprised many. I wondered why the Church, which had a platform for civic engagement and participation on the basis of faith, had not been able to avert this crisis. In 2010, together with other Christians, I drew on an Old Testament curriculum, with the theme of justice, called the Hatua study, to conduct land policy workshops in Eldoret town, a key location of the violence. In 2012, I worked with other Christians to conduct peace tours in public universities across the country. Since then, I have also used these biblical teachings on justice to train women leaders of the Anglican Church of Kenya in Anglican dioceses across Kenya. Overall, Hatua has begun to establish a national footprint and to expand the audience of churches with a social justice agenda.[4] Hatua Trust as a woman led movement of social activism came into being within the broader context of a time of significant upheaval for the nation of Kenya.[5] Throughout this chapter, I will draw insights on the emergence of women's leadership in the public sphere.

The History of the Isoko

In his overview of the history of the Isoko, Barrington-Ward examines the decentralised, patriarchal structure of Isoko society.[6] The ruler or *Ovie* of each separate grouping was expected to return to the palace

---

3 Adrian Hastings, 'Were Women a Special Case?' in Sheila Ardener, Fiona Bowie, and Deborah Kirkwood, eds, *Women and Missions* (Oxford: Berg, 1993), 109–125; cf. Dana L. Robert, 'World Christianity as a women's movement', *International Bulletin of Missionary Research* 30, no. 4 (2006), 180–188.
4 Linda Ochola-Adolwa, 'A Study of the Macro, Social and Psychological Factors that Influence the Civic Participation Practices of Christians at Mavuno Church, Nairobi, Kenya' (Fuller Theological Seminary, Doctor of Intercultural Studies Dissertation, 2017).
5 'Hatua' is a Swahili word that means to make an action or take a step.
6 Barrington-Ward, 'Spirit possession as redefinition', 455–464.

of the Oba of Benin – which was where the Isoko had migrated from to settle in Nigeria – to recognise his father's skull and to receive his state sword. The skulls of previous rulers were sent to Benin. This new ruler then ruled with a council of elders drawn from the whole society of recognised adult men.[7] New independent groupings often broke away to make new settlements, and all these groupings would owe their allegiances to same central divinities, notably, the founder and ruler of the group. Although there was a special cult of mothers for wives and daughters, the society was patrilineal.[8] The *Ovie* or male ruler, was ritually possessed at an annual festival by one of the Spirits of his forebears. The priest of the land, also male, would be possessed during the blessing of the land at the beginning of the dry season.

From the historical accounts, it is clear that women for the most part did not occupy public roles as far as the social structures of the Isoko were concerned. Barrington-Ward's view of the Isoko community as basically patriarchal and patrilineal has been echoed by others. Patrick Edewor, writing in 2006 on 'Changing perceptions of the value of daughters and girls' education among the Isoko of Nigeria', comments: 'The Isoko society is, basically, a patriarchal and patrilineal one characterised by the dominance of men in virtually all spheres of life. Women in traditional Isoko society were expected to be subservient to their husbands. Men's views on family matters and reproduction took the upper hand over those of women.' He notes that the 'social norms which supported these gender relations were culturally transmitted from one generation to another through the process of socialization'. A girl grew up to become an 'obedient' and 'good' wife. 'Female autonomy was virtually non-existent.'[9]

In 1906, the British established their own administrative structure in Isokoland, creating a new protectorate called the Colony of and Protectorate of Southern Nigeria. This protectorate was further broken down into provincial and divisional headquarters, without reference to the Isoko and other local communities, and what is important to note is that these administrative units introduced numerous challenges in the relations between communities. Obaro Ikime observes this in his 'Thoughts on Isoko–Urhobo Relations'. It is also important to note that from 1900–1930, the British set up native courts which

---

7   Barrington-Ward, 'Spirit possession as redefinition', 455.
8   Barrington-Ward, 'Spirit possession as redefinition', 456–457.
9   Patrick Edewor, 'Changing perceptions of the value of daughters and girls' education among the Isoko of Nigeria', *Union for African Population Studies* 21, no. 1 (2006), 55–70.

replaced the existing systems of justice among the Isoko as well as among other communities.[10]

Economically, the coming of the British brought about equally radical changes. Before the coming of colonialism, palm nut collection was a seasonal activity, controlled by a council of elders whose duty it was to declare the season open or closed.[11] Extraction involved the cooperation of a man, his wife and children, and possibly the extended family. Palm oil was processed to meet domestic consumption needs as well as social obligations, such as paying dowry, and for occasional luxury items like gin and gun powder. The entire process required the use of locally manufactured goods, from ropes for harvesting, to earthen pots for boiling palm fruits, as well as the use of tree trunks for building and palm fronds for fodder. The commercialising of oil production therefore disrupted the economic way of life of the Isoko and other communities through the use of other non-traditional items like basins and cutlasses and through the land ceded for the plantation system that was designed to increase production. It is these changes that Barrington-Ward describes as the shaking of central institutions, and in particular the power and authority of the elders and rulers as well as the ancestors and spirits.[12]

As a way of redefining society, whenever the Isoko arrived in a new environment, new phenomena and new social groupings were a frequent occurrence. From time to time, new spirits would disclose themselves through possession. Through dreams, visions, and voices, these new spirits would declare their intentions to the individuals they were seeking to possess. The effect was the creation of new categories which accounted for new phenomena and also gave identity to new groupings. Barrington-Ward makes the case that new spirit cults seemed to multiply at the points of greatest social and conceptual confusion where the boundaries of society were weakest. From this came the need for redefinition.[13]

Ibribina, Kimpa Vita and Njinga of Matamba

With the coming of European influences to Isokoland, the missionaries arrived, some in the company of foreign traders. However, a Christian movement was spread through a woman, Ibribina, from

10 Obaro Ikime, 'Thoughts on Isoko-Urhobo Relations', in Peter P. Ekeh, ed., *History of the Urhobo People of Niger Delta* (Buffalo, NY: Urhobo Historical Society, 2007), 427.
11 Samuel Ovete Aghalino, 'British colonial policies and the oil palm industry in the Niger Delta region of Nigeria, 1900–1960', *African Study Monographs* 21, no. 1 (2000), 19–33.
12 Barrington-Ward, 'Spirit possession as redefinition', 459.
13 Barrington-Ward, 'Spirit possession as redefinition', 460.

another culture, Ijaw, who had been seized by the Spirit while listening to the CMS missionary Henry Proctor.[14] Ibribina had been a zealous medium of a peripheral spirit among the Ijaw, and ceased her allegiance to other Ijaw spirits. Under Ibribina, a new movement proclaiming 'Jesu Krisi' flourished without the supervision and interference of formal organisational structures at a time when Europe itself was in turmoil.[15] Ibribina proclaimed a new message of love that was all encompassing, bringing together the young people of many different communities, kinship groups and quarters. Through the proclamation of a message of all pervasive power through the Spirit and the fellowship of humanity across cultures and ethnic groups, thousands flocked to be a part of the new society. Although Ibribina's ministry did not fit the structures of the mission churches, her encounter with the Spirit led to a massive expansion of the church.[16]

Ibribina's experience is to be set within the context of social upheaval and the influence of these circumstances on the emergence of women and men as leaders in Africa.[17] In Africa and parts of the Pacific in the twentieth century, the confrontation between the claims of Christianity and indigenous systems of power encouraged the emergence of leaders, particularly those with a prophetic character.[18] A notable example of a female African leader in the early eighteenth century, is Kimpa Vita, also known as Dona Beatriz (1684–1706).[19] She arose in the Kingdom of Kongo to restore order in the midst of the chaos caused by both the Portuguese colonial domination and the civil war that was pitting the heirs to the throne against one another. This young 22-year-old prophetess came into prominence in 1704, at a time when Mbanza Kongo, the spiritual and political capital of the Kingdom of Kongo, was in trouble. She had been initiated as a traditional priestess, but had also been educated in the Catholic faith and tradition. While seriously ill, she saw a vision of a friar dressed

---

14 Barrington-Ward, 'Spirit possession as redefinition', 461.
15 Simon Barrington-Ward, 'My Pilgrimage in Mission', *International Bulletin of Missionary Research* 23, no. 2 (1999), 60–64.
16 Barrington-Ward, 'My Pilgrimage in Mission', 61.
17 There were also, of course, new male leaders. Robert O. Collins, ed., *Documents from the African Past* (Princeton, NJ: Markus Wiener Publishers, 2001), notes that between 1905–1907, the Matumbi of South Eastern Tanganyika experienced upheaval brought about by the coming of colonial rule in terms of their political, social and economic way of life. Unable to resist the Germans because of their decentralised societal structure and their lack of military strength, the people silently endured the situation until they rallied around the prophet Kinjekitile Ngwale, a man, in 1904. Kinjekitile was possessed by the spirit of Hongo. The medicine conferred by Hongo would confer prosperity and health, as well as protection from famine and sickness, guaranteeing a good harvest.
18 Brian Stanley, *Christianity in the Twentieth Century* (Princeton & Oxford: Princeton University Press, 2018), notes that prophetic leaders rose up at times of great crisis or danger. Examples include William Wade Harris in the Ivory Coast in 1914, John Chilembwe in Nyasaland (Malawi) in 1914–15, Garrick Braide in Eastern Nigeria in 1915–16 and Simon Kimbangu in the Belgian Congo in 1920–1.
19 Aurélien Mokoko Gampiot, 'Kimpa Vita', in James Crossley and Alastair Lockhart, eds, *Critical Dictionary of Apocalyptic and Millenarian Movements* (Brighton: Centre for the Critical Study of Apocalyptic and Millenarian Movements, 2021). Retrieved from http://www.cdamm.org/articles/kimpa-vita 5 June 2021.

as a Capuchin, who identified himself as Saint Anthony. He had been sent to her by God to bring healing to her people and restoration to the kingdom of Kongo. Kimpa Vita experienced what she described as the possession of her body by Saint Anthony, who spoke out of her mouth, speaking against white missionaries who were an obstacle to the restoration of the Kingdom of Kongo.[20]

Both the case of Ibribina and the case of Kimpa Vita are consistent with other charismatic movements, sects and similar groups operating under the Christian banner. Like Ibribina and Kimpa Vita, Njinga of Matamba, also referred to as Njinga of Angola, arose out of a drastically changed order in society. The Ndongo forces were unable to withstand the Portuguese armies with their firearms and the local warriors they had recruited. At the height of the crisis Njinga was selected by her brother, who was the ruler of the Ndongo at that time, to lead a diplomatic mission to Luanda to make peace with the new governor Joao Correira de Sousa.[21] On the invitation of the governor she prolonged her stay in Luanda to learn more about Christian faith, and was baptised at the age of forty. On her return to Kabasa, she harnessed the prestige that Christianity offered as well as the traditional rituals to consolidate her position. Upon the death of her brother she seized the opportunity to entrench her position by sending a letter to offer peace with the new governor inviting missionaries into Ndongo to baptise those of her people who wished to be converted to Christianity. Njinga died as a Christian who had reconciled to the church although questions still remained about the depth of her commitment to Catholic Christianity.[22]

Although questions remained, Andrew Walls, citing C.C. Okorocha, notes that the rapid response to Christianity by Africans for multiple reasons cannot be relegated to the secular sphere since Africans always connected religion with the acquisition of power.[23] Unlike Njinga, whose conversion did not revolve around an initial encounter with the Spirit and whose conversion became an instrument to keep the peace with the Portuguese, the case of Ibribina and the case of Kimpa Vita began with extraordinary encounters with the Spirit, as well as patterns of prayer and worship that included physical and spiritual

---

20 Aurélien Mokoko Gampiot, 'Kimpa Vita'.
21 Linda M. Heywood, 'Queen Njinga and Her Faiths: Religion and Politics in 17th Century Angola', in Dana L. Robert, ed., *African Christian Biography: Stories, Lives, and Challenges* (Pietermaritzburg: Cluster Publications, 2018), 127; cf. Linda M. Heywood, *Njinga of Angola: Africa's Warrior Queen* (Cambridge, MA: Harvard University Press, 2017).
22 Heywood, 'Queen Njinga,' 131.
23 Cyril Chukwunonyerem Okorocha, *The Meaning of Religious Conversion in Africa: The Case of the Igbo of Nigeria* (Aldershot: Avebury Gower, 1987), cited in Andrew F. Walls, *The Missionary Movement in Christian History: Studies in the Transmission of Faith* (Maryknoll, NY: Orbis Books, 1996), 89–90.

healing. However, all three of these women leaders emerged within circumstances in which many people were uncertain, unsettled, and threatened in their lives at many levels: socially, economically, morally and spiritually.[24]

Conclusion: Understanding Women's Leadership

These cases suggest that a link exists between the emergence of women's leadership and the contexts of social and political upheaval such as those described by Barrington-Ward among the Isoko in the 1880s, and those experienced in the kingdoms of Kongo in 1684–1706 and in Ngola from 1624–1663. These situations of upheaval were an important factor in the emergence of women's leadership, precisely because the mostly patriarchal traditional institutions were in disarray. As Barrington-Ward notes, societies and communities, not just among the Isoko redefine themselves in significant moments of transition within the social and political contexts. The impetus for societies to redefine themselves comes from the shaking of central institutions and the breaking of the conceptual and social nets of the culture, as described by Barrington-Ward. In the cases looked at, and in other cases, new religious movements arise in which women are prominent.[25]

The emergence of a woman as the agent of the spread of Christianity among the Isoko is particularly significant given the patriarchal character of the Isoko community. Besides the encounter with the Holy Spirit experienced by Ibribina, the upheaval experienced by the community through the coming of colonisation and Christianity is an important factor to consider. The changes occasioned by the new currency, wealth and power and new technology broke through the conceptual and social nets of culture resulting in the emergence of new social groupings as well as the emergence of the leadership of a woman from a different culture as a spiritual leader among the Isoko. In all the three cases, of Ibribina of the Isoko, Kimpa Vita of the Kingdom of Kongo, and Queen Njinga of the Matamba, in addition to their personal encounters with the power of God and the message

---

24 Laurenti Magesa, 'Charismatic Movements as "Communities of Affliction"', in Mika Vahakangas and Andrew Kyomo, eds, *Charismatic Renewal in Africa: A Challenge for African Christianity* (Nairobi: Acton, 2003), 27–44.

25 A study conducted by Damaris Seleina Parsitau discusses the proliferation of women leaders within Pentecostalism in Kenya and notes that the emergence of women leaders within the Pentecostal church as founders, healers and prophetesses has not been replicated in Kenyan life more broadly. [At the time of writing this article in 2021, Kenya has just appointed the first woman Chief Justice, Her Excellency Martha Koome and just before this, the Anglican Church in Kenya elected Emily Onyango, first woman Bishop in Kenya.] Parsitau, Damaris Seleina, '"Arise, Oh Ye Daughters of Faith": Women, Pentecostalism and Public Culture in Kenya', in Harri Englund, ed., *Christianity and Public Culture in Africa* (Athens, OH: Ohio University Press, 2011), 131–148.

of the gospel, women leaders were propelled by the social upheaval to act as agents of change in circumstances that were highly unusual and unstable.

What Barrington-Ward contributes to in several important ways is our understanding of the incarnation of the gospel in a specific social context. He does this by putting a female prophetic leader at the centre of his experience of African Christianity and of the work of the Holy Spirit. In this he takes into account the work of the Spirit in the lives of women in the account of world Christianity. Dana Robert has taken this further, speaking of world Christianity was a 'women's movement'.[26] Having served as a chaplain at Magdalene College, where he himself had been a student, and then accepting the call to serve as a lecturer at the University of Ibadan in Nigeria, he sheds light not just on a society in turmoil, but also on a prophetic female leader whose ministry impacted him profoundly.[27] While contributing to our understanding of the real impact of the gospel on the people of Nigeria, he at the same time expands our understanding of the emergence of female leaders through the account of Ibribina, a female prophetic leader who emerged to proclaim the message of Jesu Krisi in the societal upheaval of colonialism.

---

26 Robert, 'World Christianity as a women's movement', 180–188.
27 Barrington-Ward, 'My Pilgrimage in Mission', 60–64.

CHAPTER 10

Hegel and Holiness

James Orr

Introduction

FEW OF THOSE FORTUNATE ENOUGH to have known Simon Barrington-Ward, in the course of his long life and endlessly fruitful ministry, will forget how often and how piously he would invoke the shade of Hegel, whenever a conversation began to take an intellectual turn. It often seemed as if he believed that philosopher's vision could encompass any problem and overcome any paradox. On one point, at least, he would have agreed with Derrida: 'we have never finished with a reading or rereading of Hegel.'[1] For him, Hegel's capacious and intricate body of thought was not, he insisted, a 'system,' since that begged the question against those who recognised, as Barrington-Ward did, that his philosophy was not sealed in a silo of finitude, but always pointed beyond itself towards horizons of transcendence that he spent so much of his life exploring and shaping to his vocations as a missionary, as a theologian, and as a bishop.

Yet for many of his detractors Hegel's dialectical account of the slow efflorescence of consciousness in the unfolding of history is a long and lugubrious parlour game designed to dissolve every seemingly settled conclusion. At its worst, his philosophy licenses a slightly more sophisticated historicised version of relativism that is as easy to eliminate from one's philosophy as it is difficult to dislodge from one's psychology. For my own part, as his son-in-law, I found Barrington-Ward's reliably regular recursions to Hegel endlessly invigorating precisely because it did mean that no conclusion, however definitive it might seem, ever quite counted as finished business; more often, it was simply a sign that it should be scrutinised afresh.

---

1   Jacques Derrida, *Positions* (Chicago, IL: University of Chicago Press, 1981), 77.

Hinterland of Devotion to Hegel

In a world still recovering from the baleful transposition of Hegel's thought to the dialectical materialism of Karl Marx, the most famous 'Left Hegelian' of them all, or in the more recent fusion of Hegel and Marx in the critical theory of the Frankfurt School, Barrington-Ward's devotion to Hegel was charmingly countercultural, theologically defiant, and spiritually galvanising. I came to regard him in philosophical terms as one of the last living links to the great tradition of British Idealism that dominated the Anglosphere in the final third of the nineteenth century. Barrington-Ward's father, whose early death in 1948 led him to reflect seriously for the first time on Christianity, was a practical man who thrived on the complexities of public policy and current affairs.[2] But although he showed scant interest in any of the religious or philosophical questions that would occupy his son, whenever pressed on such questions in discussion he would routinely describe himself as a 'Hegelian'. No doubt a response like that would be treated in most quarters today as an invitation to move swiftly on to other things and, given his notorious reticence in spiritual and philosophical matters, perhaps that stance was as much a strategy of deflection as anything else. In truth, though, there is every reason to suppose that Barrington-Ward's father was no less intoxicated by Hegelianism than so many others of his generation were in the twilight years of British Hegelianism, whose beating heart in Oxford was Balliol College.

Bernard Bosanquet, who had been an undergraduate at Balliol, delivered a set of Gifford Lectures from 1910 to 1912 that would come to mark one of the last gasps of British Hegelianism, which by that point was reeling from the devastating critiques of G.E. Moore and Bertrand Russell at the turn of the century.[3] Still, the legacies of the two legendary Balliol tutors T.H. Green and Edward Caird who, together with Bosanquet, made up the triumvirate of Oxford Hegelians, would have left its mark on any undergraduate studying Literae Humaniores in that period. J.H. Stirling's *The Secret of Hegel* (1865) exercised a mesmerising effect on a generation of British philosophers and inaugurated the tradition of British Hegelianism that dominated the last quarter of the nineteenth century. But it was the great Balliol tutor T.H. Green whose ideas provided the principal mo-

---

2   Having devoted his time and energies at the Oxford Union, which culminated in his election as President in the Trinity Term in 1912, Robert Barrington-Ward took a Third at Greats at Balliol in 1913.

3   T.S. Eliot's doctoral dissertation at Harvard on Bradley was never published.

mentum to the movement by inspiring a collection essays edited by R.B. Haldane and A. Seth Pringle-Pattison, *Essays in Philosophical Criticism* (1883).

These were the Hegelian hinterlands in which Barrington-Ward *père* recalled being formed. Barrington-Ward *fils* confessed that at the outset it was filial piety that led to his interest in the *Phenomenology of Spirit*, but he slowly came to discern in its author a provocative dissatisfaction with the platitudes of the *Aufklärung* (Enlightenment), whether in the form of the dualism between matter and spirit, inaugurated by Descartes, to the apparent dissolution of the self in Hume at the pinnacle of the British empiricist tradition. He cites approvingly Hegel's sharp dismissal of the 'empty babblers of the Enlightenment' (*Schwätzer der Aufklärung*),[4] a phrase that comes in a fragment of his early writings from the Tübingen Period (1788–1793) in which the affective character of the religious life is affirmed in terms that diverge strikingly from the hyper-rationalistic renditions of theological claims that so dominant at that time.[5]

Attraction and Interpretation of Hegel

Hegel's attraction for Barrington-Ward could be summarised in a handful of insights. He extracted from his writings the conviction that the life of faith as dynamic and fitful process of coming to resemble God through the ongoing negation of sin. Moral failure brought home to him the preciousness and possibilities of redemption. Barrington-Ward recognised that Hegel's vision was underpinned by a basic conviction that should scarcely amount to more than a platitude for the Christian believer – or, for that matter, the most weakly committed Abrahamic monotheist or the nostalgic Neoplatonist – namely that the foundational metaphysical ingredient of reality, the very wellspring of being as such, is not matter but mind – though he would also stress, within the realm of contingency, 'no talk of matter without talk of mind; no talk of mind without talk of matter'. If that convergence between spiritual abstraction and concrete materiality seems banal, it is worth recalling that it would have been an increasingly surprising and provocative stance to maintain during the

---

4   Simon Barrington-Ward, "Redeeming the Time," unpublished lecture, Wycliffe College, Toronto (1994b), 5.
5   The fragment Barrington-Ward quotes from Hegel's *Jugenschriften* is on folk-religion and Christianity ("Volksreligion und Christentum") and is from the so-called Tübingen Period, which spanned a time during which revealed religion seemed to have been wholly subsumed in rationalism. Hegel entered the Tübingen Stift (the seminary connected to the University of Tübingen) in 1788, which was the year in which Kant published his *Critique of Practical Reason*, and left after receiving his Konsistorialexamen in 1793, the year in which Kant published *Religion Within the Limits of Reason Alone*.

period in which Barrington-Ward first immersed himself in German Idealism. For it was then that the headwinds of Marxism – that standing antithesis to idealism in all its guises – that swept most violently across so many parts of the institutional landscape of the West. Even Magdalene College, Cambridge, a happy home and refuge for him throughout his life, was not fully shielded from these developments.[6]

Formation in faith was, he would joyfully and endlessly intone, a process of 'failing towards,' a 'saving phrase' he learned from the philosopher Gillian Rose.[7] By this he meant that the life of faith should involve framing moral failure against a horizon of hope for restoration and reconciliation. That approach took seriously the reality of sin while keeping in view the redemptive possibilities that always lay open beyond it. Barrington-Ward did not, of course, accept that propensity to sin was intrinsic to the human condition in its primal created purity, but he was drawn to the Pauline idea that providence presses evil into the service of the good and it was in Hegel's writings above all that he found these rhythms of reconciliation and redemption most powerfully expressed in the register of secular philosophy. For Hegel, after all, fallenness and finitude mark the great antithesis to the transcendent perfection and infinity of God, an incongruity that opens a rupture (*Entzweiung*) within a human subject forever torn between a longing for promised reconciliation and the chaotic actuality of his contingent circumstances.[8]

Holiness

The horizon of moral perfection, forever alluring but forever unattainable this side of biological death, involves a *process* of fitful steps of spiritual formation and here too Barrington-Ward drew on the reading of Hegel that did not construe his thought as a definitive system sealed off from novelty and transcendence, but rather one that saw it as open and unfinished. For him, Hegel's rendering of divinity as *Geist* (Spirit) distilled the sense of dynamism that marked the spiritual life and of divine self-disclosure in the quotidian complexities and messy particularity of pastoral life. Above all, he saw in the process of sublation – the process by which the conflict between two opposed ideas is resolved by the emergence of a new idea – and reconciliation

---

6 Ronald Hyam, "In Memoriam: Simon Barrington-Ward KCMG" in *Magdalene College Magazine* 2019–2020, 14. See Chapter 2 above.
7 Simon Barrington-Ward, "Sermon for Farewell Service, Coventry Cathedral," unpublished manuscript (28 September 1997), 2.
8 G.W.F. Hegel, *Lectures on the Philosophy of Religion, Vol. 3: The Consummate Religion*, Peter C. Hodgson, ed. (Oxford: Clarendon Press, 2007), 310–11.

a pneumatological pulse, even if his rootedness in hesychastic practice (the Jesus Prayer), and his lively sense of orthodoxy, ensured that he did not confuse the Holy Ghost with Hegelian *Geist*. Moral failure was always and everywhere subsumed in the light of Christ into a dynamic orientation towards a divinisation, through the rhythms of prayer and the practice of holiness. Barrington-Ward's attentiveness to the shattering effects of human sin was seared into his first religious awakening amidst the rubble and shattered cityscape of Berlin in the early 1950s. Among a Christian prayer and bible group in a village church, that was founded by the Lutheran theologian Martin Niemöller, one of the founders of the Confessing Church, and was attended by former Nazis, his fledgling faith was forged.

Barrington-Ward returned again and again in his diaries and homilies to the theme of the "Great Exchange" – that gleaming thread of Christology woven through the anthropology of Irenaeus and Athanasius that God became human that human beings might become divine.[9] For all the controversy that clouds Hegel's Christology as he unfolds it in the *Lectures on Philosophy of Religion*, in Barrington-Ward's view it represented one of the most titanic and at least partially successful effort by a major philosopher to tread the delicate tightropes of Chalcedonian Christology. Humanity as an abstract universal is sublated into *this particular* human being to usher in a human condition that is rescued from finitude and redeemed from fallenness.

Hegel showed how the radical dualism that undermines any Christology attempting to conform to the strictures of Kant's transcendental idealism could be overcome. Barrington-Ward believed in other words, based partly on his reading of Hegel, that in the event of Christ's incarnation, death, and resurrection a definitive reconciliation of divinity and humanity, a reconciliation that in itself marks a perfect and timeless state of resolution within the trinitarian life of God, whereby a distinction that emerges within God sublates itself and, in transcending that distinction, reconciles human beings to God. Barrington-Ward recognised, in other words, that, properly appropriated, Hegel offered a metaphysical justification for steering a path between docetism and Arianism, a philosophical account of how divinity could be uniquely and definitively distilled into one particular historical figure, however shocking that claim might appear:

---

9   e.g. Irenaeus, *Against Heresies*, §448: 'The Word of God became man, that you may learn from man how man may become God'; Athanasius, *On the Incarnation*, §93: 'He indeed assumed humanity that we might become God, etc.'

It is not enough that the concrete moment in God should be known, for it is also necessary that this representation of God should be known as tied to humanity; it should be known that Christ was an actual man. That is the tie with humanity in its *thisness*. The moment being *this one* is the great moment of shock in the Christian religion; it is the binding together of the most shocking antithesis.[10]

Political Engagement

At various points in his work as a missionary and bishop, Barrington-Ward was caught up in questions of a social and political dimension, notably on the debates about the Sunday trading. He inherited from his father a liberal instinct in politics, one that was developed in the course of his lifelong friendship with his Eton contemporary, Jeremy Thorpe. Here too there were Hegelian fingerprints on his thinking, especially in the threefold distinction between family, civil society, and the state that constitutes Part III of Hegel's *Elements of the Philosophy of Right* (1820). Barrington-Ward always claimed that his suspicion of Thatcherism arose from his liberalism and the threat that market reforms and the diminution of public services posed to the most vulnerable in society. Yet those reforms – notably the later passing of the Sunday Trading Act 1994 under John Major's Government, a move that Barrington-Ward vigorously opposed from the pulpit and in print – were self-consciously liberalising reforms that placed a premium on individual autonomy and drew their intellectual impetus from Hayek. It is perhaps more accurate to construe his disquiet at the neoliberalism of Thatcher and Reagan as the conservative critique that liberal autonomy breeds social atomism by weakening the organic bonds of faith, family, and flag that sustain our *Sittlichkeit*, Hegel's term for the social norms and moral traditions that structure a society's common life.

In contrast to liberalism's contractarian conception of the relationship between self and state or what he saw as Fabian socialism's suffocating statism, Barrington-Ward held fast to the insight that a philosophy of individualism was the most effective way of erasing the individual. It undermined the mediating function of civil society (Hegel's *bürgerliche Gesellschaft*), the many and various forms of interdependence and social belonging from which individuals derive

---

10 G.W.F. Hegel, *Lectures on the History of Philosophy 1825-6: Medieval and Modern Philosophy*, Peter C. Hodgson, ed. (Oxford: Clarendon Press, 2006), 27.

their sense of self-worth and existential significance. For him, it was the communities of faith at Taizé, or on Iona, or at the Monastery of St John the Baptist at Tolleshunt Knights in Essex, places he visited as often as he could, that were most effective at facilitating what he understood Hegel to mean by *Sittlichkeit*, that ethical form of communal life, rooted in tradition but free of atavism and open to transformation but only where repentance demanded it:

> The constant rhythm of the life of such communities and of the dynamic which they generate amongst others is a rhythm of repentance and forgiveness, of death and resurrection, of acknowledgement of failure and weakness and need but of constant faith in the struggle for change ... Using the term forgiveness does not suggest that we are thereby saved from confrontation ... but it does mean that within and through that confrontation there is always the hope of breaking through to a fresh recognition of possibilities ... I see the root of our understanding of the gospel in Hegel's insight that we proceed from miscognition to miscognition constantly experiencing a *metanoia*, a change of heart and mind and being free from the entail of the past.[11]

In this lecture delivered at Wycliffe College, Toronto, Barrington-Ward described his pleasure at being introduced by a friend in Cambridge, on his return from a stint as a university lecturer at Ibadan University in Nigeria, to German philosophy of the late eighteenth century, in particular Friedrich Schiller's *On the Aesthetic Education of Man in a Series of Letters* (1794) and Hegel's early political writings. He saw striking parallels between the intense philhellenic longing for an idealised political culture of the Greek *polis* and the yearning of his friends in Nigeria for a time when their culture had not yet been affected by the family breakdown and widespread social fragmentation that appeared to be symptomatic of the country's exposure to Western influence.[12] Barrington-Ward argued that Schiller and Hegel had witnessed in their own time social pathologies that he diagnosed in Western modernity. He cited a sentence from Hegel's early political writings that echoed the title of Chinua Achebe's acclaimed novel *Things Fall Apart* (1958) set in an idealised pre-colonial Nigeria (the phrase itself of course is taken from Yeats' 'The Second Coming'):

---

11 Barrington-Ward, 'Redeeming the Time', 13.
12 Barrington-Ward, 'Redeeming the Time', 2.

'Every centre of life has gone its own way and established itself on its own; the whole has fallen apart.'[13] He described the social instability and existential dislocation induced by the shock of industrial and commercial revolutions that swept through Europe in the late eighteenth century and Africa a century later.

Gillian Rose

Barrington-Ward was convinced, then, that Hegel offered the most subtle and integrated diagnosis of the individual and social fragmentation he had witnessed in Berlin, Nigeria, and Coventry. Nowhere was that conviction more vividly reinforced than through his precious and unexpected friendship with the Jewish social philosopher Gillian Rose. The phrase 'failing towards' was, as he recalled in his farewell sermon at Coventry Cathedral in 1997, 'given to me and to us all through one of the most remarkable encounters of my life.' Rose's writings reinforced for Barrington-Ward the ways in which Hegel's thought offered a conceptual framework for social progress. As he put it, '[s]he had a clear sense of the goal that lies ahead of us all, of an integration of society, a final wholeness.'[14] Barrington-Ward was struck first and foremost by Rose's charisma and remained forever in awe at the breadth and density of her work, though he worked hard to grasp the thrust and themes of her great trilogy, a task in which he was helped by Rowan Williams and Andrew Shanks, who, together with John Milbank, were largely responsible for convincing theologians in the English-speaking world of the salience of Rose's work.[15]

He drew from her work a dazzlingly erudite endorsement of an intuition that had been with him since the beginning of his intellectual life as a reflective Christian: Hegel's legacy was not a threat to Christianity but, if carefully appropriated, a revivifying tonic both for the spiritual life, for life in community, and, in virtue of its diagnostic power, for society as a whole. Yet it was clear that, as he came to know her in person, he began to discern in her a spiritual yearning and it was one that he patiently but persistently persuaded her could be satisfied by looking beyond the broken space of politics and culture between this life and the next. In the end, perhaps it is more accurate to say that Rose drew still more from Barrington-Ward's in-

---

13 Barrington-Ward, 'Redeeming the Time', 2
14 Barrington-Ward, Farewell Sermon, 2.
15 Rowan D. Williams, "Between Politics and Metaphysics: Reflections in the Wake of Gillian Rose," *Modern Theology* 11(1) (1995), 3–22. Andrew Shanks, *Against Innocence: Gillian Rose's Reception and Gift of Faith* (London: SCM Press, 2008). John Milbank's qualified appreciation of Hegel's legacy in *Theology and Social Theory* owes much to the influence of Rose (see John Milbank, *Theology and Social Theory* (Oxford: Blackwell, 1990), ch. 6.

fectious spirituality than he did from her complex and highly allusive writings in metaphysics and politics.

Rose's singular achievement, amidst the whirling tide of interpretations of Hegel, was not only to transcend the dusty dichotomy of Left Hegelianism and Right Hegelianism but also to refuse the view so dominant in postmodernist – and, in particular, Francophone postmodernist – reception of Hegel that treated his thought as a closed system sealed in immanence and sequestrated from the absolute. In what is now perhaps the most well-known, and theologically acute, early treatments of her work, Rowan Williams drew attention to 'the philosophical importance of error and the recognisability of error' as a crucial concern in Rose's critique of the fashionable reification of 'the Other' in postmodern ethics.[16] From 'absolute knowing' to recognition of a broken middle, by which Rose meant the conceptual space of an ultimately aporetic conflict, or 'agon', between an abstract transcendental formalism and the concrete demands and constraints on social and political action. The broken middle was also intended to capture the chronic tensions between the realm of law (Hegel's *Moralität*) and the domain of ethics (*Sittlichkeit*).

For all her criticisms of post-structuralism's reification of the Other, Rose's philosophical style is burdened with all of the maddening and muddy allusiveness and energetic bursts of midrash across a dizzying array of texts in continental philosophy. Her hermeneutical style makes it difficult to distinguish constructive proposals from the specific text she is interpreting.[17] An example of this is when those underlying texts are themselves as speculative as those of Hegel or of Kierkegaard, for it is the alleged *consensus* between these two figures that dominates *The Broken Middle*, though Rose assumes without argument what is a highly contentious claim, namely that it is their philosophical stances that should frame any inquiry into political and ethical matters. Sifting Rose's prose for a cogent argument is often more taxing than it should be and accounts, no doubt, for why she has had less impact than her defenders claim she deserves. But what can be said is that, so far as Rose was concerned, Hegel was a philosopher who delighted in contradictions wrestling to reconcile abstract ideas to the concrete constraints of ordering the public square towards a horizon of justice.

---

16 Williams, 'Between Politics and Metaphysics', 9.
17 V. Lloyd, *Law and Transcendence: On the Unfinished Project of Gillian Rose* (London: Palgrave MacMillian, 2009), 239, notes in an otherwise appreciative treatment of her legacy, 'Rose's texts wallow in…paradoxes to the point that they unwittingly approach the style and substance of the deconstructionists she takes herself to be supplanting.'

Her central insight was that it was futile to suppose that a smooth integration was achievable between the universal and the particular and that any instantiation of a universal moral principle would involve unsatisfactory compromise, when refracted through the fragility and fragmentation of everyday life. There could be no 'holy middle' to enact, be it in the form of Milbank's allegedly nostalgic *ressourcement* of Christendom,[18] or of the self-consciously anarchic landscape that Mark C. Taylor envisions as emerging from the ruins of institutional Christianity.[19] She suggests that both visions mistakenly suppose that there could ever be some final or definitive theological settlement between tradition and modernity or between sacred and secular.

But although Rose's conviction was in the intrinsic instability of the Hegelian oscillation between law and ethics in any political order, as her mortality confronted her she came to see and to hope for an ultimate resolution of the broken middle. She came to recognise this construed as the existential predicament of a single soul in search of meaning and, in her very last days, in the conviction that participation in the divine life beyond biological death was possible. The intention of taking the formal step towards the Christian faith had begun to form in her mind for some time beforehand, but as it became clearer that the end was approaching she quickly decided to be received into the Church of England, in what was (inevitably) a hastily improvised affair. Barrington-Ward performed the ceremony around 6pm on 9 December 1994, just a few hours before she died. In what would appear to be the last words she wrote, she sketched the moment she informed him of her plans for baptism, confirmation, and communion in anticipation of Barrington-Ward's return from Tolleshunt Knights:

> And now Simon Barrington-Ward has been to see me and
> heard the Good News and will hold my Baptism Confirmation
> Communion around a text from Dante's *Paradiso* on Saturday
> at 6.0 pm. He will drive back in time from retreat at St
> Sophrony's St John's Tiptree and everyone will be able to
> be here. I shall write out the Guest list first thing tomorrow.
> Simon asked me about the final stages along the way.
> 1.   The Grieve 'experience'
> 2.   A's letter

18 Gillian Rose, *The Broken Middle: Out of Our Ancient Society* (Oxford: Blackwell, 1992), 280–4.
19 Rose, *The Broken Middle*, 279–80.

3. David Robinson's ministry
4. Julian Green, *God's Fool* (St Francis)
5. E

'Keep your mind in hell and d[espair] N[ot].'[20]

The gnomic anonymised list leaves it unclear what impact each of these five stages meant to her, but it seems clear enough that the final phrase was pregnant with significance for her at the threshold not only of baptism but also of death. Inscribed as the epigram of *Love's Work*, her last work and undoubtedly that for which she is best known today, the phrase is almost certainly one she learned from Barrington-Ward, who deployed it frequently as a potent pastoral prescription. The words were inscribed beside his desk beneath a portrait of one of Barrington-Ward's revered spiritual counsellor and friend, Archimandrite Sophrony (1896–1993).[21] In the end, then, what Rose learned most vividly from Barrington-Ward, and from those other faith-filled Christians providentially constellated around her in those painful and precious last days, was this. Grace sublates brokenness and resolves it into blessing, and the Hegelian rhythms of formation in holiness, animating the breaking and remaking of self through repentance and forgiveness, attain a moment at the threshold of death when love's true work attains its final consummation. In *Love's Work*, Rose observes that Barrington-Ward drew her forward towards faith with a quiet humility, which she captures in a touchingly comic description of his visit to her in hospital:

> Only the Bishop of Coventry, my bemused, stumbling friend, who came to help me push gently forward, had more inviolable authority bestowed by the nurses on to him and his pathetic posy of fragrant garden flowers, which nestled humbly among the hosts of assertive bouquets.[22]

Although he was by no means the only one involved in catalysing Rose's slow spiritual awakening to Christianity, in his handling a demanding and complex pastoral situation with skill and sensitivity Barrington-Ward displayed that infectious sense of the hope he had as

---

20 Gillian Rose, "The Final Notebooks of Gillian Rose," *Women: A Cultural Review* 9 (1) (1998), 6–18, 18.
21 Sophrony was canonised by the Ecumenical Patriarchate of Constantinople in 2019 and had edited the writings of St Silouan the Athonite (1866–1938), to whom the phrase, 'Keep your mind in hell and despair not,' is attributed. See Chapter 12 below.
22 Gillian Rose, *Love's Work* (New York, NY: Shocken Books, 1995), 81.

a Christian for that ultimate reconciliation when the human person's existential sense of inhabiting a 'broken middle', between birth and death, is finally overcome.

Conclusion

Was Barrington-Ward a Hegelian? Since it is not at all clear that *Hegel* was a Hegelian that is hardly a straightforward question to answer. Notoriously, Hegel's philosophical legacy was taken up in dizzyingly divergent ways immediately after his death and, like Kant's, continues to be one that can be deployed to sharply incompatible ends. Among many theologians in the twentieth century, he has been pressed into the service of dialectical pantheism, especially in the fashionable, but now largely defunct, versions of process theology, while Eric Voegelin and, more recently, Cyril O'Regan, view him as a key inspiration in the return to gnostic ways of thinking in contemporary thought, a connection that Barrington-Ward certainly found plausible, judging from a number of his handwritten notes on works by these authors.[23]

Hegel has also been appropriated to buttress highly revisionist – even antinomian – approaches to the development of doctrine, according to which credal orthodoxy is 'sublated' into modernity's metaphysical schemes in a way that promises a 'development' of doctrinal commitments in Newman's sense, but in fact dilutes and dissolves them. That he never let himself succumb to these fashionable currents, despite his immersion in Hegel's writings, testifies not only to Barrington-Ward's theological good taste but also his passion for putting the pursuit of repentance, forgiveness, and reconciliation at the centre of all that he did, virtues that he always recognised Hegelianism could frame but never sustain. Despite all that he profited from his lifelong quarrying of Hegel's work for enduring insights into self and society, Barrington-Ward's admiration of him was always qualified by a deeper commitment to those ancient credal truths that he seemed, so effortlessly, to incorporate into the life of faith through devotion to Christ.

---

23 Eric Voegelin, "On Hegel: A Study in Sorcery," *Studium* Generale 24 (1971), 335–68; Cyril O'Regan, *Gnostic Apocalypse: Jacob Boehme's Haunted Narrative* (New York, NY: State University of New York Press, 2001).

CHAPTER 11

Ecclesiology, Grace and Brokenness

Andy Lord

Gospel Communities

SIMON BARRINGTON-WARD lived a very communal approach to the Christian life. This chapter explores the nature of his ecclesiology, the understanding of the community of the church. It also suggests that his ecclesiology was exploratory in constantly seeking how it might be renewed and draw others in. Although not an academic theologian Barrington-Ward articulates an integrative narrative ecclesiology around key concerns for gospel, community, spirituality and transformation. Running through each of these is the theme of multifaceted grace found in varied broken contexts and this is rooted in a renewed understanding of the gospel. This is a contextualised gospel that arises from his British evangelical background combined with his encounters with the world church and charismatic renewal. A good way into how Barrington-Ward approaches ecclesiology is by means of an example. In 1980 after his attendance at both the World Council of Churches (WCC) and Lausanne conferences on world mission he writes a personal story:

> The scene was the fringe of a South American city, one of those *favelas, bustees,* shanty towns which form makeshift outskirts of more and more of the growing cities of the Third World... The man stopped to speak to a group who were working on a dilapidated car. He discovered they were Pentecostal Christians, helping each other through sharing the little they had and their individual skills. They invited him in to one of the shacks to join in the Breaking of Bread. One of the workers donned a simple white robe and there, with children peeping in through the window, my friend was welcomed into the kingdom of

Jesus in the midst with simple and joyful dignity and courtesy. Here was the heart of that little group's caring and sharing: they knew more than any of us the secret of the gospel.[1]

Here we have faith, community, spirituality and transformation all together in a fragile context with the gospel summarising what is happening.

Barrington-Ward argues for an integrating gospel that revolves around the cross and resurrection of Jesus Christ. Here the evangelical focus on the cross becomes an appreciation of the brokenness of the world seen in those who live on the fringes and margins of poverty and exclusion. It is in places of the cross that the resurrection is experienced in forgiveness, reconciliation, healing and, above all, grace. The gospel is about resurrection in places of the cross: about the fullness of grace in brokenness. This happens through the work of the Holy Spirit through individuals and communities. The church needs to be the vine rooted and grounded in love, in the cross of Christ and by the Spirit.[2] This resonates with the significant work of Michael Ramsey who argued that the meaning of the church becomes most clear when studied in terms of the gospel of the death and resurrection of Jesus.[3] It is in dying and rising with Christ that the meaning of the church is found. The centrality of the Cross highlights the imperfection of the church, which it must face as it seeks to live and express the death and resurrection of Christ. Ramsey goes on from the Cross to consider questions of unity and institution from his Anglo-Catholic perspective whereas Barrington-Ward pauses to consider mission communities in a world context. His more evangelical approach checks the rush to institutional questions in order to give greater space to speak of resurrection grace in small Christian communities of faith.

Broken Communities

The renewed gospel must be lived out in small communities and it is here that Barrington-Ward situates the church. This arises out of his experience of such communities in post-war Berlin, post-colonial and revival touched Nigeria, charismatic renewal in Cambridge, and mission training in Birmingham. He often returns to the stories of

---

1 Simon Barrington-Ward, *Love Will Out* (Basingstoke: Marshall Morgan and Scott, 1988), 43.
2 Simon Barrington-Ward and Brother Ramon, *Praying the Jesus Prayer Together* (Oxford: Bible Reading Fellowship, 2001), 87–89.
3 Michael Ramsey, *The Gospel and the Catholic Church* (London: SPCK, 1956, 1990 reprint), vi. 5–7.

Berlin from the 1950s, a city divided in which he discovered people seeking a new way of being society, and Nigeria where he discovered a prophetess who discerned in Jesus the source of power that enabled new way of being church. In a world often divided by a focus on individualism or dictatorship, the Christian vision is of a personal experience of grace that is 'never merely individual. Far from it. It is the very motive energy that will bring into being and multiply groups, communities, "cells of dissent", of the kind which alone will serve to transform society.'[4] These are comprised of people who are 'unlike', former Nazis and those resisting Hitler in Berlin, those from different tribes in Nigeria and different cultures in Birmingham. Yet there is still a 'family likeness', which Barrington-Ward describes as a 'transfiguration in an extraordinary mingling of suffering and joy'. It is an 'energy of the Spirit' that brings 'that lovely balance, the equipose of grace' in which there is a 'juxtaposition of opposed qualities miraculously fused'. It is the Christ-like face of those living the gospel in community that transformed Barrington-Ward's faith.[5]

This Christ-like community that is personal and corporate does not arrive at this ideal without a process of transfiguration that is empowered by the Spirit of grace. It is not separate from our brokenness but rather it is through 'our very weakness, failure and sadness, our emptiness, the Spirit flows, the light breaks. We will learn to live solely from grace, until "grace upon grace" surprises us.'[6] Barrington-Ward was painfully aware of how the world processes of war and colonialism shaped and broke communities, yet how in these places the new life of the Spirit could grow. The contextual setting of communities is important and we might see something of the classic Church of England focus on the parish system influencing Barrington-Ward here.[7] One of the contemporary debates is as to whether the parish system should be central to Anglican ecclesiology or discarded altogether.[8] Barrington-Ward would seem to side with the latter but we need to take care of his context and concerns. He is writing out of an engagement with world Anglicanism rather than the Church of England and this maintains a concern for the local and contextual, sometimes called the parish *principle*, without concern for parish structures. He speaks of how love connects differing people in communities and also connects different communities together within the

---

4 Barrington-Ward, *Love Will Out*, 38, 61–66, 107.
5 Simon Barrington-Ward, *Why God?* (Oxford: reprint, 1993, Lion, 1997).
6 Barrington-Ward, *Love Will Out*, 63.
7 Andrew Rumsey, *Parish: An Anglican Theology of Place* (London: SCM Press, 2017).
8 Andrew Davison and Alison Milbank, *For the Parish: A Critique of Fresh Expressions* (London: SCM, 2010).

kingdom of God. So Barrington-Ward, who was shaped within the parish system, represents more of a transformational approach that speaks of varied community and connections in love related to places rather than parishes. This avoids the temptations of forcing uniformity on to church life and of leaving communities isolated from each other.

Graceful Communal Spirituality

In more recent years Barrington-Ward has become known for his teaching on spirituality, as Philip Seddon explores in this book. It is worth noting here that his deeply personal approach rooted in the Jesus Prayer was discovered in a corporate setting in a Russian Orthodox monastery in Essex.[9] This was at a time when he was seeking a better way of integrating the diversity of his experience in prayer. He saw 'so many glimpses of the way people were living and striving and suffering... some kind of universal struggle... at every level in my life and in whole of human society.' He understands this in terms of Romans 8 and 'a kind of passion of the Holy Spirit, God himself, suffering and yearning within us as we struggle in our weakness'. There is an underlying pneumatology of love and passion that spans the world and history. There is an overlap here with approaches to the church that were emerging from the charismatic renewal of the time. Notably, Barrington-Ward's friend David Watson was developing practical approaches to community with holistic discipleship rooted in experiences of being filled with the Holy Spirit.[10] We might suggest that ecclesiology is simply a lived spirituality.

Barrington-Ward's exploration of ecclesiology also grew within the context of his predecessors at CMS, Max Warren and John V. Taylor. In different ways they explored kinds of spiritual ecclesiology, an understanding of the church rooted in the Presence of God and the Go-between Spirit, always reaching out in friendship to all. Warren had long involvement in the ecclesial tensions within both Anglicanism and the missionary movement, seeking forms of church that value people drawn together by the Spirit in mission.[11] Later he pioneered 'Christian presence' in a world of many faiths, exploring God at work in non-Christian cultures. Taylor spoke of the church 'being given to

---

9   Simon Barrington-Ward, *The Jesus Prayer* (Oxford: Bible Reading Fellowship, 1996), 8–16. See Philip Seddon, Chapter 12, 'Orthodoxy and Prayer'.
10 David Watson, *I Believe in the Church* (London: Hodder & Stoughton, 1982) 2nd Edn, reprint, 1978.
11 Andy Lord, *Network Church: A Pentecostal Ecclesiology Shaped by Mission*, GPCS 11 (Leiden: Brill, 2012), 116–17.

the Spirit' in order to then 'embody Jesus Christ in the world'.[12] He holds up small communities of still prayer in living out God's work of mission. Barrington-Ward can be seen as seeking to integrate some of their insights with those of the charismatic renewal. His distinctive, in regard to CMS, was in pioneering *exchange* to ensure that these communities grew through personal sharing across cultures.[13] The sharing of Spirit-graced gifts could bring transformation in the light of the gospel of Christ. He established a CMS 'Britain region' which began to recognise a greater equality in mission, away from power being held in the West for mission elsewhere.[14]

In the background have been the writings of Dietrich Bonhoeffer, which were influential from his time in Berlin (as they were also for John V. Taylor).[15] Bonhoeffer sought to develop spirituality and community in ways deeply Christological and communal. Jesus is known in 'in the humble silence of the worshipping community' and we can say that 'Christ is the community by virtue of his being *pro me*'.[16] More than this, Jesus is the centre of history with the 'meaning of history found in the humiliated Christ' on the cross.[17] Barrington-Ward explored these links in conversation with Bonhoeffer at a number of points in his first five years at CMS, although less after then. Christology highlights for him the personal centre of Christian faith which draws a diversity of people together around the crucified one.[18] In Bonhoeffer's later writing Barrington-Ward finds support for the critique of the church in its limits 'to stand up for what is good and just in the world'. The church needs to be transformed and renewed to rediscover Christ for the world and all of this is part of mission.

In many ways Barrington-Ward was exploring how ecclesiology might be spiritual, evangelical, charismatic and Orthodox, thus enabling a process of Christ-centred and Spirit-enabled *theosis* that brings new creation for all.[19] This is mission!

---

12 John V. Taylor, *The Go-Between God: The Holy Spirit and the Christian Mission* (London: SCM, 1972), 133–134, 237–243.

13 John Clark, 'CMS and Mission in Britain: The Evolution of a Policy,' in *The Church Mission Society and World Christianity, 1799–1999*, Keith Ward and Brian Stanley, eds (Cambridge: Eerdmanns, 2000), 335.

14 See Jocelyn Murray, *Proclaim the Good News: A Short History of the Church Missionary Society* (London: Hodder & Stoughton, 1985), 268–71. It must be admitted that this was only a step in the right direction and its limits left some rightly frustrated. Later, Tim Dakin encouraged the development of CMS Africa and others to better share power and responsibility across the nations.

15 Simon Barrington-Ward, email to Andy Lord (4 July 2008); cf. David Wood, *Poet, Priest and Prophet: Bishop John V. Taylor* (London: Churches Together in Britain and Ireland, 2002), 47–68.

16 Dietrich Bonhoeffer, *Christology*, trans. John Bowden (London: Collins, 1966), 27, 59–61.

17 Andreas Pangritz, 'Who is Jesus Christ, for Us, Today,' in *The Cambridge Companion to Dietrich Bonhoeffer*, John W. Gruchy, ed. (Cambridge: Cambridge University Press, 1999), 138.

18 See his *CMS Newsletters* 414 (1977) and 429 (1979).

19 Simon Barrington-Ward, *Jesus Prayer and the Great Exchange*, Grove Spirituality Series 124 (Cambridge: Grove Books, 2013), 17–19, 23.

World Transformation

Ecclesiology is set, for Barrington-Ward, within a world movement of the Spirit in which grace transforms in brokenness. How is this worked out in ecclesial practices? Here we might expect more than we get! Rather than an emphasis on social, political and peace initiatives Barrington-Ward focuses on prayer and witness through community.[20] In this there are prophetic challenges to be given through workplaces and amidst the philosophies of the day, rather than retreat into abstract spiritual half-worlds. Here is a 'humble prophet' pointing to ways forward, seeking to be a catalyst rather than leading initiatives from the front.[21] Spirituality and world transformation overlap in the practice of intercession which is 'a remembering of people and situations within the Presence, a discovering of them deep in the heart of the love of God in which we have become immersed'.[22] It should embrace our enemies and so change the approach in places of division. This prayerful way of being should also give rise to a 'spontaneous communication' that seeks to share 'the one source of all compassion and delight', Jesus. Communities of the unlike with deep spirituality witness to and share the transformation that is possible in Christ. There is an assumption that social, political and peace work only make sense if embodied in transformed communities.

These communities are contextual by nature but in a more organic way than seen in the movements of liberation that Barrington-Ward is cautious about.[23] He is more true to his evangelical roots in proposing a translation approach where a core gospel is planted and grown in different contexts through community.[24] This has been taken up more recently by those supporting Fresh Expressions within the Church of England. There are a number of weaknesses with this approach, particularly in its focus on a pure message prior to, or separate from, an embodied faith. Yet for Barrington-Ward the contextualisation of the message and the focus on core gospel elements enables him to recognise that 'religious systems are not total systems'. There is a need to engage with the varieties of faith that are shaped by, but not precisely defined by, core commitments and beliefs. This also allows a greater

---

20 This is perhaps not a unique problem in Anglican theology from William Temple to the 1980s, as noted in Malcolm Brown, *et al.*, *Anglican Social Theology: Renewing the Vision Today* (London: Church House Publishing, 2014).
21 CMS, 'The Humble Prophet,' *Yes*, March–May 1986, 5.
22 Barrington-Ward, *Love Will Out*, 33, 37–38.
23 For all that the church exists for others in the world, Barrington-Ward is surprisingly silent on its political nature and involvement. He gives significant support to the spirituality of Ken Leech at the end of his CMS years but does not engage his liberation approach, with only brief negative mentions of liberation movements, Simon Barrington-Ward, 'No Other Name,' *CMS Newsletter* 471 (1985), 4; Barrington-Ward, *Love Will Out*, 84.
24 Barrington-Ward, *Love Will Out*, 40.

admission of weakness and brokenness in the Western church which encourages an approach to world transformation from a place of gracious trust rather than powerful dominance. As Barrington-Ward notes, 'we are all minorities now' and so have to be vulnerable and trusting in God's leading.[25] The issue of changing power systems is a significant one in his ecclesiology and has wider relevance today.

Remaking Institutions

As he was embarking on his ministry as a Bishop, Barrington-Ward noted how we cannot avoid the 'poor old battered, insulated, much-failing and fumbling institutional churches'.[26] Yet, rooted in charismatic renewal he was always seeking new patterns of church life within God's movement of the Spirit that brings renewed life and mission.[27] It was through what Vincent Turner called 'communitas' that the structures might be renewed.[28] After ten years as a Bishop, speaking at the opening of the Centre for Anglican Communion Studies Barrington-Ward notes how the occasion 'speaks to the strangely ambiguous feelings that I have...in response to the notion of Anglicanism. Like all our inheritances from the mixed and shadowed history of the Church it is a vessel containing a strange fusion of what is richly good and nourishing combined with what is alas sinful and has a bitter aftertaste.'[29] The Anglican church is seen as a broken church that often gives in to destructive extremes and hinders mission. Yet it is also a place of grace inasmuch as it is able to surrender its life to God that it may be remade. The testimony of his friend Janani Luwum, later a martyr in Uganda, pointed Barrington-Ward to the reality of this. Individuals, churches, denominations and communions need to 'die to live' in the redemptive way of Christ. Churches are reshaped through revival and renewal to better witness to Christ, although further study is needed to evaluate the impact of his time in Coventry diocese.

Barrington-Ward muses that perhaps 'the real significance of the Anglican church lies in this, that it is, of all denominations, the most obviously provisional, the most apt for death, or indeed, as I must then say, for life through death'. It is here that he touches on the wider theme of provisionality in Anglican ecclesiology. Historically

25 ibid., 127, 138.
26 Barrington-Ward, 'No Other Name,' 3.
27 Wallace Boulton, 'Living with Questions,' Yes, April–June 1980, 4; Simon Barrington-Ward, 'Foreword,' in Renewal: An Emerging Pattern, Graham Pulkingham and Jeanne Hinton, eds (Poole: Celebration Publishing, 1980), 9–10.
28 Barrington-Ward, Love Will Out, 183–97.
29 Simon Barrington-Ward, 'Dying to Live: The Vocation of Anglicanism,' ANVIL 12, no. 2 (1995), 106–8.

the Church of England was provisional in the sense that it never saw itself as the church universal but rather something that awaits a better universality in the future. This has sometimes prevented Anglican ecclesial development – why bother if it will become something else in the end. Yet it has also been the motivation for seeing the church as something humble, 'ever hoping to express something of the gospel of Christ'.[30] Barrington-Ward combines humility and faithfulness to the gospel of Christ with living the way of the gospel: a way that will allow for the unmaking of existing denominations and communions before they are remade more like Christ. A radical ecclesiology that has perhaps reached its moment as the Church of England struggles in part to face a 'good death' in the hope of renewal.

Conclusion

We might conclude as we started with a story of the Eucharist, this time that of Bishop Lakshman Wickremesinghe, amongst people of different traditions and faiths:

> As he broke bread and offered the cup, I was strangely reminded of Melchizedek, bringing forth gifts from beyond into the flux. Lakshman's fine face was absorbed, his form trance-like, his hand moved in the characteristic gestures of taking, giving thanks and breaking and distributing... His central action now seemed to affirm the reality of the infinite presence and power of God's love, released in the midst of our striving and pain in the most ordinary human and material form. Glancing at the faces round us there was no doubt anywhere that this essential brokenness of the God–man on the cross undergirded and strengthened the hold of all of us upon faith and life and opened up for all a way through meaninglessness and death.[31]

Here again is grace in brokenness, a passion for love seen in Jesus through the cross, the powerful presence of the Holy Spirit drawing the church into transformation, opening it out to the world. The gospel is not so much a message or pattern so much as a lived experience of grace discovered together in brokenness. The essential reality of parish life is a community rooted in contexts of the broken, of different nationalities and faiths. Liturgical practice is placed within a

---

30 Mark Chapman, 'The Church,' in *The Vocation of Anglican Theology*, Ralph McMichael, ed. (London: SCM, 2014), 221, 230.
31 Barrington-Ward, 'Dying to Live,' 109.

world-wide movement of the Spirit experienced as glimpses of grace within the groaning world. World transformation is motivated from spiritual integrity with an acknowledgement that Christians often speak from a minority position in contrast to some historically formed assumptions in Anglicanism. The provisionality of Anglicanism is deepened into the radical way of life through death.

Theologically we might articulate Barrington-Ward's ecclesiology as rooted in a pneumatology of loving movement and a Christology of the personal and incarnate One both shaped around themes of brokenness and grace. This resonates with the work of Dan Hardy, particularly in his exploration of a 'moving ecclesiology'.[32] It is an approach that brings a challenge to Anglican ecclesiologies that avoid the theme of brokenness. These might be the idealised blueprint ecclesiologies that Nicholas Healy notes or simply those that stress the goodness of past or the glories of pioneering forms of church.[33] An unchanging parish system and a 'new is better' fresh expression would both receive critique. The theme of grace is also vital, challenging some approaches that analyse the brokenness without giving equal weight to the grace that is changing things. A question posed might be: how are all forms of church broken and how might the Spirit be graciously leading us to Christ that they may be remade? The emphasis on God's active grace strengthens a hopeful journey through such questions to see renewed Christian communities engaged in mission in the world.

This chapter has explored the ecclesiology of Barrington-Ward, appreciating his exploration of the multi-faceted nature of God's tri-une grace that is revealed above all through the varied brokenness of this world. It is an approach to the church that is deeply embedded in its time and yet helped pave the way for more recent developments. As the church in the West continues to face deep challenges, Barrington-Ward speaks to us of an enduring hope that might carry us even as our structures and patterns are broken. Through this re-making we continue to be a people of love for others, living Christ in the reality of the Spirit to the glory of the Father.

---

32 Daniel W. Hardy, Deborah Hardy Ford, Peter Ochs, and David F. Ford, *Wording a Radiance: Parting Conversations on God and the Church* (London: SCM, 2010), 86–93.

33 Nicholas M. Healy, *Church, World and the Christian Life: Practical-Prophetic Ecclesiology* (Cambridge: Cambridge University Press, 2000).

CHAPTER 12

Orthodoxy and Prayer

Philip Seddon

Lord Jesus Christ, Son of God: have mercy on us.[1]

The Monastery of Stavronikita, Mount Athos

Looking up at the tall buttressed walls that reach right down to the rocks by the beach and harbour, Simon and I walk up and alongside an ancient aqueduct, and are welcomed at Stavronikita in true Greek monastic style: coffee, biscuits, water, loukoumi *(Greek Turkish Delight) and* tsipouro *(Greek raki). Simon is in his element, elated; this pilgrimage to Mount Athos in Northern Greece – the spiritual home of the Jesus Prayer – is the climax of his life. I am incredibly privileged to share this visit with him; it is a homecoming for Simon; it will re-sculpt both of us.[2]*

We are sitting under a trellis of vines, with vegetable beds falling down the hillside. We can see why the monks call Mount Athos 'The Holy Mountain' and 'the Garden of the Mother of God [the Theotokos].' A young Australian monk, Fr Seraphim, is sitting in the shade, weaving a komboskini *(prayer-rope). We ask him, since this is our quest, 'What can you tell us about the Jesus Prayer?' 'I just like saying it,' he says. 'Just say the prayer, concentrate on the prayer, and the Lord will give or not give, as He wants. Say it peacefully , without anxiety.' Sancta simplicitas.*

By contrast, we soon talk to Fr Palamas, formerly an architect, but now consecrated to live, pray and die here. He is right on Simon's wave-length, since, even on the plane and bus, Simon was reading up

---

1   This is the Jesus Prayer; but the words can be amended to 'upon me,' with 'a sinner' added, if so desired.
2   Simon and I visited Mount Athos in September 2011. The Revd Paul Hunt, who gave so much to Simon at several stages of his life, should have been with us, but distressingly had to withdraw following serious back surgery.

on St Maximus the Confessor (580–662) and St Gregory Palamas (1296–c.1371). When Fr Palamas brings out the monastery's own original copy of the Works of St Gregory Palamas, we gasp as we are whisked back into the fourteenth century. Fr Palamas's name links us with his namesake St Gregory Palamas, the great authority on the Jesus Prayer. Past and present merge.

Later on, we meet Fr Ephrem, an icon painter, his white artist's apron spattered with multiple colours, and Simon launches into our quest, talking about Gregory Palamas and Maximus the Confessor. In a rare, smiling rebuke, pointing to his own heart, Fr Ephrem says, 'This is what matters more.' The irony is not lost on us: Simon has been longing for some clues from the homeland of the Jesus Prayer for uniting head and heart in prayer, but his insatiable enthusiasm is very gently put down in favour of the quiet, still, 'Prayer of the Heart.'

Recapitulation: Breaking and Remaking[3]

Berlin, 1953

To the outside observer, Simon was the consummate, engaging, aristocratic cleric. In reality, before he reached the age of fifty, Simon's life was broken and remade three times in a series of critical cruciform moments. He shared the pain and gift of the Cross and Resurrection, and drank in the Spirit and the gift of tears.

The first of this sequence of sink-holes was located in the flattened city of Berlin. Full of hope, after graduating from Magdalene, his own vaguely Christian Idealism was demolished by his fellow-lodger's Nietzschean onslaught, and his own internal ruins mirrored the external. But out of – and into – the crisis came a revelation of Cross and Resurrection which overwhelmed him and re-shaped his life and thought. This is Simon's testimony:

> I met as never before with the Living God in Christ. Here was Christ the *Mitmensch*[4] in whom we could truly be grasped by God in the fullness of His Love, not the God of idealism or of romanticism, but the God who, when all meaning was stripped

3   Simon Barrington-Ward, 'My Pilgrimage in Mission', in the *International Bulletin of Missionary Research*, Vol. 23, No. 2, April 1999, p. 60, the opening paragraphs. See Chapter 13.
4   lit. the 'with [us] Man],' i.e. God with us in the person of Jesus Christ.

away and all lay in ruins and devastation, could draw alongside us in a wounded, broken human being ... Now I had discovered or been dis-covered ... I could truly begin to be broken and remade. I had seen my life's work, to join in bringing all into the redemptive movement of this love which alone could save us![5]

God came close in Christ and grasped him personally. A small community of reconciled enemies in Berlin – former Nazis and members of the resistance to Hitler – powerfully expounded the 2 Corinthians 5:21 verse that reshaped Simon's world:

'For our sake God made him [Christ] to be sin,
so that in him we might become the righteousness of God.'

He saw that an almighty reversal had taken place in the death of Jesus Christ: God had taken our place, reversed roles, exchanged *his* life for ours. He was ruined that we might be resurrected.[6]

During this time, the words of a rhapsodic early Christian text also captured Simon's imagination – the *Sweet Exchange*, extolling God's unimaginably beautiful embrace of humanity's ruins:

O the sweet exchange, O the inscrutable creation, O the unexpected benefits, that the wickedness of many should be concealed in the One Righteous, and the righteousness of the One should make righteous many wicked![7]

What gripped Simon was not just that he personally had been saved, but that God had acted in Christ to redeem *the world*. He never analysed theories of the Atonement, but emphasised the absolute priority of God's immense love and inventive goodness as revealed in the death and resurrection of the person of Jesus for the blessing of the whole creation. His tired deist doctrine of God was replaced with an adamantine conviction of a universe securely held in God's love. He also studied the early Greek Christian thinkers Irenaeus, Clement and Athanasius, who from now on constituted the wallpaper of his visionary thought-world, setting in motion in him the themes of the restoration, reintegration and 'recapitulation of all things' in Christ.[8]

5　Barrington-Ward, 'My Pilgrimage in Mission,' following the original script, which differs considerably from the published version noted above. See Chapter 13 for the full original script.
6　Karl Barth, *Church Dogmatics* (Edinburgh: T & T Clark, 1956), IV.1, para. 59. 2, 'The Judge judged in our place.'
7　Anon, *Epistle to Diognetus* 9.3–5. Simon Barrington-Ward, Goshen College, Indiana: Commencement Address, 2012; Simon Barrington-Ward, *The Jesus Prayer and the Great Exchange* (Cambridge: Grove Books, 2013). Spirituality Series, 124), 5, with added capitalisation.
8　Barrington-Ward, *Goshen Commencement Address; The Jesus Prayer and the Great Exchange*, 6.

Ibadan, Nigeria, and Magdalene College, Cambridge, 1960–1969

Ten years later, in a second death-to-life moment, Simon experienced the renewal of the Holy Spirit when he returned to Magdalene after three years' teaching and research in Ibadan, where anthropological exploration, personal alienation and spiritual reconfiguration all overlapped. His research among the Isoko of the Niger Delta had introduced him to the spirit-possession movements of African Traditional Religions, specifically to a 50-year old memory of a spirit-prophetess Ibribina speaking in the 1910s of 'Jesu Krisi' and prophesying a cleansing from evil powers, a 'new love, a new all-pervasive Spirit power ... a new heaven and a new earth.'[9] This had fired him up, and given him new perspectives.

In a later academic article, he wrote: 'a quest for clarification and integration, grappling deep with reality, can be overwhelmed as if from beyond itself ... A parallel process can take place in one's reconceiving of one's identity and one's relationship.'[10] These research observations, and the title of his article – 'the centre cannot hold' – provided a fascinating lens on his return to Magdalene in 1963, when, as Dean, he was indeed shaken and broken; his own personal centre was rocked. Simon often confessed his shock and confusion on returning to an empty chapel in the alien cultural world of his own 'beloved Magdalene', and being reduced to total *aporia*.[11]

But in these fresh personal ruins, as suggested by the sub-title of his article, 'Spirit possession as redefinition,' he was overwhelmed by the same spiritual reality he had studied in Nigeria. With unconscious prescience, he experienced a fresh re-configuration: the Nigerian Pentecostal themes came home to Simon, giving him a whole new language of the Spirit, through the ministries of David Watson, David du Plessis and John Collins.[12] 'I received my re-making, an infilling of the Spirit,' he wrote. This was his Pentecost – the gift of living water was poured into him, his ministry was renewed, and the 'new love' of Berlin and Nigeria constituted his new identity in Cambridge.

This was when I first met Simon – as my supervisor in Early Church History, studying the theologians who were his life-blood. Full of the Holy Spirit, overflowing with generous love, with a sparkling mind

---

9 Brother Ramon and Simon Barrington-Ward, *Praying the Jesus Prayer Together* (Oxford: The Bible Reading Fellowship, 2001), 106.

10 Simon Barrington-Ward, "The centre cannot hold ...' Spirit possession as redefinition', in Adrian Hastings and Edward Fasholé-Luke, eds, *Christianity in Independent Africa* (London: Collins, 1978), 445–470, where 'melting down', 'overwhelmed,' reintegration' and 'a new vision' all appear on 464, and 'reconstituting' on 465.

11 Barrington-Ward, 'My Pilgrimage in Mission,' 62. cf. Dr Ronald Hyam, 'In Memoriam Simon Barrington-Ward, KCMG, Honorary Fellow,' https://www.magd.cam.ac.uk/news/magdalene-college-magazine-2019-20 (and personal correspondence). See Chapter 2. *Aporia* refers to a state of puzzlement.

12 Barrington-Ward, 'My Pilgrimage in Mission,' 62. These were notable leaders of the Charismatic movement at that time.

and irrepressible *joie-de-vivre*, he talked of Ibribina, of 'being gripped' by God, of the multiplication of love, of a synergy between God and creation, and of a mysterious St Silouan, whose instruction 'Keep thy mind in hell, and despair not' baffled me and drew him even then.[13]

Bethlehem, the late 1970s

... in that first, simple, starting place [the crypt of The Church of the Nativity], I was overwhelmed by uncontrollable and un-stoppable tears. And the phrase that welled up with the tears, and kept being repeated within me, was, 'If only we could begin all over again ... If only we could begin all over again!' What a mess we had made of it all! 'If only we could begin all over again.' In the end, quite quietly, gently and insistently, at last a voice seemed to respond, 'But you *can*, you *can* begin all over again, 'That is why I came. It was for this that I was born.' Stumbling back up the steps out of there afterwards, I somehow knew that this central theme of breaking and re-making was the pattern of our pilgrimage into the divine love, and always had been![14]

This third simultaneous breaking and remaking took Simon to still deeper caverns of longing. Simon told of the tears of Bethlehem, shortly after taking up his post as General Secretary of CMS in 1975, with typically matter-of-fact lack of pretension; but the tears did not primarily concern an individual sense of failure, psychological fragmentation or personal moral short-fall. Rather, a greater beauty and a new vocation was excavated out of this desolation, which was never annihilated but re-composed in the gift of tears. A moment of universal vicarious repentance and radical confession had taken him right back, through the Nativity in Bethlehem to Adam – 'If only we could begin all over again!'[15] The call to continual and deeper repentance never left him; every cul-de-sac became a turning-point. 'But you *can*, you *can* begin all over again.'

The Cross, the Spirit and the tears were all now integrated in a

---

13 Archimandrite Sofrony [*sic*], *The Undistorted Image. Staretz Silouan: 1866–1938* (London: The Faith Press, 1958), 103–106. Simon was always recommending and giving me books–Abbé de Tourville, *Spiritual Letters*; Fr Jim Borst, *Witness to the Spirit and Charismatic Renewal*; Anon. *The Way of a Pilgrim*; Valentine Zander, *Seraphim of Sarov*.

14 Barrington-Ward, 'My Pilgrimage in Mission,' original script, 1. Chapter 13.

15 A parallel to Simon's summons down to deep caves of repentance can be found in Arvo Pärt's *Adam's Lament* of 2009, which follows the Russian text of *The Undistorted Image*, 137–144, and itself is dedicated posthumously to Sophrony. Simon and Pärt share a common debt to Fr Sophrony and the monastery at Tolleshunt Knights: Simon's paring down of thought into the Jesus Prayer paralleling Pärt's *tintinnabulation*; music and prayer both arising out of a profound silence; each sharing a common debt to 'East' and 'West'; Pärt's 'it is enough when a single note is beautifully played' corresponding to Orthodox 'pure prayer'. 'If you want to understand my music,' said Pärt, 'read this' (i.e. *The Undistorted Image*). See Peter Bouteneff, *Arvo Pärt. Out of Silence* (NY: St Vladimir's Seminary, 2015), 16, 99.

desperate but wonderful gift, which gathered up all his cruciform moments.[16] His basic orthodox Christian faith would then be extended within the framework of Eastern Christian Orthodoxy, in which he would soon meet Fr Sophrony.

The Monastery of Pantokrator, Mount Athos

In the spacious sun-lit courtyard of the Pantoktrator monastery, dedicated to the Transfiguration, time stands still, scoops us up, lifts us backwards and forwards, fusing time and eternity.

The radiant Fr Theophilos and Simon meet and greet one another; a transfiguration beckons. Not merely does Simon's face beam, but hearts are enraptured, as he says to Theophilos, 'It is so lovely to see you,' gazing at his peaceful, sanctified face. Theophilos replied, 'I am so happy,' adding, 'It is enough for me to see you, honoured father.'[17] A profound love hovers over them, envelops them. Theophilos sees in Simon the charismatic monastic; we see Christ in Theophilos. The Cloud of the Presence seems to overshadow them. It is good for us to be here.

In Theophilos an ancient monastic greeting first addressed to St Anthony in the fourth century leaps into the twenty-first in a rare, visible, palpable holiness. They are one in recognising the inner light shining out of the other, God-bearers each, deeply embedded in Christ. Through Simon, Theophilos feels in touch with Sophrony; 'I can see the blessing of Sophrony in your face.' But Theophilos makes no claims for himself. 'We are so far,' he says – meaning, we are all so far off the mark. He repeats that, and tears at the depth of his humility and holiness flow freely down my face.

Simon recorded Theophilos' words: 'The Jesus prayer is a Spirit-given gift of love which will draw us into the infinite peace of the new creation in Christ, who draws us into union with himself through this prayer, and open up though his cross the risen life into which he invites us.'[18] – Like St John the Evangelist, whatever Simon imbibes he remodels into his own Spirit-inspired language.

Afterwards, we ascend the winding staircase in the huge tower via

---

16 See Andy Lord, *River of the Spirit. The Spirituality of Simon-Barrington-Ward* (Oxford: Fairacres, 2021), a work of which I was only made aware after writing this chapter.

17 Fr Theophilos wrote – very personally – in Simon's diary, Ἀρκεῖ μοι τὸ ὁρᾶν σοι, τίμιε Πάτερ, slightly differing from the original Greek: Ἀρκεῖ μοι μόνον τοῦ βλέπειν σε. See the ET in Benedicta Ward, *The Sayings of the Desert Fathers: The Apophthegmata Patrum: The Alphabetic Collection* (Cistercian Studies Series, 59), 1975: St Anthony, saying 27.

18 Barrington-Ward, *The Jesus Prayer and the Great Exchange*, 16. Chapter 15.

a combination of ancient bolted doors and modern electronic security codes, reaching the fifth floor. An icon of Theophanes the Cretan stands out, glowing. From a heavenly blue circle, a square and an asteroid behind Christ, gold and silver light streams out from the Transfiguration into the universe. Is that what I saw happening earlier to Theophilos and Simon?

The Monastery of John the Baptist, Tolleshunt Knights, Essex: Father Sophrony[19]

This is my Pentecost! Come, Holy Spirit! Draw me through the Lord Jesus Christ, crucified and risen, into the triune love of Father, Son and Holy Spirit! ... Lord Jesus Christ, Son of God, have mercy upon me, a sinner![20]

1982 was the year when Simon met Fr Sophrony, and his life took a new turn.[21] Simon was again feeling under pressure, lacking spiritual energy in leading CMS, and longing for renewal – not that anyone who read Simon's life-giving *CMS Newsletters* would have guessed. A new colleague at CMS, Paul Hunt, spoke to him about Sophrony and his monastery in Essex, and the power of the Jesus Prayer. Simon instinctively said, 'Paul, I need that. I must come.'

In his account of his first visit to Sophrony, Simon wrote lyrically of the 'natural energy of still movement ... held together by the steady, rhythmic beat' of the Jesus Prayer, and then, typically, of being 'drawn in,' 'caught up,' 'grasped', 'gripped,' 'discovered or [having] been dis-covered,' 'broken and remade.'

It is no accident that these are all passive verbs, speaking of the initiative of God's own prior longing, desire and (in the Orthodox tradition) *erōs* in wanting to be known and loved by his creation, in a way that corresponds to our own hopes and yearnings, rather than to a distant God of deism, the Enlightenment God of Idealism or the God of sublime romantic feelings. Here, for instance, four times in a single paragraph, is Simon's sense of the dynamic forward movement of our life in Christ through the work of the Spirit:

---

19 In order to avoid confusion, I use here the term by which most people commonly referred to Fr Sophrony, even though, since his canonisation in 2019, he is now referred to ecclesiastically as 'St Sophrony the Athonite'.
20 Barrington-Ward, *Goshen Commencement Address; The Jesus Prayer and the Great Exchange*, 9–10.
21 In *The Jesus Prayer and the Great Exchange*, 7, the year is given as 1984; but this was an incorrect memory.

I found myself drawn increasingly deeply into this way of praying... almost as though we all really were converging more and more on the living Lord, who was summoning us ever closer to himself...
'[the] prayer not only drew us nearer to its source and goal in the Lord... it was reaching out further and further, all-embracingly... so greatly moved was I and caught up...
I was being drawn on and on, as we all were, into a movement that seemed shaped by the power of the Holy Spirit... alway still drawing us and all things ever more fully... [22]

In personal terms, what made for such profound love and respect between Simon and Sophrony, so that nearly thirty years later, on Mount Athos, when Simon saw a portrait of Sophrony, he beamed, rooted to the spot, as if in heaven?[23] Formally, Simon, General Secretary of an Anglican missionary society, had approached an Orthodox Elder (the Russian *staretz*)[24] for spiritual guidance, never before having ventured such a form of spiritual mentoring; but now he readily apprenticed himself to Sophrony. Simon and Sophrony caught fire; Simon was profoundly drawn to the wisdom and prayer of 'my beloved Sophrony', and longed for a fusion of Western and Eastern Christian traditions. Accordingly, he visited Tolleshunt regularly over the years with his wife Jean, and Sophrony and the whole monastic community at Tolleshunt loved him.

Fundamentally, Simon was always longing for a greater unity of heart and mind. As an intellectual and a theological historian, he wanted to know God more truthfully, especially in prayer, fusing a seeking heart with a fertile mind. The Jesus Prayer which he began to learn from, and with, Fr Sophrony precisely offered the path to 'pure prayer,' still silence, the inner quiet of *hesychia*, prayer 'with the mind in the heart;' but also, in reverse, lifting up the heart to pray with the mind. From then on, Simon took the unitive path of 'standing before God with the mind in the heart.'[25]

There was also a 'double click' with Sophrony on both the philosophical and theological levels. Simon had long been fascinated with Hegel, and perhaps his attempt to find through him a great philo-

---

22 Barrington-Ward, *The Jesus Prayer and the Great Exchange*, 8–9.
23 Barrington-Ward, *Goshen Commencement Address; The Jesus Prayer and the Great Exchange*, 7–11, 12–13.
24 Sophrony was indeed Russian – Sergei Simeonovich Sakharov. Sister Gabriela, *Seeking Perfection in the World of Art, The Artistic Path of Father Sophrony*, Stavropegic Monastery of St John the Baptist, 2014 (2nd ed.), 9, 21ff.
25 Igumen Charito of Valamo (compiler), trans. E Kadloubovsky and E M Palmer, ed. with an Introduction by Timothy Ware, *The Art of Prayer. An Orthodox Anthology* (London: Faber and Faber, 1966), 17, 63, 89, 93, etc.

sophical–theological structural framework was now to find a point of synthesis through Sophrony's own thought-world, philosophy and spiritual experience. Indeed, Sophrony had himself been a philosopher – and was now a philosopher of prayer. 'Prayer,' he wrote, 'is infinite creation, far superior to any form of art or science ... Prayer is an act of supreme wisdom, of all-surpassing beauty and virtue ...In its essence [prayer] transcends our plane of existence.'[26]

At the level of Simon's tears of repentance, there was a close kinship: his cataclysm of tears in Bethlehem was matched by the 'ocean of tears' into which Sophrony had been plunged.[27] Simon knew of Sophrony's own years of 'sorrowful repentance,' of his 'furnace of fiery repentance,' and his 'inconsolable repentance.'[28] I don't think Simon experienced the depths of Godforsakenness that both Silouan and Sophrony knew; rather, he had been thoroughly immersed in the Spirit who drew him into 'the immensity of the Divine Love.'[29] Was it this that kept him back from being drawn into the terrifying depths of abandonment that St Silouan and Sophrony knew?[30]

Equally, Simon shared Sophrony's quest for the Living and Personal Absolute. 'Here was a man in search of absolute truth,' wrote Jean-Claude Polet;[31] it was only the discovery that the Absolute was Personal that held Sophrony together: 'Truth is revealed to us as Personal Absolute ... as I AM'[32] or even, in Archimandrite Aimilianos's vivid phrase, 'something absolutely absolute!'[33] Exactly so for Simon, being drawn into their vision; in an undated letter to Paul Hunt, he wrote: 'I felt the need ... to emphasise this personal communion (with all the transcendent depths of the mystery in each and every 'person' and of the personal God) in the Jesus Prayer...' Truth is Personal; divine truth triply so.

Finally, Sophrony was for Simon a 'visible icon': a focus of evangelical and charismatic monasticism. There in front of him was the disciple of the great St Silouan the Athonite (1866–1938) of whom he

---

26 Archimandrite Sophrony, *On Prayer* (Tolleshunt Knights by Maldon, The Patriarchal Stavropegic Monastery of St John the Baptist, 1996), 9, 11.

27 Archimandrite Sophrony, *We Shall See Him As He Is* (Tolleshunt Knights by Maldon, The Patriarchal Stavropegic Monastery of St John the Baptist, 1988), 59.

28 Sophrony, *On Prayer*, 53; Sofrony, *The Undistorted Image*, 27, 29, 49; Archimandrite Peter, 'The Birth of the Word of God in the Heart of His Saints. The Example of St Sophrony the Athonite,' in the *Friends of Mount Athos Annual Report*, 2020, 18, 23; Sophrony, *We Shall See Him As He Is*, 67, 81.

29 Georges Florovsky, in the Foreword to Archimandrite Sofrony, *The Undistorted Image*, 6.

30 Nicholas V. Sakharov, *I LOVE, therefore I AM. The Theological Legacy of Archimandrite Sophrony*, Crestwood, NY: St Vladimir's Seminary Press, 2002, 'Godforsakenness': pp, 171–197.

31 In the Introduction to Sister Gabriela, *Seeking Perfection in the World of Art, The Artistic Path of Father Sophrony* (The Patriarchal Stavropegic Monastery of St John the Baptist, 2014 (2nd ed.)), 10, 11.

32 Sophrony, *We Shall See Him As He Is*, 65, 158, 207, etc.

33 Archimandrite Aimilianos, 'Addresses Delivered During the Enthronement Ceremony at the Holy Monastery of Simonos Petras,' in *Spiritual Instructions and Discourses. 1. The Authentic Seal* (Ormylia Publishing, 1999), 98.

had known for so long through Sophrony's *The Undistorted Image*. As Sophrony to his *staretz* St Silouan, so now Simon to his *staretz* Fr Sophrony, Simon at just fifty-two, and Sophrony eighty-six; but in Sophrony, Simon not only forged a personal reverence for his own *staretz*, but also intuitively travelled back through the millennia to the origins of the Gospel and the monastic vibrancy of the Desert Fathers and Mothers, in a living and monastic succession of prayer which mattered tremendously to him.[34] Once again, as in Bethlehem, he moved forward by going backwards; he had met 'a monumental saint.'[35]

The Jesus Prayer encapsulated all Simon's longings to know God with a single heart and mind, in a life-long process of recapitulation with repeated, insistent reduction, distillation and intensification, as if these ten words (in English) said all that was needed.[36]

'Lord Jesus Christ, Son of God: have mercy upon us.'

Our whole life could be condensed in this Jesus Prayer, converting us into an arrow-head prayer of transparent doxology and contrition, the shortest prayer yielding an immense vision, the greatest concentration embracing the greatest expanse.[37]

The Monastery of Koutloumousiou, Mount Athos

We meet in Fr Chrysostom's comfortable study-cell, lined with books. He is an enthusiastic dialogue-partner, epitomising a wonderful Christian integration of intellect and love that draws us both. Thought and prayer, philosophy and theology all intermingle. Our questions float on the flood of wisdom offered by Chrysostom. He offers an anthropological critique of the fragmentation of the person in modern society; by contrast, he says, true prayer integrates all the powers of the soul, becomes a universe held in the love of God; by becoming more integrated we become more universal. 'We need to find the lost pieces of ourselves, and give ourselves to God: from fragmentation to unification.' This is a life-long discipline, he added

34 Simon Barrington-Ward, *The Jesus Prayer* (Oxford: The Bible Reading Fellowship, 1996), 9, 37–60.
35 Fr Seraphim Aldea, The Orthodox Monastery of All Celtic Saints, Mull, 'What I've learnt from St Sophrony (Sakharov) of Essex. Monk and Artist - the MONUMENTAL Saint.' https://www.youtube.com/watch?v=vOuX7UIAGEQ
36 See Chapter 2 on Magdalene College: Professor Nicholas Boyle, https://www.magd.cam.ac.uk/news/magdalene-college-magazine-2019-2020 (online).
37 Khaled Anatolios, *Deification through the Cross. An Eastern Christian Theology of Salvation* (Grand Rapids, MI: Eerdmans, 2020). Five of his eight chapters are shaped around the theme of 'doxological contrition'.

– 'Hesychia *is internal intensified activity.*'

   Chrysostom continues: 'Contemporary man has lost his true axis, his true self; we have a variety of possible selves with which we can play – wife, work, children, leisure. But without true introversion and self-knowledge, we cannot find God, because we cannot find our-selves. We cannot find God deep within, because we do not know what 'within' means. In this case, our relationship with God simply becomes one of a series of rôles and relationships.'

   He changes up a gear: 'We may feel a sense of the absence of the Presence, but we are with God all the time. *So we hold fast to God. We want to be part of Jesus' prayer to the Father, and so we hold fast* to God so that we lose everything, so that we gain everything. *Prayer is not a capitalist investment opportunity. We have to give everything. We give our blood; we receive the Spirit. We bear the cross of life in our everyday lives. This is blood also.' This is* Discipleship.[38]

   Simon records Chrysostom's words: 'Since, according to Gregory Palamas, God's energies and activities are always at work in and all around us ... St Gregory himself affirms that we can be constantly helped to dare to reach out to attain that goal of theosis, *of being drawn into an ultimate union with the triune God, however far away we may feel ourselves to be from it. This is attained through the con-stant, infinitely encouraging gift of the still, ever more graciously initi-ated, increasingly developed, ever unchanging and steadfast practice of the Jesus Prayer, constantly and penitently renewed deeply with us by the Spirit again and again!'*[39]

Recapitulation: *Theosis* and Synthesis

Theosis

Theosis is a difficult concept for Western Christians. For many, the very language of 'deification' sounds blasphemous, as though we were trying to achieve equality with God (Philippians 2:6!). But that is to misunderstand: the term was coined by Gregory of Nazianzus in the same century that the Nicene Creed was formulated;[40] *theosis* is built entirely on a Trinitarian theology of *grace*, by which we are ad-opted into, united with, conformed to Christ in the Spirit, as we enter

---

38 I deliberately insert the original single-word title of Bonhoeffer's famous work, *Nachfolge*, published in 1937.
39 Barrington-Ward, *The Jesus Prayer and the Great Exchange*, 19.
40 Stephen Finlan and Vladimir Kharlamov, eds, *Theôsis. Deification in Christian Theology* (Cambridge: James Clarke, 2006), 1.

and share the life of God. In short, *theosis* is participation in Christ.[41] Simon was captivated by this vision.

At its most basic, *theosis* is a single all-embracing term for the entire process of salvation, from regeneration and salvation, forgiveness and justification, confession and sanctification (to use the varied terms of Western theology) right through to our ultimate union through death with Christ in God. Its focus is on the prayer of Jesus the True High Priest in John 17 that we may fully 'oned' with him in the Spirit and the Father, being made 'partakers of the divine nature,' while equally being drawn into Christ's self-emptying, which requires *our kenosis* ('emptying'): '*Kenosis is theosis.*'[42]

At its most majestic level, it presents our destiny as that of being drawn fully into the eternal beauty and communion of the Trinity in the light of the limitless scope of the Incarnation of the Word. Ironically, then, the Eastern Christian tradition of *theosis* takes the body more seriously than one might expect,[43] often choosing the language of transfiguration for our Christian life, and – if we can put it like this – placing full responsibility for the recapitulation of all things in Christ with God.

Simon loved quoting the foundational patristic texts on this theme, Irenaeus being the chief source for his theology of recapitulation – the gathering up, the reintegration of everything in Christ: Irenaeus of Lyons (125–200): 'The Word of God, our Lord Jesus Christ, in his immense love became what we are that we might become what he is;' Clement of Alexandria (150–215): 'God became human that we might become divine;' Athanasius (296–373): '[The Word of God] became human that we might become God.'[44]

This was the theme that Simon explored continually following his first meeting with Sophrony, for his early language of 'being drawn' was caught up to reach its apogee in the Jesus Prayer and the doctrine of *theosis*. *Theosis* explicitly includes the *telos* – the end of Christian living – in our Christian hope (cf. Romans 8:28) rather than being 'tacked on' at the end, as a bonus or an afterthought; Simon used the

---

41 I am grateful to Prof Paul Gavrilyuk for alerting me to a 'brilliant' recent article by Mark McInroy, 'How Deification Became Eastern: German Idealism, Liberal Protestantism, and the Modern Misconstruction of the Doctrine,' *Modern Theology Month* 2021, John Wiley & Sons Ltd, 23 February 2021 (online: DOI:10.1111/moth.12700), where McInroy shows how F.C. Baur and A. Ritschl misread *theosis* in a false polarising way, rendering it alien, 'Eastern' and sub-Christian. McInroy refutes all the charges – see also Simon's *The Jesus Prayer and the Great Exchange*, 26, note 4.

42 Michael Gorman, *Inhabiting the Cruciform God. Kenosis, Justification, and Theosis in Paul's Narrative Soteriology*, Grand Rapids, Eerdmans, 2009, 37 and *passim*; Sakharov, I LOVE therefore I AM, 'Kenosis,' 93–115.

43 Timothy Ware, *The Orthodox Church* (Harmondsworth: Penguin, 1964), 54, 3; cf. Simon B-W, *The Jesus Prayer and the Great Exchange*, 6 – Athanasius: 'he embraced our humanity that we might embrace his divinity.'

44 Irenaeus, *Against Heresies*, 5; Athanasius, *On the Incarnation*, 54, 3; cf. Simon B-W, *The Jesus Prayer and the Great Exchange*, 6 – Athanasius: 'he embraced our humanity that we might embrace his divinity.'

word theosis six times in *The Jesus Prayer and the Great Exchange*.[45] It is not a mantra or vain repetition; rather, the two lungs of the Jesus Prayer juxtapose doxology and contrition, praise and lament, heart and mind, intellect and love – Alleluia and Miserere – or, as Simon puts it, 'a cry for help and a cry of longing to be grasped in his great love'; both 'I am sorry,' and 'I love you.'[46]

Synthesis

There is an Orthodox saying that 'the true theologian is one who prays'. I would believe this includes also 'the true philosopher'. That is to say that out of our prayer our philosophy emerges.[47]

But at the same time that Simon was entering more deeply into the Jesus Prayer[48] and *theosis*, he was no less eagerly interweaving his life-long spiritual yearnings with renewed philosophical vigour. He studied Hegel from the 1960s. Amazingly, Simon owned a complete recent set of the *Works* of Hegel – in German; and even more amazingly, he and Jean, on their visits to Tolleshunt, discussed Hegel with Sophrony and the community from 1982 up to Sophrony's death in 1993. The monks and nuns revelled in these philosophical discussions with 'our wonderful friend Bishop Simon.'

Simon was constantly searching for a synthesis, of philosophical and theological visions, of Western and Eastern Christian theology; but above all he seemed convinced that Hegel could provide a Western philosophical framework for his own theology of *recapitulation*, shaped by the early Christian writers and sharply focused in the Jesus Prayer.

His deep personal, philosophical and theological engagement with the philosopher Gillian Rose during his time as Bishop of Coventry had a profound effect on them both (1985–1995), especially under the threat of her inoperable cancer. In a moving sermon, he says:

> I had already felt there was some connection between [Hegel's] great work *The Phenomenology of the Spirit* and the [Jesus] Prayer, but I couldn't quite see what it was.[49]

Their discussions, as described in this sermon, revolved around a 'redemptive process' requiring a 'continuous repentance of reason,'

---

45 Barrington-Ward, *The Jesus Prayer and the Great Exchange*, 6, 11, 13, 18–19, 21.
46 Barrington-Ward, *The Jesus Prayer*, 19, 68, 82.
47 Simon Barrington-Ward, in Anna Jeffrey, ed., *Five Gold Rings* (London: DLT, 2003), 7.
48 Helen Orr, https://www.youtube.com/watch?app=desktop&v=PxttrnyBC40: The Jesus Prayer with Bishop Simon Barrington-Ward.
49 See Gillian Rose, Sermon, Little St Mary's, on the First Sunday in Lent, 29th February 2004. Unpublished sermon. Chapter 16.

very much in line with Simon's own earlier discoveries, but also, in a now famous phrase, a 'failing towards' our goal, which also fitted in with Simon's repeated narratives of 'breaking and remaking' combined with constant longing for God. Simon described how he had spoken to Gillian Rose about St Silouan, and the famous and terrible phrase given to him by God, 'Keep thy mind in hell and despair not,' in response to which she determined that that phrase, which spoke so powerfully to her, would be the epitaph for her book, *Love's Work*.[50]

At last, Simon said, forgiveness fully entered her; and he baptised her, a Jew, at her insistence, as a movement '*within* not beyond Jewish faith.' She died within two hours, the Jesus Prayer having acted – like an icon – as a 'spring-board,' or as a 'trampoline' to lift her into eternity.[51] Whatever the intended content of the title of Gillian Rose's book *The Broken Middle*, there is no doubt that, for Simon, it evocatively matched his own convictions about 'the Wounded Man in the Heavens,' who had first found him in Berlin, and whose brokenness had met his own and restored him to life.

Simon's quintessential literary alchemy thus epitomises this call to *theosis* in Christ:

> It is not just our personal participation in that movement, in a constant *interchange* of God the Father in Christ coming to us in the Spirit, and our constant growth into him through the Spirit. It is all part of the movement of the whole creation towards its final fulfilment. God in Christ, through the Spirit, keeps coming to us in his infinite love and compassion, and in his mercy. In this way of faith and prayer, he draws all of us who are willing to participate, willing to let ourselves be drawn into the movement of his Spirit within us, and within those whom we seek to serve all round us, always moving on with them towards the ultimate finale – the goal and fulfilment of this present creation, and of the new creation to come, the risen life, towards which and into which we are already being more nearly drawn.[52]

This was movingly at the heart of our last meeting with Simon and

---

50 Sophrony, *On Prayer*, 50, distinguishes 'two types of despair: the one, purely negative, destroys man, first spiritually and then physically. The other is a blessed despair. It is about this second form that I never stop talking.' It would be an intriguing study to compare St Silouan's and St Sophrony's writings on despair with those of Søren Kierkegaard in his *The Sickness unto Death* (1849).

51 Sophrony's language, as expounded in Sister Gabriela, *Seeking Perfection in the World of Art. The Artistic Path of Father Sophrony* (The Stavropegic Monastery of St John the Baptist, Essex: 2014, 2nd enlarged edition), 155, 179.

52 Barrington-Ward, *The Jesus Prayer and the Great Exchange*, 11.

Jean in their Care Home on 17th October 2019. As soon as Simon came in, supported by two assistants, he confided to me intimately and with great vigour that he had been given 'a new revelation' of the new creation that would replace the old; out of the ruins and destruction of the old a new world would be born in Christ. Incredibly, with his tired mind, Simon's final vision in Cambridge was recapitulating his first revelation in Berlin sixty-seven years previously, as his own now frail body evoked the ruins of Berlin, while he also still lived in 'confident hope' of the resurrection. Simultaneously, he was also in his puzzled mind back in Magdalene, wondering why strip lights had been brought in, when 'the old candles were much nicer.' That was when he accidentally coined the beautiful neologism of Magdalene's 'Mellowship' ... The College and the Cambridge he had loved and that had given him so much, but where his foundations had once been shaken, was in the end a place of comfort, rest and delight – and the gate of heaven.

Six months later, he was praying his way into and through death with the Jesus Prayer on – of all days – Holy Saturday, the day before Easter, full of decay and collapse, but fuller still of promise and glory. All the denominational and theological traditions which he had entered, drunk from and transcended were behind him; his phenomenally enquiring mind and his heart refined by love had done their work. Now he was reaching out towards the true fulfilment of all his longings, as he was drawn towards death in the hope of winning Christ, the goal of all his yearning, his true End.[53]

The Monastery of Simonopetra, Mount Athos

Fr Averchios has just welcomed us at the port of Daphni, saluting Simon warmly as 'Bishop Simon of Cambridge.' We enjoy the joke. Averchios drives us along a rough track on the hill-side in a Landrover. What a spectacular view! – the jagged peak of Mount Athos rising sharply into the sky, with the monastery itself built on a 1,000 ft granite cliff abutting directly on to the azure sea.

Like hungry woodpeckers, we seek out the sap and grubs; like miners, we drill down into deeper seams of gold in a truly charismatic monastic community. We sense the influence of Elder Aimilianos whose own experience in 1973 of God's 'Uncreated Light' literally

---

53 Barrington-Ward, *The Jesus Prayer and the Great Exchange*, 22.

turned his night and darkness into day, and took him to Simonopetra as Abbot. Simon is caught up, profoundly moved in the Spirit. He recalls Sophrony's words when they first met, saying, of the cross on his prayer-rope, 'This is my Pentecost.' Now he learns that Elder Aimilianos described Simonopetra as 'the upper room of a permanent Pentecost.' 'Was it for this we came?'

Not for the first time, we are exhilarated by the vigorous, enthusiastic singing in the Liturgy, with exquisite swoopings up and down, as though the beaming monks were in heaven. There is virtuosic, kalophonic extravagance, like honey-bees sipping nectar, as in our excited conversations. We are treated like royalty, shown to the front seats. They love Simon; he is brimming over with joy, laughter, love, learning; he embodies Christ's own longing and generosity.

We talk with Fr Makarios, an intelligent, scholarly monk, on the balcony over the sea, relishing the coffee, biscuits, water, loukoumi *and* tsipouro. *Our topic is not the* problem *of prayer, but the* gift *of prayer. 'The Jesus Prayer,' he says 'is love; a "work of love".' 'Prayer is participation in God; the presence of Jesus in the Jesus Prayer is the hidden presence of the One who will be revealed at "the end of all things"; so praying now is not only praying in the light of the End, it is praying the End.' It carries within it the transfiguration of our humanity and of our deep identity in Christ.*

Our pilgrimage to Mount Athos and on the Holy Mountain, is ending. Our pilgrimage has not ended. Even a climactic experience of prayer, or the Spirit, or the Trinity, is not the end. God is our End. As Simon says, '[W]e must start our journey, like our prayer, at the end.'[54]

'Lord Jesus Christ, Son of God: have mercy upon us.'

---

54 Barrington-Ward, *Five Gold Rings*, 7.

His Own Words

CHAPTER 13

My Pilgrimage in Mission[1]

Simon Barrington-Ward

The Birthplace

ONCE, NOT LONG AFTER I had become General Secretary of the Church
Missionary Society, I went on a visit to Jerusalem, that strange ful-
crum of the world's struggles, longings and frustrations. As Donald
Nicholl once said, adapting Proverbs:

> For silver, the crucible; for gold, the furnace; for the testing of
> hearts, Jerusalem.

A friend, a remarkable monk, took me through the city, somehow deep under all the clutter of centuries of conflicts, along a submerged *via dolorosa* that ran from the 'Pavement' where prisoners
were scourged outside Pilate's quarters to the dungeon of Caiaphas's
house.

In the afternoon we went further back and deeper down still, to
the cave stable under the great church in Bethlehem, where, from
the earliest remembered times, pilgrims have knelt before the reputed
birthplace of Christ. It feels itself womb-like and dark and hidden. I
was glad that, for once, there was no one else there when we came
but my friend to kneel alongside and to pray, oblivious of me. I was
glad because, ridiculously, as I knelt there, before the guttering flame
of a lamp beside the silver star showing where the birth had been, in
that first, simple, starting place, I was overwhelmed by uncontrollable
and unstoppable tears. And the phrase that welled up with the tears,
and kept being repeated within me, was, 'If only we could begin all
over again. If only we could begin all over again!' What a mess we

---

1   The text of this Chapter is published for the first time here. It is Simon's original, fuller, more allusive text, from his
    computer, and differs intriguingly from the edited version published in *The International Bulletin of Missionary Research*
    23.2 (April 1999), 60–64, which may be read online: 1999-02-060-barrington-ward.pdf (internationalbulletin.org).

had made of it all! 'If only we could begin all over again.' In the end, quite quietly, gently and insistently, at last a voice seemed to respond, 'But you can, you can begin all over again. That is why I came. It was for this that I was born.' Stumbling back up the steps out of there afterwards, I somehow knew that this central theme of breaking and re-making was the pattern of our pilgrimage into the divine love, and always had been!

Shadow Over Regent's Park

The first enactment of that pattern had come to me as a child born into the 1930s. I lived in the secluded world of Regent's Park, a lovely part of London, first in one of the cream stucco Nash terraces that surrounded the park and then moving to another. The sound of the animals being fed at daybreak in the Zoo, the bicycle rides to the Infants' School in the park, the gleam of the street lights on the ceiling at night, went with the sense of the God of whom my mother told me stories, who was in his Heaven and who shone through the flowers and trees and lawns holding me and everything and everyone, park keepers, gardeners and shopkeepers who gave their wares so kindly to us, in a mysterious unity. I imbibed the sense of human progress and the safety of the ordered world of modernity, with all wars and violence including that in which my father had fought, and of which he said little, were in 'the olden days.' Even when I saw a newsreel of Japanese bombing houses in China my father reassured me that it would not happen here.

But in spite of that assurance from one who was then an informed journalist (we had to be quiet when he was writing his Leaders), fingers of darkness stabbed their way into this precarious world. We had collected money, and prayed, for a whole family living in one damp tenement room in Liverpool. Why? From Germany, people speaking of war and fleeing from terror visited my father. Soon the shadow had spread over the park. Shelters were being dug there. The intimate cast-iron railings were removed to be melted down, they said. The new air raid sirens were being tested. By the time, on our summer holiday, my father told us war was declared, we were not to return to London, but ended up in Boarding-school and then in a village gathered round the radio listening to Churchill growling that we would 'fight on the beaches' and half expecting invasion. The new vision for the post-war future in which we were to trust was of the Welfare State to which my father was dedicated, the future federation of Europe and a stronger successor to the League of Nations. Modernity and progress had gone. Now at school and at home and then, after my father's death and at University, we were to trust in the invisible spiritual framework which sustained those Western values, which he had still always embodied for me and for which the war was fought. I decided I wanted to 'help people' and opted for ordination as a possible way of doing this, though I was somewhat vague about its basis. The shock of that first breaking remained with me. Perhaps the 'remaking' was less clear.

Resurrection in the Ruins

After Cambridge I went out to Berlin to teach those 'Western values' of democracy and the rule of law as a *Lektor* in the Free University in the Western Sector of the city.

Here the 'breaking', the disintegration, was more rapid and far more complete. As the plane curved over the city, it was the 17th June 1953, and from the grey moon landscape of ruins to the horizon stretched out beneath us there rose up a column of smoke from the East German Trade Organization building. Workers had risen against the regime in a revolution which was to last one day. But in the midst of the scene the Brandenburg Gate clearly to be seen looked like a door from nowhere into nowhere.

I was to wander amid the ruins on both sides, to visit the massive totalitarian facades of the *Stalinallee*, and to be confronted by the rise of capitalist commerce in all its brash new vulgarity in the Western *Kufürstendamm*. The West was infinitely preferable to the police state of the East from which so many were fleeing, but the West itself raised more questions than it could answer. I became lonely and depressed, wandering on solitary walks in the rubble. My fellow lodger, a former member of the Hitler Youth, enlisted in the defence of Berlin and inspected by a sullen, electrifying Hitler before he fled, and now himself a refugee from the East, was an economist, studying the rise of the great future multinational companies which were to arise in the 'German miracle.' He was also a nihilist, making sceptical use of Nietzsche and demolishing my confused idealism easily. I began to feel the ruins had entered into me!

It was then that a devout neighbour, a housewife, recruited me to come and join in a poetry reading in the pastor's house. It was the first sustained welcoming group I had met with and the house was warm and convivial, full of works of art and furniture the Pastor had

165

designed and made. I joined to my surprise in a weekly Bible study and daily prayers and pretty soon I was hooked. They took me to work in refugee camps. They had a vision for the future of the city. I went to meetings about this and visited the Lutheran Seminary and heard the lectures of Martin Fischer and Heinrich Vogel, a Lutheran Barthian. Above all in this extraordinarily ordinary, all-age, all-class group of disciples, forgiven and forgiving, self-confessed Ex-Nazis alongside those who in Pastor Niemöller's former church had been secretly resistant to Hitler, I met as never before with the Living God in Christ. Here was Christ the *Mit-mensch* in whom we could truly be grasped by God in the fulness of His Love, not the God of idealism or of romanticism, but the God who when all meaning was stripped away and all lay in ruins and devastation could draw alongside us in a wounded, broken human being. Now I had discovered, or been discovered by, a third way stretching far beyond East and West. I could truly begin to be broken and remade. I had seen my life's work, to join in bringing all into the redemptive movement of this love which alone could save us! I was free to enjoy the rest of my time in Berlin and to share the new insights I had been given in a variety of ways (including visits to the Brecht ensemble acting great plays in the East and to sceptical political cabaret in the West, and the writing of a play about forgiveness which the students in the University performed).

I returned to Cambridge to study theology at Westcott House, an Anglican theological College I had heard of (knowing nothing of church parties), where I learnt much of the Anglican sacramental tradition but above all more of God's *agape* love, and I went on to become a very young Chaplain of my former college, Magdalene, and to work in the vacations in the 'New Town' being built round Hemel Hempstead near London. In both I saw a dramatic response to the message and Master that had laid hold of me, not least through Billy Graham's visits to Cambridge and to London, seeking to draw Christians and unbelievers alike into a 'new love,' the key to college life and to community in an urban desert!

Aiyetoro

One day Charlie (C.F.D.) Moule, our great New Testament Professor, sent for me and asked me, in response to a letter he had had, to go out to teach Church History at Ibadan University in Nigeria. So I came to be projected suddenly in response to what seemed to come as a quite unexpected call into the great world beyond Europe and into

Africa where there would be so much to learn and re-learn. As I came to encourage the students working with me to explore the history of the church in their own areas and to learn to care for them pastorally across the University under an African lecturer, I was filled with a passion, in that vital, warm colourful scene in the halcyon days before the first coup, to explore the meaning of the gospel to them and their forbears as it came through indigenous preachers and mass movements. In the Western Delta among the Isoko people where I stayed in the villages and studied their story, guided by social anthropologists such as Robin Horton and, later, Godfrey Lienhardt, I stumbled upon an amazing early (1910–20) vision of Christ which had never been fulfilled but the tradition of which had persisted.

I was struck by the sense of alienation and sadness of some of my finest informants, a kind of nostalgia for vanished hopes. It seemed that in the 1880s and even earlier the old order was disrupted. The powers that were in the 'clans' were increasingly shaken, and the spiritual forces that undergirded them were weakened by new political and commercial pressures from outside which undermined their authority. The central cults lost their hold while the peripheral multiplied among women and younger men. New leaders arose overnight and brought in a succession of spirit cults in waves, intending to fill the vacuum. At this moment a prophetic woman leader, Ibribina, a trader, emerged with a message which had possessed her in the back of a mission church far away up the Niger. She introduced new songs and dances, waving a Bible, but what is more she went back and had instruction from the CMS Missionary which gradually enabled her to read and translate the gospels.

She saw in 'Jesu Krisi' a new love, a new all-pervasive Spirit in power, the possibility of a new people, a fellowship of the unlike, bonding together all 'tribes', ethnic groups, black and white, into a new society, in which the rich cared for the poor, the strong for the weak in what was to be a new Heaven and a new Earth. Other leaders joined her and eventually thousands of people flocked in. It was wartime in Europe and only one inspired young missionary could make occasional visits. The movement grew until after the war white missionaries could come in and tidy it up and institutionalise it. Ibribina was assigned a role as a College matron, many of the inspired leaders were sacked for having more than one wife, and the CMS shaped and trained the new church to fit in with the wider colonial world. A much more individualised, spiritualised faith fitted better and of course a more compartmentalised church.

I thought of Ibribina when I visited Aiyetoro, ('the happy city'), a town on stilts near Lagos where a 'Pentecostalist' group, so called, had set up a community which had all things in common. It lasted for three generations before quarrels brought it to an end. For Wole Soyinka, arguably one of the greatest African writers, that place transformed into an idealised, pagan grouping became the only source of hope for African society in his novel *Season of Anomy*. But he took it from a purely Christian source which truly embodied Ibribina's vision. Who understood the gospel better – she or the missionaries? Ever since her, African prophets and church movements in that area have been trying to recover her original version of Christ's model for humankind.

An *Agape* Revival

I returned to Magdalene, Cambridge, with my wife-to-be, Jean, who had been the (Scottish, former CMS missionary) Medical Officer in Ibadan and with whom I had struggled to bring healing and wholeness to the students as we worked together with others in the Graduate Fellowship on the staff. There the whole society of the young had changed, and at first I was broken-hearted at finding myself unable to get through to them at all. It was only through my encounter with David Watson, then a Curate in the city, that we met with the beginnings of the Charismatic renewal and once again, through the hands of David du Plessis on a missionary visit to London, I received my re-making, an infilling of the Spirit. Gradually, in that Utopian culture, I was able to see the meaning of our Nigerian experience; to develop a form of Chapel community which seemed to offer to many the 'Ibribina' possibility; to point their generation to the hope of a new humanity, a new way of being God's people in the Spirit.

Then came a further opportunity of working this out. John V. Taylor whom I had come to know at CMS where I had chaired their Africa committee, invited me to go and start a new CMS Training College at Selly Oak, which I wanted to call Crowther Hall, after the great Nigerian Bishop consecrated under CMS auspices through Henry Venn's farsightedness in 1864. He had died of a broken heart, after being deeply hurt by a new arrogant generation of young missionaries, at a time when CMS had forgotten much of its earlier vision. In Selly Oak, I was to lecture on how CMS had started in 1799 as a movement of reparation for the evils of the Slave Trade and East

Asian commerce, to bring the hope of a new gospel life to Africa and the East, and how after Venn's death it lost its way. But then again, under the recent leadership of Max Warren and John Taylor, the society had begun once again to work out a mission of repentance for the sins and failures of Western missions in the first half of the twentieth century, the hope of working out a new relationship with the churches it had helped to found in African and Asia. How I prayed also that we could at Crowther Hall itself start an 'Ibribina'-style revival community of the Spirit in which to train the new 'mission partners'!

But that was not quite how it worked out. My first fellow member of staff had come back to Britain from the experience of the East African revival. Early on she began to confront me about certain failings in the organisation of the new college and in its inner relationships. A Ugandan pastor who came to stay helped us in prayer and practice. As the community developed I began to discover whole new facets of the action of the Holy Spirit. *Metanoia*, turning to God, conversion, opened the door not only to the initial knowledge of God in Christ, but also constantly and continuously to growth into life in the Spirit at every stage. The Dove was released through the Cross, wholeness through repeated brokenness. Indeed the real test of the presence of the Holy Spirit was whether there was genuine growth in love.

We began to grasp more of the lessons the Corinthians had to learn about power in weakness. The fullness of the Spirit is here and potentially available, but yet it is also still incomplete and we have as much to receive from our own frustrations and sufferings as from any triumphant miracle. One of our number, a remarkable community health worker, began to urge us out also into the inner city not far away, so that we could learn from the poor and, as we worked alongside them, find our capacity for sacrificial loving, 'long-term loving' as Max Warren had called it, be tested and be thrown back more deeply on grace, in our own co-operation and in our struggles to help change the injustice of our society. The goal that Ibribina had glimpsed would only begin to be reached along the way of the Cross. And yet a sense of resurrection breakthrough and of the release of the Spirit's healing among us kept being rediscovered. We began to sense more of the meaning of the notion of an *agape* revival through continuous forgiven-ness and repentance, as the only way left in mission. As one of our Mission Partners, a psychotherapist working with Pathan people in a mental hospital in Peshawar put it, 'we are being enabled to demonstrate a language of love which is what crosses all cultural barriers.'

The Redemptive Process

The sudden and unexpected summons to attempt to step into the great shoes of Max Warren and John Taylor as General Secretary of CMS gave me an opportunity of exploring more of the universal implications of this corporate discovery. Through a varied, sensitive and gifted network of people strengthening our relationships with fellow Christians in churches in many parts of Asia and Africa, and through my own journeys visiting those churches and their leaders, I was given so much over ten years. I became quite convinced that the world missionary task has to be tackled together between all the churches and not just from one-sided initiatives from the West or in the West.

An agency like the CMS with its long history and widespread network is well placed to be part of an international grouping of enthusiasts for the communication of the gospel to our world. Much of the task seemed now to involve linking growth points world-wide. Everywhere I was struck by the way in which the crisis through which the Isoko people were passing at the time at which Ibribina emerged as an evangelist is a crisis shared by people of all faiths and cultures. Everywhere religious patterns and institutions are beginning to be or will be faced with crisis and upheaval. The Islamic movements which some have termed 'fundamentalism' are all symptoms of this crisis, as are movements of Hindu or Sikh nationalism and parallel soul searchings and questionings in the Buddhist worlds of Thailand or Sri Lanka. China is becoming a great 'laboratory of the Spirit' as is Africa, and Japan is passing through radical self-questioning and searching. Spiritual aggression and self-assertion in these arenas as much as in religious bodies in the West point to a crisis of identity. We are moving towards a melting pot in the next Millennium, a kind of breaking and remaking of humanity.

In such a situation the greatest experiences of all for me lay in my many encounters with pilgrims on the edges and frontiers of many worlds of faith, amongst wounded 'original inhabitants' like the Australian Aborigines in their dreaming, or in the heart of great frameworks of faith like the Hindu kingdom of Nepal, or among Muslims in Northern Nigeria, in Khartoum or Omdurman or in Pakistan. Again and again I would find spiritual pioneers, pointers to the strangely hidden centrality of Jesus Christ to the struggles of

so many peoples, 'watchers on the walls.' They would often be leading small movements of fellow seekers converging on the story of a
wounded and broken God/Man, whose teaching and action, death
and resurrection had captured their hearts and imaginations, often
through dreams and visions. I came to the conclusion that this is a
story whose hour has come, if we do not hinder it, but rather are
content to become broken and remade alongside Christ and in the
power-in-weakness of the Spirit that flows from Him.

Call to Mission in Partnership

There and in Coventry when I went there to that great broken and
remade Cathedral with its theme of reparation and reconciliation, I
realised increasingly that we are being called to mission in partnership with all who will join gently in this deeply humbled and repen-
tant, Celtic-style *agape* revival mission. I felt it was our visitors there
whom I invited from South Africa, from the Caribbean, from Jinan in
China, from India, from Wales and North America who brought this
message home to us. The Archbishop of Canterbury has described
much of the Church in the West as bleeding to death and there is truth
in this. But I also found in many churches, especially in desert-like
housing estates in the cities and struggling villages in the country, the
Spirit was moving and fresh initiatives were putting out shoots. We
began a movement of prayer and repentance and love wherever we
could and numbers of people joined in. We had a marvellous small
team of workers with youth children, and a fine Mission Adviser, who
all shared the same vision and vision-symbol based on the Mercian
cross.

Everywhere the theme seemed to be leaping out, of forgiveness
and repentance: at Stratford where, as a Trustee for Shakespeare's
birthplace, I preached on Shakespeare's development of this theme,
especially and miraculously in his late plays; at Warwick University
where the then Professor of Social Thought, Gillian Rose, helped me
to explore the movement of what she called 'failing towards' in Hegel
and Kierkegaard. Tragically, she was struck down with cancer, which
she fought bravely, and in the course of the struggle worked through
her insight until the point at which I had the privilege, on her death
bed—though neither of us knew it was to be that—of baptising her.
I was drawn further and further at this time into the practice of the
Orthodox Jesus Prayer on which I wrote a small book. This prayer
had over the years at CMS become a rhythm of life for me. But now I

seemed to be drawn through it into a sense of the cosmic redemptive process to which in the world church, by being broken and remade together, by entering deeply into an *agape* revival we will be enabled in the new Millennium to reach out into all the broken worlds of humanity with Christ's healing, and to seek to engender a culture of forgiveness in our whole society and globe, constantly 'failing towards' God's goal for us.

For me this is a theme to be pursued in Cambridge, where I am now back in my old college after twelve years in Coventry and Warwickshire. Here I want to turn more and more to the study and the contemplation of this task now confronting the world missionary movement. We must seek to draw all into that movement into which God in Christ draws us on his Cross as He is lifted up. That we might through CMS and other agencies reach out across all churches to work everywhere with those who will, 'by their tears, by their love and by the giving of their lives,' seek to be changed and to bring change 'until the kingdoms of this world become the Kingdom of our God and of his Christ.'

CHAPTER 14

The Christic Cogito: Christian Faith in a Pluralist Age

Simon Barrington-Ward

IN THE 1960s, coming back from Nigeria to Cambridge to be Dean of Chapel at Magdalene was a cultural shock. I had been studying other people in deserted shrines and new movements in Africa. Now I was to be plunged into the falling apart of my own culture.

Peter Baelz, coming to give the Lent Addresses in our Chapel, was a reassuring figure. He loomed over us in the candlelight and seemed to proffer a thread to guide us circuitously through the shadows. He hinted at a 'metaphysic of love'.[1] We in the West should have begun not from that lonely and self-dividing 'cogito' of Descartes, 'I think therefore I am', but rather from a fresh laying hold on our true source and theme in Christ, 'I am loved therefore I am'.

At the time we were experiencing a sudden fresh spiral of the enlightenment and of romanticism like that first devastating encounter with Descartes' great 'turn to the subject' and the slide into sceptical relativism that followed. People were losing their bearings in a flux of possible visions and yet the gulf between the surface of life and any overarching meaning was increasingly hard to bridge.

Peter's words inspired me to search for resources to bring that essential relatedness in Christ alive in this new context.

Poets and artists seemed to help more than theologians. One voice that suddenly won a dramatic response was that of Gerard Manley Hopkins. Readings of his poems opened up a new perspective. No doubt this was partly because of his own peculiar spiritual pilgrimage, breaking tragically with his family, rebelling against the mechanised materialism of his times, and championing the endangered natural world, like so many round me.

---

1 In Peter Baelz's books, *Prayer and Providence* (London: SCM Press, 1968) and *Christian Theology and Metaphysics* (London: Epworth, 1968), he develops allied themes.

But the real reason is more significant. Hopkins, in his famous sprung rhythm as his fellow poet, Geoffrey Hill,[2] points out in one of the finest comments on him, was grappling with the deepest issues of his time. At one level he was going with the new tempo he could sense, the turbulent drift and disintegration of the society. But at another level Hill suggests he was pressing back against it.

Wordsworth,[3] in the *Intimations*, had used a change of time signature, breaking with his resigned iambic meter, laden with the burden of his times:

Heavy as frost, and deep almost as life!

to the sudden movement of

O joy that in our embers,
Is something that doth live.

Hopkins himself called this 'a magical change' and Hill sees it as a key point in 'the developing life crisis of the nineteenth century'. 'Wordsworth transfigures a fractured world.' Far from being, as critics suggest, 'an injury sustained' it is 'a resistance proclaimed'. Hopkins himself is engaged in the same redemptive resistance.[4]

He uses brief phrases to mediate between a primal cry of agony and an exclamatory prayer, '(My God) my God' in 'Carrion Comfort', or the drowning nun calling out in the 'Wreck of the Deutschland', 'O Christ come quickly' in which cry, like the whole poem itself, she 'christens her wild worst – best.'

Nicholas Boyle[5] similarly illuminates the Christian poet's sacrificial task Hopkins seeks to 're-penetrate the secular subject matter of the experiencing self' with the grace of Christ. He plunges into the flow and fragmentariness of experience and there discerns the instress of Divine Presence, of flashes or glints which fuse Divinity and the created object and which become 'moments in the life of Christ the God–Man'. To do this Hopkins must be immersed in the pain of the very loss and distance from their true destiny of his family, friends and contemporaries. In loneliness and failure he comes to utter, out of the depths of his weakness, poems that with great power break through

---

2   Geoffrey Hill, *The Lords of Limit* (London: Andre Deutsch, 1984), 'Redeeming the Time'.
3   ibid., 87.
4   ibid., 98–9; 101.
5   Nicholas Boyle, 'The Idea of Christian Poetry,' 436, Vol. 67, No. 798, October, 1986 (special issue for Kenelm Foster O.P.). It will be seen that I am heavily indebted to this article and its author. He links Hopkins with a development in which also Erich Auerbach and Hegel figure and he indeed led me to both. I don't want to lay any blame on him, however, for the use I have made of this linkage.

to a reintegration, a resurrection until 'this Jack, Joke, poor Potsherd, patch, matchwood, immortal diamond, is immortal diamond!'[6]

This struggle for coherence and integrity in the midst of an unprecedented freedom and diversity becoming both spiritual and social is strangely contemporary all over the world. Werner Kretschel, Superintendent and Pastor in East Berlin, has described the vast crowds of demonstrators at the time of the silent liturgy of their marches, gathering in a congregation larger than he had ever seen and singing refrains that were hymns. Many of them were workers, many young. Few had ever been in a Church before. Looking out over that diverse throng, sensing their hunger for meaning, their hanging on his words as had no other congregation before, he longed for a new word, a new pattern. He longed to reach back to the beginning and start all over again.

When Werner described this I thought of Erich Auerbach's incredible evocation in his 'Mimesis' of the Gospels as a new literary form.[7] Auerbach saw in them an astonishing new phenomenon from which sprang the whole development of Western realism he went on to trace, a previously unknown intermingling of the sublime and the humble. Between Eastern and Semitic religion there came into being here a new 'ground of becoming', in which the sacred seemed to enter and in-dwell the secular, the Spirit penetrates the material. Shepherds, fishermen, prostitutes, tax gatherers and ordinary people enact a response to a tremendous composition of human and divine. Out of this Judaeo–Christian source flows a new revelatory mode, in which the Eternal purpose is embodied, in the seemingly inconsequential and contingent histories and actions of particular human beings. A fragmentary succession of detail, almost incidental encounters, actions, gestures, are clothed with everlasting purpose and significance.

It was in the West that this earthing and historicising of Spirit was to take on the freest and most far-reaching form. Auerbach examines its effect in the birth of Western medieval art and literature.

The climax of his story is Dante's 'Divine Comedy', where, as on the facades of Chartres, allegorical and typological figures take on a new human expressiveness, almost breathing and moving, forever held in the characteristic attitude of a living moment. Through Beatrice herself the most passionate human responses and bodily desires are

---

6   Gerard Manley Hopkins, 'That Nature is a Heraclitean Fire and of the comfort of the Resurrection Poems' (Oxford: 1948), 111.
7   Erich Auerbach, *Mimesis: Representation in Western Literature*, trans. Willard Trask (Princeton: 1953), ch. 9, 'Farinata and Cavalcante'. Charles Williams, *The Figure of Beatrice: A Study in Dante* (London: Faber, 1953), 101.

drawn up into the ascent into divine fulfilment. After this high point of balance and interplay of spiritual and material, Auerbach suggests there is a breaking free of the secular. Out of the tension of the central nexus of divine purpose and the free and varied flow of earthly life, were to arise the natural sciences and the beginnings of Western democracy. Finally, through Renaissance and Reformation comes the Enlightenment, as an almost necessary alienation and estrangement, as if its rational and empirical and individualistic impulse had to break free into a final movement towards relativism and pluralism to secure real human liberty. But although the enlightenment was a vital, critical process, the catastrophic distortions of the central spiritual/material nexus at the heart of Christian history continued. Anti-Semitism, the crusades, the aggressive expansion of Europe, two world wars, the holocaust, nuclear destruction. *Corruptio optimi pessima!* The corruption of the best is worst. But we still have, at the blocked spring of the genuine Christian tradition, with Werner Kretschel, to reach back to the beginning and to find and be found by the essential movement of Divine love, in a story and a person whose 'hour has come'. At the apparent source of some of the world's greatest problems and conflicts we could then rediscover the real means of their ultimate resolution and cure.

If Dante provided the climax of an earlier phase, I believe that it is Hegel who can give us the clue to a new beginning now. Hegel set out to think through the movement of the Divine Spirit into its opposite, into the material, the temporal, and the relative, its willingness to be identified wholly with it, poured out into it and broken by it, and thus to overcome it and to draw it back into a genuine communion. Hegel set out to think through the unfolding of nature and history 'in Christ'.[8] Trinity, Incarnation and Cross provided his new 'Cogito', developed this time not at the outset but in the by-going. 'Hegel', H.S. Harris declares, 'does for the age of knowledge what Dante did for the age of faith.'[9] Indeed the *Phenomenology of the Spirit* is a vital re-working of the central mediation in Christ between infinite spirit and finite life which Dante also sought to express. But human society has undergone a sea change. The world now has broken more free and Spirit, following the trajectory of Incarnation and Cross, has to

---

8 Even J.N. Findlay in *Hegel, A Re-examination*, in one of the more 'secular' interpretations of Hegel, acknowledges this: 'In the Christian study of the Incarnation, Passion and Resurrection of Christ, Hegel comes to see a pictorial expression of his central thesis: that what is absolute and spiritual can emerge only in painful triumph over what seems alien and resistant. Hegel may, in fact, be said to have used the notions of Christianity in the very texture of his arguments, and is almost the only philosopher to have done so!', *Hegel a Re-examination* (London: George Allen & Unwin Ltd, 1958), 30.

9 H.S. Harris, 'Hegel's Image of Phenomenology,' 106, in Cho, K.K., ed., *Philosophy and Science in Phenomenological Perspective* (Dordracht/Boston/Lancaster: Martinus Nijhoff, 1984).

pervade the created order more precariously and vulnerably still, to draw an ever richer and more complex world back into relation with its divine source.

The Enlightenment had seen Descartes' 'turn to the subject'; that moment when the philosopher withdrew into himself, shutting his eyes, closing off his senses, determined to accept as true only what had inner evidence in consciousness. Stephen Houlgate has brilliantly outlined the whole story of what followed and of Hegel's response.[10] Traditional Western metaphysical thinking had always seemed to posit a series of opposites set against each other, such as infinite, finite, God and the soul, spirit and material, but now they appeared severed permanently from one another. Once empiricism had culminated in Hume, the last connections were cut between sense perceptions and those necessary connections between observed events such as causality, which had always been assumed to be contained in experience. If these universal determinations were just assumption and habit, then the last links between our subjective experience and any overall meaning were destroyed. God faded away and even the self was dissolved. Even Kant's great analysis of our processes of thought and perception could not, for sure, restore what had been lost. Kant demonstrated that the world, as we understand it, emerges from a synthesis of the basic categories of our thinking with our sense perceptions which yields a sense of continuity and objectivity. But even he kept the Humeian idea that these categories cannot be said necessarily to apply to reality in itself. Beyond all our knowledge lies a reality we can never know or grasp in the 'noumenon'. Our categories, generated by our minds, remain subjective. Their contradictions could never apply to what must be the perfect consistency of reality, whatever that may be.

Hegel went with the flow of this whole movement of thinking a long way. He accepted the turn to the subject, the emphasis on our own inner consciousness. He accepted Hume's view that sense perceptions cannot yield universal, necessary, causal connections. He took gratefully Kant's description of the basic categories and forms of human thought with which our sensory experience must be synthesised. Indeed, he took the argument further and said that these categories

---

10 Stephen Houlgate, unpublished paper presented to the Society for Systematic Philosophy, APA, Washington, December, 1988. Hegel Society of Great Britain, Oxford 1989: 'Thought and Being in Kant and Hegel', 11–12, Houlgate here quotes, *The Philosophical Writings of Descartes*, trans. John Cottingham, Robert Stoothoff and Dugald Murdock (Cambridge: Cambridge University Press, 1984), II, 24. My argument at this point is taken entirely from this paper and the development by Stephen Houlgate of elements of the same argument in *Hegel, Nietzsche and the Criticism of Metaphysics* (Cambridge: Cambridge University Press, 1986), 100–18.

were in themselves one sided and must needs give rise to a process of continuous contradiction. If the categories are this one sided and contradictory, they cannot be used to produce the abstract notion of reality 'in itself', the mysterious 'noumenon', at all.[11]

But, in fact, all we have to do is to render our own thought more explicit and allow the categories to develop, through a constant dialectical process of thought, through a kind of continual death and resurrection. As each contradiction and opposition is over-reached and taken up into a more comprehensive whole, we realise that the structure of our consciousness *is* the structure of being itself. Thought and Being are one. The process of our thought is the process of life. *There cannot be a 'noumenon' beyond our knowledge since we cannot even comprehend at all a reality which is inconceivable.* Rather, as we reflect on our own consciousness and understanding and grasp its continuous cruciform movement we find not even a way to bridge a real gap between thought and being. We simply see that gap 'collapse and disappear'.[12] Our consciousness becomes the point at which Being is conscious of itself.

Hegel sees Spirit through the continual flux of human thought and consciousness developing and refining an ever subtler and richer complexity. Nothing is lost. Each thought, each entity in life, as it gives itself over to that which over-reaches it is transfigured by it, into a greater whole and preserved and fulfilled as a part of that whole.

This is the law of human self-consciousness and of human interrelationships and of the emergence of human society itself. 'Human self-consciousness comes to be by negating or dying to partial modes of itself and by growing into a fuller identity.' So, 'what Christians worship in Jesus Christ is the incarnation of man's true character, identity and determination, an identity which brings fulfilment if it is accepted, but, which 'damns' man, if it is rejected.'[13]

This is how Hegel sees the Spirit working through the whole disintegrating process of the Industrial Revolution and the emergence of a plural market society of free and autonomous individuals. He lamented that we could not get back to the ideal community of the Greeks. But this led him into a quest for a form of society combining individual freedom and mutual commitment which is strangely appropriate to our universal concern at the present.[14]

---

11 Stephen Houlgate, *Hegel, Nietzsche and the Criticism of Metaphysics*, 118.
12 Stephen Houlgate, 'Thought and Being in Kant and Hegel'. For the whole argument, see 15–17.
13 Stephen Houlgate, *Hegel, Nietzsche and the Criticism of Metaphysics*, 98.
14 There is much here of relevance to the struggle, in this country and worldwide, for ways of evolving a genuine 'social market', where no-one is marginalised and all are equipped continually to take part and to benefit. Hegel, over against

Hegel has often been read as the developer of some total rational system in much too literal and shallow a manner. For Hegel, reason yields itself to work its infinitely patient and hidden course through unreason, through the mass of contradiction and chance occurrence. What he is depicting is a movement not of inexorable progress, but of something nearer to the process in the natural world envisaged by scientists like Prigogine[15] or Paul Davies[16] where order emerges continually through, and out of, chaos into an ever-increasing complexity. The Universe thus has a 'pluralistic, complex character'.[17] Structures appear to break down and are subsumed into richer, more highly elaborated structures in 'a creative act taking place through time'. The unfolding organisation has less the character of a mechanism than of 'a work of art, involving change and growth,... rejection and reformulation of the materials at hand, as new potentialities emerge.'[18]

Nietzsche, like many of his disciples since, misread Hegel, seeing him only as the author of a 'fixed and discredited system'. In contrast he reverted to the scepticism of Hume and became, with his brilliant and wayward creative imagination, a philosopher of total pluralism and fragmentation without remainder. His great claim was to face the reality of a life stripped of all meaning with either Dionysiac ecstasy or, in another mood, heroic defiance.

But neither he nor his disciples seem to have grasped the fact that Hegel had already faced this reality, and discerned, within the dynamic pulse of thought and life itself, an emergent meaning and unity, a resurrection beyond the death of God.[19]

Thomas Mann saw Nietzsche as the source of German irrationalism in which ultimately he found the context of Fascism. Adrian Leverkuhn in Faust is certainly, like many of his Cambridge equivalents in the 1960s, a Nietzsche figure. He clearly 'lives in a period pervaded by Nietzsche's thoughts on culture and society'.[20]

I have always seen the less attractive, more seemingly bourgeois

Marx, who misread him, is coming into his own as a social philosopher. Compare *Hegel An Introduction*, Raymond Plant, with the development of Plant's own thought in Kenneth Hoover's and Raymond Plant's *Conservative capitalism in Britain and the United States* (London: Routledge, 1989) (and 'Faith in the City: Theological and Moral Challenges,' Diocese of Winchester, SO23 9GL, an implicit critique of recent Christian social thought).

15 Ilya Prigogine and Isabelle Stengers, *Order out of Chaos* (London: Heinemann, 1984).
16 Paul Davies, *Cosmic Blueprint* (London: Heinemann, 1987).
17 Prigogine and Stengers, *op. cit.*, 9.
18 Louise Young, *The Unfinished Universe* (New York: Simon & Schuster, 1986), 15 quoted in Paul Davies, *op. cit.*, 6.
19 There is scope here for a careful critique of deconstructivism, and of what seem misreadings of Hegel such as that of Jacques Derrida and of his fascinating and stimulating theological disciple, Mark Taylor (e.g. Mark C. Taylor *Erring: A Postmodern A/theology* (Chicago: Chicago University Press, 1981). Don Cupitt less plausibly shares some similar approaches in *The Long Legged Fly* (London: SCM, 1987). For a trenchant critique of Nietzsche from a Hegelian viewpoint cf. Stephen Houlgate, *Hegel, Nietzsche and the Criticism of Metaphysics*. See Note 10 above.
20 Thomas Mann, *The Uses of Tradition* (Oxford: T.J. Read, 1974), 367ff.

Zeitblom, his faithful friend and companion alongside him, with his dogged devotion to truth and morality, as a kind of Hegel figure. The possibility remains of a far more open reading of Hegel than that of Nietzsche and his followers allows, of the fullest possible acceptance of the chaotic flux of thought and life and the continuous dream-like appearance and shifting, collapse, and reintegration of religions and philosophies. But through it all Hegel discerns most subtly a movement of order and purpose and continuous growth into wholeness genuinely symbolised in the death and resurrection of Christ and in the corporate experience of his risen life in the Spirit. Hegel's philosophy becomes itself a 'metaphysic of love'. It is the divine love which pours itself into our creation, which makes itself vulnerable to our self-assertion and self-alienation, and which, at cost, re-penetrates the heart of our existence in order to draw us back, and, with us, the whole created order into an ultimate reunion with itself. As we give ourselves in love and as we yield ourselves to this love, so we discover that it is the truth of everything. 'I am because I am loved.' This is the Christic Cogito which I believe is still to emerge in and through the intermingling of faiths, ideologies and cultures in the melting pot of the coming century.

The enlightenment has been effectively exported along with modern technology to every part of the world. Every faith has now for some time been undergoing the same crisis that first befell Christianity. The Christian task now is to let the Cross of Christ through the action of the Spirit be planted deep within the consciousness of all faiths. But the only way to do this is above all to plant the Cross again in the heart of the consciousness of Christians themselves. We need a more far-reaching repentance and a self-criticism, a deeper humility, a costlier readiness for long-term loving. We need to learn what it means to take up the Cross and follow, to be 'crucified with Christ' as we are 'plunged into the life' of worlds in crisis. To such a witness (martyria) these worlds are open.

Much of Africa, for instance, is a vast, open 'laboratory of the Spirit', where traditional localised spirit worship and reverence for fathers and mothers, and for founders of the community or the family, have increasingly given way to more wide-ranging new cults, offering healing, witchcraft cleansing and the promise of new belonging. Intermingling with these are many varieties of new churches or praying groups, often founded by a visionary healer, woman or man, who may well have begun from some kind of vision of Christ, as

Himself either a supernatural healer and intermediary or as some kind of spirit power. But as these leaders have developed their grasp upon Christ and deepened their vision, sometimes they have come nearer and nearer to the Christ of whom the missionary poet Arthur Shirley-Cripps wrote in the 1930s:

The black Christ with parched lips and empty hands, A black Christ bowed beneath a heartbreak load.

Gabriel Setiloane wrote long ago of:

This Jesus of Nazareth, with holed hands
And open side, like a beast at a sacrifice;
When he is stripped naked like us
Browned and sweating water and blood in the heat of the sun,
Yet silent
That we cannot resist him.
How like us He is, this Jesus of Nazareth,
Beaten, tortured, imprisoned, spat upon, truncheoned,
Denied by his own and chased like a thief in the night.[21]

The fullest expression of this vision comes in African oral tradition, in folk sermons and spirituality and in dreams and visions. The whole story of Simon Kimbangu[22] and the symbolism of his being seen as the black Simon who carries the Cross behind Jesus, and the many liturgies associated with the movements which have converged in Kimbanguism in Zaire are typical. Similarly the deepest and richest fruit of the East African revival in people like Archbishop Luwum show a very profound perception of Jesus's suffering lordship, where His sacrificial blood offers an internal cleansing which restores trust and dedication. Janani Luwum, hunter,[23] warrior, dancer, who gave his heart and life to Christ and then suffered for his resistance to injustice, is still one of the most powerful icons or reflections of this black Christ, bearing the pain and struggle of the people. As Christ penetrates more and more deeply into the consciousness and imagination of African spiritual creativity, new black theologies and visions have still to unfold.

The crisis in Islam is bound up with the question as to what is the true nature of Islam itself, an issue frequently debated over the years

---

21 Kwesi A. Dickson, *Theology in Africa* (London: DLT, 1984), 196.
22 Marie-Louise Martin, *Simon Kimbangu* (Oxford: Blackwell, 1975).
23 Margaret Ford, *Janani Luwum: Making of a Martyr* (Lakeland, UK: 1978).

in, for instance, the press in Pakistan. Must its identity depend upon the imposition of Sharia Law and a total Islamic society within an egalitarian theocracy, or will other ways have to open up beyond the present Iranian model or the Wahhabi[24] inheritance of Saudi Arabia? There is the question raised long ago by Dr Muhammad al Nuwaihy,[25] 'Can Islam find its way to a discovery of transcendence which allows, indeed necessitates, a suffering identity with creation and humanity?' He found this suffering identity in the Qur'an itself. Others, crossing a sufist bridge, have begun to find it in the person of Jesus, sometimes discovered first through the Qur'an and later through a reading of the Gospels. There are little groups and individual pilgrims, often led by dreams and visions as well as by detailed study of the New Testament, coming into being in tiny ways in the very heartlands of Islam. Among them is one such leader whom I met in Pakistan, who has meditated profoundly over the radio on the agapé love of Christ and whose group, meeting and worshipping, chant fragments of the New Testament as they might chant the Qur'an. Many of the scattered Christians in Iran itself have stories of this kind and may well be preparing the way for a future reaction.

These, of course, are well outside any Church and are mostly people developing their own movement on the very fringes of Islam itself and in relation to it, though discovering the Cross and Risen Presence of Jesus as transcending and replacing the Islamic Law. One Sufist theologian, Hassan Askari,[26] drawn first by Bach's Matthew Passion when he was in Germany, and, studying the Cross as the heart of Jesus's whole life and teaching, increasingly has seen the relationship of the Cross to Islam itself. For him 'Christ becomes a sign for all of us'. 'There is no Cross but the Cross of Jesus.' And again, 'The Cross is a sign in the realm of relationship between God and humanity for people of all faiths today.' It may yet be that the Person and Cross of Christ will be enabled to penetrate from within to the heart of the Islamic consciousness, just as Christians begin to recognise the Jewish–Christian inspiration which lies behind Muhammad, and his genuine prophetic calling.

In the crisis which Indian religions and Buddhist patterns are also confronting in the face of the modern urban industrialised world,

---

24 For one exploration of this question see, Edward Mortimer, *Faith and Power, The Politics of Islam* (London: Faber, 1982).

25 In an unpublished lecture given in Cairo Cathedral in May, 1974. This is a theme richly explored by Bishop Kenneth Cragg, more than any other, recently in *Muhammad and the Christian* (London: DLT, 1984), *Jesus and the Muslim* (London: George Allen & Unwin, 1985), and, more generally, *The Christ and the Faiths: Theology in Cross-Reference* (London: SPCK, 1986).

26 Hassan Askari, *Inter-Religion: A Collection of Essays* (Aligarth: Printwell Publications, 1977).

renewed questions arise as to the role of the *Sangha*, the monastic community, or indeed of sadhus and gurus, in relation to the social and political world.

There is a real sense in Eastern tradition in which it is difficult for the 'renouncer' or the *Bodhisattva* ever fully to return and grapple realistically with the transformation of this world. It is fascinating to speculate what effect it would have had even on Gandhi's own miraculous mission, if he had come nearer, as Stanley Jones longed for him to do, to the apprehension and acceptance of a fuller and richer Christology.

Certainly, again there is a wide scattering of pilgrims and disciples in the tradition of the famous Narayan Tilak,[27] the poet of Maharashtra, who became a Christian *Sannyasi*, or Sadhu Sundhar Singh, with his Sikh and Bhakti Hindu background,[28] who became a devotee of Jesus Christ through a vision. There are those who come first to this understanding through perceiving Christ as their Guru or Avatar and growing into a fuller sense that He is the presence in a newly unfolding history of the pleroma, the fullness of the ultimately transcendent in our midst. There are a host of such visionaries within and beyond the Church in India. Stanley Samartha has also pointed out how many Hindu and Muslim artists 'have been inspired by themes in the life of Jesus Christ, particularly his sufferings, death and resurrection'.[29] Christ is beginning to dawn in new ways, and within a Hindu or Sikh or Muslim milieu, He discloses elements of a new relationship with the Divine. He is not just absorbed into another way of thinking, but, within the growing interchange of faiths, begins to modify the sensibility of others.

So much of all this movement points to changes in the deep structure of human consciousness and in the imagination and perception as well as intellectual conceptualisation.

Indeed, the crisis in Christianity itself might well be said to be to do with the loss of capacity for this kind of imaginative thinking which Hegel called 'reason'.[30] A great deal of Western Christian theological writing today is Kant-ian in spirit and starts from the assumption of the relativity and limitation of all our religious perceptions so that beyond there is a kind of Divine 'noumenon'.

---

27 Plamthodatil S. Jacob, *The Experimental Response of N.V. Tilak* (Madras: CISRS, 1979).

28 A.I.J. Appasmy, *Sundar Singh: a Biography* (London: Lutterworth Press, 1958).

29 Stanley J. Samartha 'The Cross and the Rainbow' in *The Myth Of Christian Uniqueness*, John Hick and Paul Knitter, eds (London: SCM, 1987), 82–3.

30 Hegel took from Kant the distinction between 'Understanding', ordinary, objective rationalising, and 'Reason', a more far-reaching participatory activity of mind and spirit with power to enter into the real development of the structures of consciousness and being.

Many of the contributors to two recent conferences and anthologies attempting a pluralistic theology of faiths, the one presided over by John Hick and Paul Knitter,[31] and the other by Leonard Swidler, have something of the general tone given by Hick and Swidler in their introductions to the two resulting volumes. Hick's exploration of the cultural relativity of religions, like that of Gordon Kaufman and Cantwell Smith himself, essentially seems to rest on this type of Kantian distinction. Gavin d'Costa[32] in a brilliant critique of John Hick, has drawn attention to his Kant-ian roots. Kaufman[33] speaks of the various religions as 'products of human imaginative creativity in the face of the great mystery life is to us all!' Leonard Swidler talks of trying to develop some kind of 'Ecumenical Esperanto', and we all know what has happened to that particular linguistic experiment. One of the most penetrating comments in either anthology is that of Stanley Harakas,[34] an Eastern Orthodox theologian in the Swidler volume. Commenting on a long rambling paper of Cantwell Smith on the history of 'religion', he asks whether it is possible that a Western, rationalist and individualistic bias has weakened Cantwell Smith's sense of the inner cohesion and integrity of religions. Is this kind of theology, in fact, seeking the formation of a new world-wide religion 'after the fashion of that described in Isaac Asimov's novel *Foundation*?' 'Are not the methods of the history of religions somewhat anaemic for the accomplishment of such a goal in the face of the powerful revelatory claims at the source of most organised religions?' A weakened Christology[35] leading to anaemic and abstract concepts in which the proponents of new universal theologies circle round a Kant-ian void is scarcely likely to be productive. Significantly those with a greater intensity of imagination and depth of spiritual consciousness at the conferences, such as Raimundo Panikkar, came nearer in their colourful flamboyance to a Nietzschian pluralism, and in the end proved equally incoherent, retaining from their Christian

---

31 John Hick and Paul F. Knitter, ibid.; Leonard Swidler, ed., *Towards a Universal Theology of Religion* (New York: Orbis, 1987).
32 Gavin d'Costa, *Theology and Religious Pluralism* (Oxford: Basil Blackwell, 1986), esp. 39. *Scottish Journal of Theology* 39 (1986).
33 John Hick and Paul F. Knitter, op. cit., 8.
34 Leonard Swidler, op. cit., 77, 78.
35 There is usually a sublime assumption in these theologies that New Testament criticism must lead to a reduced and relativised understanding of the claim that Jesus is the Christ. 'The Myth of God Incarnate' is the necessary foundation for the 'Myth of Christian Uniqueness'. Theologians of Pluralism have made so many foolish self-destructive disclaimers about the true nature of Christ and done so much to damage the very treasure they have to bring. Other readings, however, suggest otherwise, e.g. C.F.D. Moule, *The Origin of Christology* (Cambridge: Cambridge University Press, 1977), for an earlier response. Nearer to the present argument, Gerd Theissen, *The Shadow of the Galilean* (London: SCM, 1986), evokes a great sense of the mystery, enigma and unclassifiable quality of Jesus transcending shallow judgements. The crucial point is that, even if Jesus's presentation of the Kingdom is that of 'God in Strength' (Bruce Chilton, *God in Strength*, Freistadt 1979), that strength in all three synoptic gospels and strikingly in Paul, Hebrews and John, is realised and released in the 'weakness' of the Passion.

roots only a vague and seemingly groundless optimism. Sadly they were all trying, with some degree of success, to drag Hans Küng across what was regarded as a crucial rubicon as his Christology weakened and his general abstract humanism thickened into the murky waters of their own relativism.[36]

All this conversing was a long way from the real, deep spiritual interaction in the melting pot of religions amongst people of profound prayer and faith at a time when out of the West we need to be able to bring something beyond our Western enlightenment heritage. We need not to lose our corporate hold upon the Living Christ in whom we have indeed been given the supreme disclosure of the Divine Love. The last thing that those of all faiths, who struggle with us at a profound level to find new visions and new social patterns for humanity, need is for us to lose our own testimony to the fullness of Christ. This, after all, is what, in the heart of the disintegrating movement we set in throughout the world, we still have to bring. The historical passion through which so many are passing is here comprehended in its central critical moment. The content of the faith in Christ becomes the immanent content of thought itself. The way of love and self-giving, the way of the Cross opens up a way that runs through all ways, a way in which God is finally known to be, in the confusion and through the relativity, absolute.

Quaerens me sedisti lassus
Redemisti crucem passus
Tantus labor non sit cassus
Seeking me you became weary
Redeeming me you suffered the Cross
Let not so great a labour be in vain![37]

I recall once Bishop Lakshman Wickremesinghe of Kurunegala presiding at a Communion amongst Buddhists, Hindu Tamils and Christians all working for peace and justice in his strife-torn country. He towered over us tall, refined and austere, as he broke the bread

---

36 For an analysis of Hans Küng's 'progression', see Scott Cowdell 'Hans Küng and World Religions: The Emergence of a Pluralist,' *Theology*, March 1989. But he is, in fact, still not quite submerged by the end of 'What is True Religion?' at the end of Leonard Swidler, ed. (op. cit., Note 29), although Christianity is now true 'for me' and 'cannot claim to have comprehended God', 25, op. cit. The Kant-ian 'noumenon' hovers overhead. Both Gavin d'Costa (op. cit., Note 31) and Michael Barnes's *Religions in Conversation: Christian Identity and Religious Pluralism* (London: SPCK, 1989), have recently offered lively critiques of current Christian approaches to Pluralism and propounded positive and creative approaches. Both begin to transcend the tired typology of 'exclusive' and 'inclusive' and offer good critical surveys of the main protagonists. Neither seems quite to have grappled adequately with the central Christological issue. Rahner's framework no longer seems adequate on the one hand and a dialectical pneumatology not a sufficient alternative on the other. Keith Ward's stimulating but rather static attempt to draw out an 'essence' from selected representatives of various faiths (*Images of Eternity*, London: DLT, 1987) is also lacking in this vital area.
37 From 'Dies Irae', Latin Mass of the Dead. See *Hymns Ancient and Modern* (London: Historical Edition, 1909).

and put forward the cup. I was reminded strangely of Melchizedek, bringing forth gifts from beyond and into the flux. Lakshman's fine face was absorbed, his form trance-like, his hands moved in the characteristic gestures of giving thanks and breaking. He had spoken in a way which drew upon both Buddhist and Hindu stories and legends. His central action was now such as to affirm the reality of the infinite presence and power of God's love released in the midst of our struggles, confusion and pain. Nor, glancing at the faces around was there any doubt anywhere that this essential brokenness of the God–Man on the Cross undergirded and strengthened their own hold upon faith and life and opened up for all of us a way through meaninglessness and death. The same movement which we glimpsed through Manley Hopkins, through African prophets and Indian artists and poets and devotees, through Auerbach and Dante, was there disclosed: 'the love that sways the universe and the other stars...' This is the love that in Hegel, as in Peter Baelz's 'metaphysic of love' bears all things, believes all things, hopes all things, endures all things, the love that releases life into its infinite outpouring of variegated forms and fusions, to draw all back ultimately into communion and union with itself.

CHAPTER 15

Becoming What You Are: Exploring the 'Great Exchange'

Simon Barrington-Ward

The Commencement Address for the Graduation of Students at Goshen College

3pm on Sunday the 22nd of April 2012

The First Part of the Exchange: God enters into Our Life and Death

I would like to tell you the story of two discoveries, each of them vital to me, which have somehow come to play a major part in my life.

The first is a discovery of which I believe all you will all probably have shared something, in one way or another, and that is, the discovery of God meeting with us in the person of Jesus Christ.

The second, which came to me much later, was the discovery of a way of being more and more deeply united with Jesus Christ, and, through Him, with the triune God, Father, Son and Holy Spirit. This particular 'way' of prayer, which developed possibly amongst the martyrs in the time of the persecution of Christians, so from the earliest years of the growth of the Christian church, and then, amongst the Desert Fathers and Mothers of the fourth century, and in their early communities, out of which Christian monasteries later developed. The interplay between these two discoveries I have come to see as two parts of an 'Exchange' between God and humanity arrived at through Christ.

I myself grew up from my earliest years, in a broadly Christian household. I attended church services from childhood on and at school, and from my earliest days, when I was moved by what I have come to see to have been experiences of God. My parents nurtured this awareness in me. In my last year or two at school, I came up against some other boys, who sought to attack my continuing sense that somewhere, all around us, though hidden from us, there is a divine presence. My father, a journalist, who was something of an idealist philosopher, wrote some brilliant letters to help strengthen my sense that there really were grounds for our 'innate sense' of the reality of goodness, beauty and truth in the world. He gave some real and clear support to my conviction that there is a divine reality always somewhere about us and within us, which he succeeded in showing me really was there. Eventually, I even went so far as to apply to be trained for the ministry of the Church, went before a selection panel and was actually accepted.

But two events threatened this. One was my father's suddenly devastatingly early death, just as I was applying to study history in Cambridge. The other, coming much later, when I was in my third year at the University, was the invitation of a German fellow student to go out and lecture in the English Department, at the bidding of his Professor, in the so-called Free University in West Berlin, where the famous old Berlin university was in Communist hands, in the Russian half of the divided city.

As the aircraft in which, as a young graduate, I flew to Berlin, came down out of the clouds over Eastern Germany, the bombed city which lay beneath me looked like a landscape on the moon. Crumbled ruins still seemed to stretch to the horizon, and a grey/brown river wound its way through piles of rubble, while long thin facades lining curving streets were pierced by empty windows looking into a void. But this grim, first impression was countered when a kindly, welcoming group, my smiling friend of Cambridge days and his colleagues soon took me back to a pleasant suburb, a former village close to woods and lakes, called Dahlem, with houses little damaged, where I could walk under trees from my lodging, to the smooth, white buildings of the new University.

Soon, I was meeting my new students, most of them older than I was, as they sat in the tea parties I tried to give them in my room and poured out stories of terrible experiences, fleeing with their families from the Russians, of seeing their mothers or sisters raped by the invaders, of being beaten up and lost as they struggled through to the broken city, and of guilt over German support for the Nazis. Trying to help them, I felt out of my depth, as we struggled to converse in broken English and German.

My fellow lodger, Klaus, a brilliant graduate student of Economics, had developed into a passionate, vital sceptic. As we became friends, he set to work to tear my increasingly vague Christian faith to pieces. Amid the mass of ruins, I went for long, lonely walks. Even when I ventured into the nearby woods and lakes, they seemed almost deserted. I tried attending the local church, the 'Dahlem Dorfkirche' (village–church) as it was called, and quite enjoyed services, and the lively preaching of the pastor, an exciting speaker called Daenstedt. But the most moving experience in that church, which really helped me more, was a communion service on Saturday nights, amongst what still seemed to be almost a kind of secret group, because it had been started in the wartime by the famous, previous pastor, Niemöller, who had been arrested by the Nazis, and then released by popular demand. I was especially moved by the moment when this group knelt round the altar, as Pastor Daenstedt murmured the words over us, 'Ich bin der Weinstock. Ihr seid die Reben...ohne mich koennt Ihr nichts tun!' 'I am the Vine. You are the branches ... Without me you could do nothing.'

One day, I was invited by this group to join them for an evening discussion of contemporary German poems, which then led into a study of the Bible passage, which was made to seem still more exciting! They were a striking group of people. Some worked at the University and some in local shops, but there was a remarkable sense of openness and trust between them and atmosphere of what I can only describe as 'forgiven-ness'. For instance, when one woman said to me confessing her old ideas and actions, 'You see, I was a Nazi!', I realised that no one else in the City or the University had said anything like this to me, nor would I have expected them to. But the people in this gathering were rather special. They came together fortnightly and I found myself entering into a deep, mutual acceptance and an even deeper sense of the presence of God. The Holy Spirit seemed here to be at work within us and amongst us.

But for me, the key meeting that amongst us took place was when Pastor Daenstedt expounded the real nature of the relationship with the eternal Divine Spirit into which, in the person of Jesus Christ, we had all been brought. We were studying 2 Corinthians 5, and the mysterious saying in verse 21, 'for our sake God made Him (Christ) to be sin, so that in Him we might become the righteousness of God'. When we were all puzzled by this, Daenstedt exclaimed, 'but this is the heart of our whole life as Christians!' It is saying that in the man Jesus Christ, God entered, as nowhere else, into the depths of our human tragedy, our frustration and brokenness. In Christ also, we might enter into our true destiny, our freedom, our fulfilment, our ultimate joy, our final transformation beyond death, to be made part of the new creation to come. This is 'der suesse Austausch', the 'sweet exchange' (he translated it for me!).

We talked about this 'exchange' late into the night. I had never taken in before, that the Jesus Christ, whom I had learned to think of as an example, a kind of embodiment, of goodness, was really the key to a whole new relationship with God for all humanity. Nowhere else in human history had God come alongside human beings in a human life, and entered into our sin and death. Someone in the group quoted an early Christian 3rd century booklet, written for inquirers into Christianity, entitled *The Letter to Diognetus* (a Roman seeker):

> O the sweet exchange, O the inscrutable creation, O the unexpected benefits, that the wickedness of many should be concealed in the one righteous, and the righteousness of the one should make righteous many wicked!

'You said you were baptised as an infanbilitit,' said Daenstedt to me. 'Well, this is "the exchange" into which you were brought, when as an infant you were made one with Jesus Christ in that baptism!' He continued:

> All human experiences or glimpses of God or of the Divine in all the faiths and philosophies that exist are really supported by this one happening. The reality of God, the Divine Eternal Spirit, whom many seek, is here universally confirmed as having entered into this new relationship with humankind: 'God with Us and for Us', established through God becoming a human person. Why not think about what this could mean and, if you feel so led, then just pray to Him and resolve to entrust yourself to Him?!

So I walked home in a whirl of thoughts and possibilities. I found myself sitting on my bed and saying, 'Jesus, I want to trust you. If you were wrong, I will be wrong with you.' After that I slept deeply. When I woke up into a new, sunlit, spring morning, and walked to the church for the early morning Bible Study some of us enjoyed with Pastor Daenstedt, I was borne along as if on an entirely new spiritual current, drawing me on and out into the great ocean of the Divine love, which had now opened up to me through this first part of a great exchange! The doors had opened up again into the possibility of my entering into a union with God!

The Second Part of the Exchange: We Enter into the Death of the Son of God and His Risen Life

I was soon able to explore, in talks with Daenstedt, this theme of God drawing us into an 'exchange', through coming to us in a human life, death and resurrection. He pointed me to the teaching of the early Greek Christian thinkers who shaped this notion. He quoted one of them, St Athanasius who wrote in his book, *On the Incarnation* (54), 'He [the Word of God] became human, that we might become God.' Others, before and after, had written similarly of this exchange between God and ourselves. For instance. Irenaeus, two centuries earlier, had written: 'In his immense love he became what we are, that we might become what he is.'*Against Heresies 5*. Irenaeus quoted a popular Psalm verse of the time, Psalm 82.6, 'I said you are gods and, all of you, sons of the Most High.' For him, human beings can become 'gods' through baptism, being united to Christ and growing into union with God through Him. Clement of Alexandria (150–215) had already anticipated the thought that 'God became human that we might become divine.' Our life could eventually come to be 'hidden with Christ in God,' and this can become our ultimate goal: what the Greeks were to call *Theosis*, being deified, being united by the Spirit through the Son with the triune God, becoming 'partakers of the divine nature' (2 Peter 1.4) as in the transformed life to come, the whole creation could come to be drawn into a new union with God.

Much later in my life, at a time when I was put in charge of a large, Church of England Mission Society (CMS), sending people from the UK to churches all over the world and bringing them from other parts of the world to the UK, I realised suddenly what difficulty I myself had in praying, and what a struggle I had always had, somehow, to 'get through' to God. In my new role I really needed help. A kind friend, at our CMS London Headquarters, drove me down to an Orthodox monastery he knew in Essex, where he was sure I would find help, especially from its leader, an outstanding holy man, a Russian monk, called Archimandrite Sophrony. We came to a lovely, old, former Church of England clergy house, deep in the country. It was set in a large and lovely garden, there to be met by a group of community members, women and men in white robes, awaiting us kindly, though I fear we'd lost our way and were late, but they were so welcoming.

They swept us past new buildings, glowing with vivid mosaics: one (painted with the help of children) showing animals entering Noah's Ark up a ladder, another, depicting St Nicholas in a tiny vessel at sea mastering the storm with his raised cross, and many other such. We were brought into a spacious, dimly lit but lofty Chapel. The congregation were mostly standing, but we were shown to two chairs on the men's side of the congregation, from which we could gaze at a fine screen of icons in front of us, lit by candles. All around us, the smaller icons of many saints populated the white walls, many familiar from Orthodox history and legend.

Spontaneous one sentence prayers were already starting, uttered by different voices, some intercessory, all interspersed with silence. But then a leading voice, a woman's, led into the main period of worship and the central Prayer, which, after a pause, she steadily, and powerfully repeated always the same petition, 'Lord Jesus Christ, Son of God, have mercy upon us!' After some time of this repetition we were led by another voice, this time a man's, followed in silence by the whole congregation of monks and nuns, and also a few lay visitors such as ourselves. This Prayer was spoken in the same way, as a kind of steady, earnest but confident plea, sustaining a sense of confident yearning, and inspiring what seemed to be a profound, unselfconscious unanimity in those all around us. Glancing to the left of me, near the corner, I could see, in front of a throne-like chair, Father Sophrony, as I knew it must be, half-sitting, half-standing, his steadfast gaze being framed by a mass of white hair, side whiskers and beard, surrounding him like a white cloud! His piercing blue eyes seemed to gleam, as if reflecting the light of the candles. The rest of the whole congregation stood motionless, somehow relaxed, clearly all equally intent on that single, repeated petition. After one voice had led for a time, another, male or female, then took up this Prayer, led with such a steady and natural rhythm, that it felt as if we were all a flock of birds, flying steadfastly towards their unseen goal, the figures on the icons on the walls flying together, held together by the continual, steadfast beat of the same petition. Occasionally there would be a slight variation of tone or pace, but one felt always deeply drawn into a constant movement towards our shared goal. The Prayer, which had been interspersed with silences, and taken up by a succession of varied voices, always one at a time, each eventually ceasing only to give way to another, still continued, always at the same pace, and driven on by the same energy.

I can truly say that in that setting I found myself drawn increasingly deeply into this way of praying, as though we really were converging on the living Lord, drawing us ever closer to Himself. By the time, perhaps an hour and a half later, though one was soon quite unaware of time, that the Prayer was nearing its end, one became aware of this, only through an increasingly intercessory inclusion in its form, as the last phrase turned into, 'have mercy upon us, and upon our world.' This was only spelling out something which had already been implicit, since that prayer not only drew us nearer to its source and goal in the Lord, but also now articulated what we had already sensed throughout, that it was all embracing . Other names or places could be thus included deliberately. To my amazement, I found that I wanted the whole process never to end! I was so greatly moved by it and drawn into it. What I was sensing, without then knowing it, was that I was being drawn on and on, as we all were, into a movement which seemed shaped by the power of the Holy Spirit, enfolding us like a tide, and yet always seeming to be drawing us nearer and nearer to its goal.

Suddenly, I felt as if I had rarely, if ever, prayed so strongly as this before, and as if I would want somehow always to be held in the rhythm of this movement and drawn into its flow. I didn't want it to stop. After the last voice ceased, we then stayed in total silence, letting the prayer continue within us, while others around gently slipped away. Eventually, when a tall monk, smiling gently, passed me, I suddenly dared to ask him, 'Do you think that it might be possible to meet with Father Sophrony, now?!' He smiled and said that he would see. It was certainly possible, he added, if it were feasible! With that he left me. It seemed only a short time after that, that I was being ushered into the presence of that wonderful figure whose eyes seemed to have caught mine for a moment much earlier.

When I stumbled into his presence, in a small room, he was sitting behind a table, with the monk who had spoken to me next to him, and another older one at his other side, large icons on the wall above them, of equally venerable figures, gazing down, gave me a feeling of a wider company with us! But all seemed as gentle and yet searching as Sophrony himself. I stammered out something about my longing to pray in the way that I had just, somehow, learned to do, this very afternoon. Could I dare to ask his help? With a fresh gleam, he asked me how deeply committed I was in my quest for this kind of praying. Would I be prepared to come back regularly to learn this 'way', and to enter in upon it, making of it a bond of the Spirit, uniting me with him and this community? Would I be prepared to return regularly to them, and, in the mean time, to pray regularly and constantly, daily, letting nothing else stand in the way? I said that I thought I could and would. I felt I was being searched spiritually, and was not really up to this testing commitment, but that I really must seek to continue it. 'Will you return in six weeks time to begin learning more?' he asked me, firmly but kindly. I promised.

He picked up a knotted, black, circular cord or 'prayer rope', with a tassel at the end of it, and round wooden beads at intervals, every 20 knots along it. Taking hold of the tassel between his right finger and thumb, he said, again with a humorous glint, 'This is my Pentecost! I start by holding it, and asking the Holy Spirit to pray within me, 'Come, Holy Spirit!" Then he took the cross of knots between his forefinger and thumb, saying, 'Draw me through the Lord Jesus Christ, crucified and risen, into the Triune Love of Father, Son and Holy Spirit!' He moved the forefinger and thumb to hold the first knot, and prayed, 'Lord Jesus Christ, Son of God, have mercy upon me, a sinner!'

(Only when they are all praying together, the monks and nuns just use the phrase...'have mercy on us!'). Then he told me to do the same with each knot, in turn, with a pause before moving to the next knot. 'When you come to the bead,' he said, 'keep a brief silence before moving on. Sometimes you will feel led to make that silence longer, to be as long as seems to be right. This will grow. All the time the deep prayer of your heart is to be drawn into communion with Christ, into journeying with Him to the goal towards which he is drawing us, that of dwelling 'through Him in the Spirit with the Father'. If your thoughts begin to wander, keep drawing them back, and move on. You must be constantly 'practising the presence of Christ,' sensing his being there with you, and you with Him.' He strongly emphasised this.

'In praying like this', he said, 'You are being drawn into a journey with Christ towards the goal to which, through the Spirit, He is leading us all, into the new creation, the new life to come, and eternal presence through Him, by the Spirit's power, in the Tri-une God. As you pray the prayer, 'have mercy upon me, a sinner', the Spirit is bringing home to you Christ's continuously reassuring forgiveness, cleansing you and enfolding you. He is making you His, however far your thoughts have wandered, cleansing you instantly through the shedding of His blood, drawing you away from the passions and lusts of this world, and on into union with Him, and through Him, in the Spirit with the Father. Struggle to go with Him in this.'

'After each bead, you can also pray for others equally, by name, or for any situation confronting you or them, or the world. 'Have mercy on whomsoever or whatsoever!' Here, we often pray, 'Have mercy upon us, and upon our world!' I remembered then that this was the repeated plea with which the prayers in the Chapel had ended. Fr Sophrony blessed me and said finally, 'Come back. Never give up nor despair! As you pray, you are being drawn, and others drawn with you, into an ever deepening union with God in Christ through the Holy Spirit.' He handed me the Prayer rope and blessed me!'

I did go back to my beloved Father Sophrony quite regularly, and still go to the monastery, where I still have guides, companions and friends, but supremely, the praying of that prayer. Father Sophrony, who led me, and continually taught me more and more, until, increasingly translucent as he seemed to become, he slipped into the world beyond, inspired what for me has become a lifelong journey into Christ, in the Holy Spirit, and so towards that new creation in which we shall all be fulfilled at last.

Continually we realise, and are being drawn into, the interplay of God's Journey with us in Christ through the Holy Spirit, and, in the same Holy Spirit, our journey in and with Christ to the Father. This way of praying becomes part of a continuous exchange, which can be worked out in and through us and our fellow Christians all through our life. I have also found that the sacrament of what we call in the part of the church I belong to, 'Holy Communion,' is central to this growing union with God in Christ. It is the fullest possible realisation of the same double movement, the same interchange, which I have described to you as it is realised constantly in the Jesus prayer. The 'practice of the presence of Christ,' crucified and risen, seems to draw you ever more deeply in the Spirit into a growing oneness with the Triune God, severing you more and more continuously from the distracting passions and lusts which hold us back, gradually purifying and yet deepening a truer and more freely more self–giving love for others, and Christ's cleansing and healing forgiveness keeps liberating you more effectively from the self-seeking which He keeps revealing in you! Over and over again, in all our manifest failures in love, His gracious and healing word to us still draws us into our true response as we hear Him say, 'Dwell in me, and I in you!' (John 15.4), and this becomes again our true and constant goal as, in spite of our seemingly helplessness, we keep finding our broken selves, as we repeat our prayer, 'Lord Jesus Christ, Son of God, have mercy upon me, a sinner' being cleansed, renewed and drawn back again and again into union with Him!

May those of us who are graduating here today, together with all of us who are sharing in this special moment with them, in all the situations in which they and we may find ourselves, come to know God, in Christ, through the Spirit, entering more and more into our lives, our work, and our whole being, and drawing us, through that wonderful 'exchange' of His Life and Death and Resurrection into the ever deeper and richer healing and fulfilment awaiting each and all of us as we journey on into life in Him forever!

But it is not just our personal participation in that movement, in a constant interchange of God the Father, in Christ, coming to us in the Spirit and our constant growth into Him through the Spirit. It is all part of the movement of the whole Creation into its final fulfilment. God in Christ, through the Spirit, keeps coming to us in His infinite love and compassion, His 'mercy', as we call it, in this way of faith and prayer I have described to you. Also, in and through all of us, who are willing to participate and give ourselves over to the movement of His Spirit within us, those whom we seek to serve all round us, into and towards the final goal and fulfilment of this present creation, the new creation to come, and the risen life towards which and into which we are all being drawn.

Those who graduate here today, are starting out on a great journey. It is my hope, that they might find, and that all of us here might find, with them, help from exploring more of the infinite resources which have been made available to us in the person of God in Christ, through the Spirit, and of the unsearchable riches of that 'great exchange' which are still open for us, to draw upon more and more deeply, as we grow ever more fully into union in the Spirit through Christ with God. In Him, we have received the power to respond to and to enter into the fullness of His invitation: 'Dwell in me, and in you.' (John 15.4).

CHAPTER 16

Sermon for Gillian Rose

Simon Barrington-Ward

Little St Mary's on the First Sunday in Lent
29th February 2004
A Lenten Journey

Deuteronomy 8.3 Remember the long way that the Lord your God has led you these forty years in the wilderness, in order to humble you, testing you to know what was in your heart, whether or not you would keep his commandments...

Luke 4.1–2a. Jesus, full of the Holy Spirit, returned from Jordan and was led by the Spirit in the wilderness, where for forty days he was tempted by the devil.

A Theologian in Disguise

I CHOSE GILLIAN ROSE, Jewish social philosopher, because I feel that she crucially influenced my whole life and thought and work in a strangely Lenten way. She was someone who influenced me profoundly through entering into a real exchange with me of the kind that always affects us the most because grace itself is so marvellously mutual. And I wanted to celebrate her on this Sunday especially because her life was something of a movement through Lent and Holy Week to Easter.

The story begins when I had been Bishop of Coventry for four years, after being General Secretary of CMS for ten. I had already begun to find illumination from two sources, one was a growth into the practice of the Jesus Prayer, the continuous praying of the words, 'Lord Jesus Christ, son of God, have mercy on me,' becoming central

195

to my life, the other, an effort to study Hegel to whom I had been introduced by a Magdalene friend. I had already felt there was some connection between his great work *The Phenomenology of the Spirit* and the Prayer but I couldn't quite see what it was. At that stage, one morning, a letter and a book arrived in the post from a woman who told me that she was a new professor of social and political thought in the nearby University of Warwick. Then she added, 'But I am really a theologian in disguise'. The book she sent was one she had written 'in which', she said, 'I argue against the conventional wisdom that Hegel's thought has no social import if the Absolute (his word for God) cannot be thought.' She had heard from colleagues that I might be interested in this. This book blew my mind. I had to read it twice with a damp towel round my head, it was so dense! So with some excitement I went to see her in her lovely flat in Leamington.

Her impact was immediate. She was physically quite small and compact but her intense gaze and vitality, her warmth and her at once magisterial and vulnerable hold upon one made her seem larger than life. In her mid forties she was attractive and compelling. She soon responded to my bumbling questions with a force, a clarity and a poetic unexpectedness which at once stretched the mind and the imagination to make room for new insights. No wonder she had brought with her to Warwick ten research students from the University of Sussex.

The Repentance of Reason

Through reading her books and papers, and then listening to her inaugural lecture (like all her lectures more a dramatic happening, more like a concert performance or a poetry reading than an academic occasion), I was to begin to see Hegel through renewed eyes. His description of the development of human consciousness not only set reason in a historical, social and spiritual framework, it also described a redemptive process. She outlined the first glimpse of a kind of idealised ancient Greek Eden, typical of Hegel's generation and time, which depicted a society in which nature was cherished by a culture in which all were producers at one with their products ('Odysseus carpentered for himself his great marriage bed.') There was there no separation between religion and art, ethics and law, politics and science, but an underlying unity of life and action from within which freedom was born.

But the main theme emerged through Hegel's account of the subsequent, steadily increasing fragmentation of human society with the rise of the whole institution of private property under the imperial tyranny of Rome. Then, as that broke down, came the rise and fall of a succession of cultures, ways of being and seeing, quests for new wholeness, each struggling to shape consciousness and community in new ways, but each distorted by fresh contradictions, which could only gradually be recognised and broken down to give way to further development. The Divine Spirit had poured itself out into creation separated itself from itself in consciousness, empowered ever new embodiments of its life which in turn failed. Hegel saw the post-enlightenment society of Western Europe as still, for all its pretensions to progress, an 'animal kingdom,' in which the contrast, the 'diremption,' between its claims to universal freedom and justice and its actual exclusion and injustices, still cried out for drastic change.

Through our talks I began to see that what was called for was a kind of continuous 'repentance of reason'. Gillian liked that phrase and described it for her part as a constant 'failing towards' our goal; a goal we must always be deeply committed in thought and action. Hegel had set the cross at the heart of his philosophy. Through history for him there ran a rhythm of death and resurrection, of breaking and remaking of consciousness. History, Gillian insisted, was the story of the self-loss and self recovery of the Divine, losing life to save it, and in its self-humbling a self displacement, a self emptying (*kenosis*), opening up a way for humanity into that same self-displacement through the person of Jesus, or for her through the covenant with Israel. She elaborated this teaching in her big, dense book *The Broken Middle* and her more accessible book essays on *Judaism and Modernity*.

Meanwhile, for me, the Jesus Prayer began to come into play. Gillian showed me that continuous repentance is continuous turning, going beyond one's present mindset or *nous*. There must be a kind of repeated testing of hearts and of the social structures, which shape them and are shaped by them. As a Bishop, she said, I must never confine myself to a church separated from the rest of the world. I should be leading people in that church to be a redemptive force in the whole of their society. She encouraged me to integrate the Jesus Prayer with the struggle for justice and the concern for the poor in city and country, the attempt to undo the tragic betrayal of children, to break open a way through the desert of poverty and drugs, all of these efforts becoming parts of the same quest for wholeness. The prayer must be at the heart of that quest. She was passionately concerned for my work with inner city and housing estate parishes, my message to the wealthier sections of the community and the holders of power and my work as chair of the International Affairs and Development Committee of the Synod. She herself visited Israel to work with Israeli lawyers supporting Palestinian human rights. All our attempts at reform, all our successes and failures, like our own inner struggles for healing and integrity, were frustrated by the contradictions and divides, the 'diremption,' running through our entire life, so that we keep 'failing towards' our goal.

The Power of Grace and Forgiveness

But while Gillian accepted the whole rhythm of repentance and made me read Rabbi Soloveitchik on *Penitent Man* (*Homo Penitens*), who is presented in his writings as wiser than *Religious Man* or *Rational Man*, for her, *my* understanding of forgiveness and grace coming to us in the person of Jesus as Messiah, the Christ, was still impossible. For all her many involvements with Christians and wide reading of Christian theology, she feared a Christian romanticism or sentimentality which contrasted grace with law and let us off the hook far too easily, offering only 'cheap grace,' and she preferred real attempts to bring the actual laws we live by closer to the pattern of the ultimately ethical society. I tried in vain to point to the fusion of repentance and forgiveness, the new commandment *and* the grace to fulfil given in the Gospels.

This morning's gospel portrays a Messiah who at the outset not only runs counter to the falling short and failing of the old Israel but who himself constitutes and opens up a new way of being Israel and indeed of being human to all who will seek to unite themselves with Him.

He works out that way in forty days in the desert re-presenting the forty years in which the old Israel had failed in its wanderings in the wilderness and ever since. The old Israel had failed the test, pining after the fleshpots of Egypt and demanding bread, unwilling to endure. The Devil confronts Jesus with that same temptation. He replies with the same words from Deuteronomy 8.2 which God spoke to Israel, after giving them the manna. It was given, he said, to show them that God provides and that we should learn that we live not by bread alone but by every word that proceeds from the mouth of God, by our trust in Him. Israel still failed to live in that way and Jesus the new Israel in person enacts a new obedience and opens it to those who be joined with Him.

Then again, where the old Israel might have fallen into the worship of power and national self aggrandisement, Jesus, nucleus of the new Israel invited them to follow *not* a messiah who would bring them military conquest of their oppressors and control over the wealth of the nations, but instead one who would bring them into a true worship of the only God, of the kind He had called them to offer in Deuteronomy 6.13, a worship in which He would dwell in them and they in Him, their only truly secure home. Finally, where the old Israel might fall into the temptation to manipulate God, when in the desert they asked for water and began to doubt whether the Lord was with them or not (the word *Massah* meaning 'proof' cf. Exodus 17.1–7), now they wanted to see their Messiah standing on the top point of the Temple roof, as some traditions said he would, and performing miraculous feats. But Jesus, as the Messiah and the nucleus of the new Israel, refused all such proving of God or of himself and looked to his doing the will of Him who sent him as the only assurance needed that he was the one they awaited (Deuteronomy 6.16). He thus repudiated Satan's misuse of the scriptures (Psalm 91) and gave himself to that role of a servant which would make clear who he was.

All Jesus's replies demonstrate the true way of being Israel, which will be opened up to all humankind. In his losing of self even here at the start, his self-displacement demonstrates the true becoming into which, through his final laying down of himself on the cross, he wills to draw all. So the forty days of Lent for all of us should surely be primarily a time of seeking to be held close to Him and so able to follow Him 'in the way'. For us, as for the Desert Fathers and Mothers, only the forgiveness, only the grace given through the realisation of the presence of the living Christ can give us the strength to resist the assaults of sin.

Gillian's Easter

There is no doubt that this was where the great gap opened up for Gillian. She had little real sense of grace and no recognition of Jesus Christ. One evening she rang me to tell me that she had been diagnosed with cancer. I visited her in hospital where they decided the cancer was too advanced to be operable. Enmeshed in tubes, 'What is my direction now?' she asked me, in a way that demanded an answer. I heard my voice telling her to go still further into *metanoia*, breaking beyond her previous mindset. 'I will attempt that,' she said quietly.

'You can go now!'

When she came out, now to undergo some chemotherapy, she told me she was going to write a small autobiographical book about her love affairs and her illness and its treatment. This was *Love's Work* (the title echoing Kierkegaard's *Works of Love*) which became a best seller. I had told her of St Silouan, a monk who prayed the Jesus Prayer on Mount Athos and went through a time of prolonged spiritual darkness and torment by demons, like a Desert Father. He cried out to God for deliverance and was given a rather dusty answer when God said in his heart, 'The proud always suffer.' 'How then may I be delivered from this pride?' he asked. The strange answer came, 'Keep thy mind in hell and despair *not*.' Startling me as ever, Gillian suddenly glowed and put her hands on my shoulders as if to bless me! 'I shall use that saying as the epigraph for my book,' she said.

Her love affairs in her story became a parable of our endless breaking and remaking, our quest through failure as, with each new venture, we still hope for completeness. The description of the attempts to treat her illness either through technology, a symbol of political muddling through, or through alternative medicine, which stood for her for impossible utopias, emphasised instead her attempts to live with her illness in symbiosis, a symbol of what it means 'to live, to love, to be failed to have failed, to forgive, to be forgiven for ever and ever. When I read these words in the copy she gave me, I threw it into the air and caught it again for joy. At last forgiveness had fully entered in.

Later, when she was in hospital, strongly depending upon a Christian doctor whom she trusted deeply, she suddenly wrote him a letter and sent me a copy. I quote:

> You know me to be a Jew. I am also a Trinitarian... However, while I feel held by God and the Holy Spirit, like many Jews I have a difficulty with Christ, 'to the Jews a stumbling block.' As a result of this week's experience I have gained Christ. For Christ is a stumbling block, but once you touch the hem of his robe with faith, you are healed. I shall be thanking God for this insight and gift.

Healing was now a metaphor for true mediation, that way through our own endless repentance towards our goal which in Jesus opens up from the outset, even in those calm firm words in which, in the Temptation story, he judges and breaks through the devices and illusions of this world. A Catholic friend who also received a copy of the letter, wrote back to Gillian. 'Why just touch the hem of his robe, why not seek to be united with Him?' Gillian asked me what this meant. I said her friend would undoubtedly have meant the sacrament, communion. 'Can I receive communion then?' 'Not unless you were baptised,' I said. She said, 'I want to think about that; I need to talk to a Rabbi.' I strongly agreed that she would need to think most carefully and to talk with a Rabbi. I asked the Hospital Chaplain to find one for her.

When I returned on Sunday night, she said that she had thought it all over and wanted me to baptise her. She looked pale, composed, almost regal, as she sat up in bed reading and writing. 'What about the Rabbi?' 'Oh forget the Rabbi. Any way he couldn't come.'

So at her imperious command, the time for her baptism was set for the following Saturday, when all her friends would be at the University, for a Conference she had helped to plan! During that week she seemed to have arrived at an amazing equilibrium. She had moved into the forgiveness on the far side of repentance, from mere *eros* into an *agape* love she had never quite acknowledged before. She wanted, as she had always said, to live in 'joyful mourning' (a favourite phrase of hers, from the 6th century John Climacus, 'Abbot' of St Catherine's, Mount Sinai). Gillian was now both grave and yet also elated. But, by Saturday afternoon, before the friends could arrive, she was suddenly becoming weary and sinking gently, sliding down into semi-consciousness. I was summoned urgently. When I saw the situation I took the water and the oil the Chaplain had prepared and said to her that I must baptise and confirm her *now*, and she must squeeze my hand in assent if she truly wanted this, which she duly did. I went ahead then with only her mother (already an Anglican Christian) and her younger sister there. Not long after this was done she actually slipped away from this life before the other visitors arrived. I had to break the news to them and give them the wine to drink in celebration, which Gillian had arranged to be there for them. We could not but sadly yet joyfully toast her new life.

Her baptism into Christ, she had already made clear, was for her a movement *within* not beyond Jewish faith. It was, as she made clear, a receiving of the grace by which Jesus enables us to overcome temptation and contradiction from within even now, in which we begin to move beyond repentance on its own, into the final mercy, and are united here and now with the One in whom our present journey is already our homecoming. The Lenten journey begins to open out through Good Friday's 'It is finished!' The Saturday of waiting is suffused with the glory of Easter, breaking in already; that glory in which we, here and now, even in our Lenten time, can even now rejoice with her in the 'sure and certain hope' that we shall rejoice with her forever.

ACKNOWLEDGEMENTS

As editors, we are very grateful to the wide range of people who were delighted to pass on to us their memories of Simon, and especially to all the authors of these chapters, whose names and roles are mentioned in the pages of Contributors.

The Archbishop of Canterbury was profoundly influenced by Simon when a young man, and throughout his ministry in the Diocese of Coventry, and we express our gratitude to him for such a moving Foreword.

We are deeply indebted to the family of Simon, for lending us his personal archive of papers, cuttings and computer disks, and in particular to his daughter, Helen Orr, and son-in-law, James Orr, for writing Chapter 1 and Chapter 10, and for contributing generously, with others, to the publication costs of this book.

We appreciate the work of the archivist of the Cambridge Centre for Christianity Worldwide, Philip Saunders, where Simon gave many of his books and papers in 1998.

We thank the artist, family, institutions, editors and publishers for permissions to republish the following items:

Front Cover: Peter Mennim, for his portrait of Simon, and Magdalene College, Cambridge, who commissioned it and where it hangs in the Senior Common Room.

Back Cover: The family of Simon for the photograph.

Chapter 2: Magdalene College, Cambridge, for the articles by Emeritus Fellows Ronald Hyman and Nicholas Boyle, in its alumni magazine for 2020 and Sarah Atkins, Chaplain, for her letter sent to members of the College.

Chapter 13: 'My Pilgrimage in Mission', *International Bulletin of Missionary Research* 23.2 (April 1999), pp. 60–64.

Chapter 14: 'The Christic Cogito: Christian Faith in a Pluralist Age' in D.W. Hardy and P.H. Sedgwick (eds), *The Weight of Glory: a vision and practice for Christian Faith, the future of Liberal Theology* (T&T Clark, 1991), pp. 257–270.

Chapter 15: 'Becoming What You Are: Exploring the "Great Exchange"'

The Commencement Address for the Graduation of Students at Goshen College, Indiana, USA, 22 April 2012.

Chapter 16: 'Sermon for Gillian Rose', Little St Mary's Church, Cambridge, 29 February 2004.

We want to express our thanks to Simon Barrow, Director of Ekklesia and Managing Editor of Ekklesia Publishing, for all his encouragement, insights and work on this project as well as for his own contribution, Chapter 6.

Finally, we are grateful to God, Father, Son and Holy Spirit, who draws us all together in an extraordinary exchange of gifts and to whom this book is a thank offering for the life, ministry and vision of Simon Barrington-Ward.

Graham Kings and Ian Randall

CONTRIBUTORS

Sarah Atkins has been the Chaplain of Magdalene College, Cambridge, since 2018, and read Theology there as an undergraduate (2002–5). She was ordained in 2014 and served her title as a curate at St Mary and St Michael, Trumpington, near Cambridge. She is an Assistant Diocesan Director of Ordinands in the Diocese of Ely.

Simon Barrow is Director of Ekklesia, the beliefs, ethics and politics think-tank and change network. A writer, publisher and adult educator, Simon lives and works in Scotland. He was previously Assistant General Secretary of Churches Together in Britain and Ireland and Executive Secretary of the Churches' Commission on Mission. He also worked for CMS between 1982 and 1987. His many books on religion, politics and culture include *Christian Mission in Western Society* (CTBI, 2001), co-edited with Graeme Smith.

Nicholas Boyle is the Emeritus Schröder Professor of German in the University of Cambridge. He came up to Magdalene College in 1964 and has been a Fellow of the College since 1968. His books include *Goethe: The Poet and the Age* and *Who Are We Now? Christian Humanism and the Global Market from Hegel to Heaney.*

Sarah Cawdell is a part time vicar in rural Shropshire with a passion for mission through local parish life. She studied theology at Cambridge and King's College London, with a particular interest in the mission theology of the CMS. Sarah opens the Rectory garden with the Quiet Garden Trust and is exploring mission as developing contemplation.

John Clark served in Iran with Operation Mobilisation and the Church Missionary Society, living through the Iranian Revolution. His interests in Iran and the Middle East have been maintained with CMS, first as Middle East and Pakistan Secretary and then Communications Secretary, and with the Church of England's General Synod, where he became the first Director for Mission and Public Affairs. Currently he serves on various charities committed to Christian witness in the Middle East.

Clive Handford served as Chaplain in Lebanon and Syria, was Dean of St George's Cathedral in Jerusalem, and Archdeacon in the Gulf and Chaplain in Abu Dhabi and Qatar. Returning to England, he was Archdeacon of Nottingham before becoming Bishop of Warwick. He was Bishop in Cyprus and the Gulf and from 2002 to 2007 was President Bishop of the Episcopal Church in Jerusalem and the Middle East. He is actively retired in North Yorkshire.

Ronald Hyam is Emeritus Reader in British Imperial History in the University of Cambridge, and has been a Fellow of Magdalene College since 1960. His books include *Britain's Imperial Century 1815–1914*, and *Britain's Declining Empire 1918–1968*.

Graham Kings is Honorary Assistant Bishop, Diocese of Ely, and Research Associate at the Cambridge Centre for Christianity Worldwide (CCCW). He served as Vice Principal, St Andrew's College, Kabare, Kenya, founding Director of the Henry Martyn Centre, Cambridge (now CCCW), Vicar of Islington, Bishop of Sherborne and Mission Theologian in the Anglican Communion. He has written books on mission, theology and art, liturgy, and poetry and his latest is *Nourishing Mission: Theological Settings*.

Andy Lord is vicar of All Saints' Didcot in the Diocese of Oxford, Bishops' Advisor and Visiting Lecturer at the London School of Theology. He worked for the Church Mission Society in the 1990s, has a PhD in Pentecostal ecclesiology and has written a number of books and articles on mission, church and spirituality, including the books *Transforming Renewal, Network Church* and *Spirit-Shaped Mission*.

Linda Ochola-Adolwa works as the Executive Director of Hatua Trust, a faith-based organisation whose mission is to catalyse Christians for Social transformation. She is also an ordained Anglican minister. She completed her doctorate from Fuller Seminary in Pasadena, California in 2017 and has created materials to inspire and encourage Christians to embrace their identity as Kenyan citizens, and to practically take up their civic responsibilities. Linda is married to Peter Adolwa and has two sons.

Helen Orr was a choral scholar who read theology at Magdalene College, Cambridge. She was the first Pioneer Minister at 'Michael House' (historic chapel now a reordered cafe ministry hub in Cambridge city centre), leading 'Fresh Expressions of church'. She was for twenty-five years a professional singer/songwriter before training for the priesthood. Her most recent album, 'Inspiration', is a concept album for the 'unchurched' generations. She is Vicar of the Benefices of Bassingbourn and Whaddon, Diocese of Ely.

James Orr is Lecturer in Philosophy of Religion at the Faculty of Divinity, University of Cambridge. He has written a number of articles on philosophical theology, political theology, continental philosophy, and analytic metaphysics. He is the author of *The Mind of God and the Works of Nature: Laws and Powers in Naturalism, Platonism, and Classical Theism* (Peeters, 2019) and co-editor of *Neo-Aristotelian Metaphysics and the Theology of Nature* (Routledge, 2022).

Ian Randall was a lecturer in church history and spirituality in London, at Spurgeon's College, and in Prague, and is a Research Associate of the Cambridge Centre for Christianity Worldwide and a Senior Research Fellow of the International Baptist Theological Study Centre, Amsterdam. He has written a number of books and many articles on movements of mission and renewal. He has been a hospital chaplain and is involved in spiritual direction in Cambridge.

Cathy Ross is Head of Pioneer Leadership Training at Church Mission Society and Canon Theologian for Leicester Cathedral. She is from Aotearoa/NZ and has worked as a mission partner in East Africa. She was the General Secretary of the International Association for Mission Studies for eight years. She has published in the area of mission and her research interests are in mission, hospitality and feminist theologies.

Philip Seddon, following studies in Cambridge and Tübingen, has worked and written in the fields of Christian Spirituality, Spiritual Direction and Biblical Theology in Nigeria, Nottingham, Cambridge, Birmingham and Salisbury. In addition to a life-long love of languages and music, science and psychology, and his own Evangelical tradition, he is constantly drawn by the profound freshness of the Orthodox tradition.

Justin Welby is the Archbishop of Canterbury. After 11 years in the oil industry and ordination training, he served in the Diocese of Coventry for 15 years before becoming Dean of Liverpool and Bishop of Durham. He has written *Dethroning Mammon: Making Money Serve Grace* and *Reimagining Britain: Foundations for Hope.*

BIBLIOGRAPHY

of the Main Works by Simon Barrington-Ward

Books

Love Will Out: A Theology of Mission for Today's World, CMS Newsletters 1975–85 (Basingstoke: Marshall Pickering, 1988).

The Jesus Prayer (Abingdon: BRF, 1996).

Why God? (Oxford: Lion, 1997).

With Brother Ramon, *Praying the Jesus Prayer Together* (Abingdon: BRF, 2001).

The Jesus Prayer and the Great Exchange (Cambridge: Grove Books, 2013). Grove Spirituality Series 124.

Chapters

'"The centre cannot hold..." Spirit possession as redefinition' in Adrian Hastings, Fasholé-Luke, *et al.* (eds), *Christianity in Independent Africa* (London: Rex Collins, 1978), 445–470.

Chapter One in Anna Jeffrey, ed., *Five Gold Rings: Powerful Influences on Prominent People* (London: DLT, 2003), 1–8.

'The Christic Cogito: Christian Faith in a Pluralist Age' in D.W. Hardy and P.H. Sedgwick, eds, *The Weight of Glory: a vision and practice for Christian Faith, the future of Liberal Theology* (Edinburgh: T&T Clark, 1991), 257–270.

'The Revival Through CMS Eyes' in Kevin Ward and Emma Wild-Wood, eds, *The East African Revival: Histories and Legacies* (Farnham: Ashgate, 2012), 53–60.

Articles

93 *CMS Newsletters* from 1975–1985, available at the Cambridge Centre for Christianity Worldwide and the University of Birmingham. The most significant 24 of these Newsletters were published in his book *Love Will Out: A Theology of Mission for Today's World, CMS Newsletters 1975–85* (Basingstoke: Marshall Pickering, 1988) and were entitled:

> The Personal Centre; Call to Prayer; Prayer: A Double Rhythm; Love Will Out; In Search of a Whole Gospel; Grace and Truth; A New Belonging; Fearful Symmetry; Word Out of Silence; Point of Balance; Response to Islam, I: Points of Entry; Response to Islam, II: Broken Circles; A Faith in Travail; The Dream is Over; A People Between; Credibility Test; African Mediator; Tale of Two Cities: Christians in Hong Kong and Singapore; Missionary Movements: A New Phase; The Form of a Servant; Ways Through the Ways; A Sign for All Faiths; The New Love: Christians Relating to Those of Other Faiths – An Affirmation; No Other Name.

'My Pilgrimage in Mission', *International Bulletin of Missionary Research* 23.2 (April 1999), 60–64.

'Dying to Live: The Vocation of Anglicanism', *Anvil* 12, no. 2 (1995): 106–8. https://biblicalstudies.org.uk/pdf/anvil/12-2_105.pdf

Unpublished

Simon Barrington-Ward Archive at the Cambridge Centre for Christianity Worldwide, which is currently being added to and updated. https://www.cccw.cam.ac.uk/wp-content/uploads/2017/10/SBW-Barrington-Ward.pdf

Simon Barrington-Ward Archive at the home of Helen and James Orr, Cambridge, including, 'Redeeming the Time' lecture given at Wycliffe College, Toronto, 1994.

'Exploring "The Great Exchange"', Commencement Speech, Goshen College, Indiana, USA, 2012. Published above as Chapter 15.

Audio

Kettle's Yard, University of Cambridge Museum, ReCollection, oral history archive, interviewed by Robert Wilkinson, on 26 Feb 2008, four sections totalling 1 hour 4 mins. https://www.kettlesyard.co.uk/collection/recollection/interviewee/simon-barrington-ward/

Videos

St Paul's Forum, St Paul's Cathedral, 'The Jesus Prayer', 2 October 2011, 55 mins. https://www.youtube.com/watch?v=JCwiyU3DVV4

Interviewed by Helen Orr, Simon's daughter, about The Jesus Prayer, 6 Feb 2014, 26 mins. https://www.youtube.com/watch?v=PxttrnyBC40

'Looking Towards the End: Cambridge Memories of C.S. Lewis' interviewed by Dr James Orr, Lecturer in Philosophical Theology, Cambridge, and son-in-law of Simon, 8 February 2014, 23 mins. https://www.youtube.com/watch?v=g_TPKVqvjnU

NAME INDEX

SUBJECT INDEX